COGNITION, COMMUNICATION, AND ROMANTIC RELATIONSHIPS

LEA'S Series in Personal Relationships
Steve Duck, Series Editor

COGNITION, COMMUNICATION, AND ROMANTIC RELATIONSHIPS

James M. Honeycutt
Louisiana State University

James G. Cantrill
Northern Michigan University

2001

LAWRENCE ERLBAUM ASSOCIATES, PUBLISHERS
Mahwah, New Jersey   London

An instructor's manual for this text is available to all adopters. To obtain a copy, please contact the publisher at 1-800-926-6579 or www.erlbaum.com

Lawrence Erlbaum Associates, Inc., Publishers
10 Industrial Avenue
Mahwah, NJ 07430

Cover design by Kathryn Houghtaling Lacey

Library of Congress Cataloging-in-Publication Data

Honeycutt, James M.
Cognition, communication, and romantic relationships /
James M. Honeycutt, James G. Cantrill.
    p. cm. — (LEA's series on personal relationships)
  Includes bibliographical references (p.) and index.
ISBN 0-8058-3577-6 (pbk. : alk. paper)
1. Intimacy (Psychology) 2. Interpersonal Relations. 3. Love. 4. Interpersonal communication. 5. Cognition. I. Cantrill, James G. (James Gerard),
1955-II. Title. III. Series.
BF575.I5 H66   2000
158.2—dc21   00-039383
                                                         CIP

Books published by Lawrence Erlbaum Associates are printed on acid-free paper, and their bindings are chosen for strength and durability.

Printed in the United States of America
10 9 8 7 6 5 4 3 2 1

This book is dedicated to the memory of John Boone Honeycutt. His legacy acts as a guide that positively influences expectations about the meaning of communication, commitment, love, and intimacy in close, enduring personal relationships.

Contents In Brief

Contents

ix

Series Editor's Foreword

This series from Lawrence Erlbaum Associates (LEA) is intended to review the progress in the academic work on relationships with respect of a broad array of issues and to do so in a manner that is accessible and illustrates its practical value. The LEA series also includes books intended to pass on the accumulated scholarship to the next generation of students and to those who deal with relationship issues in the broader world beyond the academy. The series thus comprises not only monographs and other academic resources exemplifying the multidisciplinary nature of this area, but also textbooks suitable for use in the growing number of courses on relationships.

As it grows, the series will provide a comprehensive and current survey of theory and research in personal relationships through the careful analysis of the problems encountered, and solved, in research, and it will also consider the systematic application of that work in a practical context. These resources are intended to be not only comprehensive assessments of progress on particular topics, but also significant influences on the future directions and development of the study of personal relationships. Although each volume will be focused and centered, authors will place the particular topics in the broader context of other research on relationships in a range of disciplinary traditions. The series will thus not only offer incisive and forward-looking reviews, but also demonstrate the broader theoretical implications of relationships for the range of disciplines from which the research originates. Series volumes will include original studies, review of relevant theory and research, and new theories oriented toward the understanding of personal relationships, both in themselves and within the context of broader theories of family process, social psychology, and communication. Reflecting the diverse composition of personal-relationship study, readers in numerous disciplines—social psychology, communication, sociology, family studies, developmental psychology, clinical psychology, personality, counseling, women's studies, and gerontology—will find valuable and insightful perspectives in the series.

Apart from the academic scholars who research the dynamics and processes of relationships, there are many other people whose work takes them up against the operation of relationships in the real world: officers, teachers, therapists, lawyers, drug and alcohol counselors, marital counselors, and those who take care of elderly people. For these professionals, a number of issues routinely arise concerning the ways in which relationships affect the people whom they serve, such as the role of loneliness in illness and the ways to circumvent it, the complex impact of family and peer relationships on a person recovering from drug-dependency, the role of playground unpopularity on a child's learning, the relational side of chronic illness, the management of conflict in marriage, the establishment of good rapport between physicians and seriously ill patients, the support of bereaved people, and the correction of violent styles of behavior in dating or marriage. Each of these problems demonstrates the far-reaching influences of relationship processes on other aspects of life that are presently theorized to be independent of relationship considerations.

The present volume is devoted to the exploration of the ways in which the emotions and behaviors in the development of relationships are strongly connected to memory, communication, and social understandings. Because relationship development is dependent on social expectations as much as on the true development of emotions and behaviors, this book carefully analyses the ways in which individuals absorb and react to social understandings about the nature of relationship growth. Such expectations come from common beliefs about the appropriateness of behaviors at particular points in relationships and are embedded in many psychological forms and structures shared not only by the partners themselves, but by others to whom they portray their relationship. Information about such beliefs comes also from the media, from observing others, and from previous experiences. The book carefully analyses the sources and the consequences of such beliefs, along with their structures and forms. The text thus offers a new set of insights into the issues of relationship development and offers some well-grounded advice on ways to understand the experiences of couples as they develop relationships. Practitioners, therapists, ministers, and others who deal with relationship preparation, relationship development, and avoidance of relationship problems will find this book as interesting as the researchers and scholars at whom it is primarily aimed.

—Steve Duck
University of Iowa

Preface

People have expectations for what constitutes appropriate behavior in different types of relationships. A memorable event from a close relationship may be pleasant, such as sharing a fun activity with a partner, or the event may be painful, such as discovering that a prospective partner is completely different in person from what was expected after a long correspondence by e-mail.

Expectations for the rise and fall of relationships are based, in part, on memories of prior relationships, on what people have learned from observing others, and from information in books, movies, television, or other media. Prior experiences affect an individual's expectations about what is likely to occur in new relationships. A range of empirical studies confirms the common belief that intimate relationships go through distinct stages of development (Duck, 1986; Honeycutt, 1993; Knapp & Vangelisti, 1996; Surra, 1990). Stage models of relational development have received a great deal of research emphasis over the past 20 years, even though these models have been criticized for a number of limitations in describing relational development.

At its heart, this book presents a cognitive approach to the development of romantic relationships and addresses many of the criticisms leveled against stage models by emphasizing the role of cognitive expectations about how relationships develop. These expectations originate in people's memories regarding relationships, some based on direct experience and others gained indirectly through reading romance novels, watching movies, soap operas, or hearing about other people's experiences.

Of course, memory is not the only thing that comes into play when researchers explore the landscape of romance. Research has revealed systematic gender differences regarding how people think about romance and relationships. In particular, women tend to recall more specific information about relational events in their marriages than men do (Ross & Holmberg, 1992). Indeed, when telling stories about events in their relationships, men often look to their female partners to fill in gaps. These kinds of differences are discussed throughout the book.

Gender differences notwithstanding, individual conceptions about the development of romantic relationships are rooted in memory. These memories about relationships, despite their dynamic qualities, are not random events. Individuals think about relationships developing in an orderly sequence that mirrors the basic patterns found in other people's reports of their own experiences. Still, individuals report that their personal relationships are somehow more unique than other people's typical romances. However, research reveals that the presumed special traits of their romantic trysts underlie the commonality found in shared memory structures (Honeycutt, 1993; Honeycutt, Cantrill, & Greene, 1989; Honeycutt, Cantrill & Allen, 1992; Honeycutt, Cantrill, Kelly, & Lambkin, 1998).

Studies demonstrating a fundamental agreement among the expectations that characterize developing romances allow the creation of a cognitive model portraying the prototypical behaviors that characterize romantic relationships. This model reveals how memory is hierarchically organized, how it is related to people's love-struck goals, and how people systematically recall discourse associated with particular scenes or events in the development of romance. The recall of these relational events creates anticipations that allow people to categorize behavior into meaningful categories (e.g., deciding if a prolonged gaze communicates intimacy or merely interest in the topic of conversation), to decide what type of relationship they are experiencing, and to anticipate where it may be headed. To use a navigational metaphor, relational memory structures serve as a gyroscope that guides people through relational space because memory provides mental maps or road signs for steering their ongoing experiences. Yet some people are better relational navigators than others because of their successes in prior relationships, perseverance, self-confidence, and motivation.

As a result of their experiences, people may believe that they are experts at creating quality relationships. Yet it can be argued that one of the worst kinds of advice is based on personal experience because that experience may not apply to others. Indeed, many television talk shows present individuals with relational problems who are then satirized for entertainment without serious therapy or understanding taking place. On the other hand, therapists, communication scholars, and relationship researchers have broad exposure to the experiences of others through their work and the studies they conduct on populations of the romantically inclined. In fact, a reliance on personal experience as a source of information is known in the cognitive literature as an availability bias. Just as it is easier for individuals to retrieve instances of their own actions, as opposed to recalling studies or reports of other people's experiences, so too do people generally rely on what they know about romance rather than taking a broader view (Tversky & Kahneman, 1974). Thus, people often find that their relational expertise is based on personal limited experiences that are not shared by others. What has worked for one person often does not generalize to other individuals, despite this belief.

A second cognitive bias that contributes to the myth of every person being a relationship expert is the vividness bias. Personal information that is vivid and stands out is seen as having more value than impersonal information, such as statistics. For example, talk shows often have individuals discussing how their relationships broke up so that the talk-show format becomes the contemporary version of a public therapy session for viewers and participants. Yet there are few shows about couples who maintain their relationships despite adversity or couples whose relationships flow along without much fanfare. Sensational cases represent vivid information that is easily accessed, and what could be more vivid to someone than his or her own failed relationship?

The vividness bias is revealed in the numerous self-help books and magazines that offer advice on how to find the right person and keep the relationship going. Yet if this advice is useful, why does advice often seem contradictory (e.g., Be assertive of your own views, and Be supportive of your mate)? The answer may be due to dialectic opposition in the form of contradictory needs. Montgomery (1993) defined dialectic opposition as the simultaneous presence of two relational forces that are interdependent and negate each other; each force defines the other while acting at cross-purposes. Relationships are inherently concerned with balancing needs for autonomy with connection, predictability with novelty, and openness with closedness. Baxter and Simon (1993) discussed the dialectic moments in which one need dominates its antithesis. For example, novelty may be desired over predictability if the relationship is seen as boring. Romantic efforts by one's partner that involve surprise and spontaneity alleviate the boredom during these moments. Yet for those who take a cognitive approach to understanding relationships, the question arises as to how these vivid periods are configured in the mind and the extent to which such memories influence the ongoing understanding of current relationships, beginning with courtship.

ORGANIZATION OF THE BOOK

The focus of this book is an understanding of the role of memory, communication, and social cognition in the development of romantic relationships and the description of that development in terms of stages of development. Chapter 1 previews a model of relationship expectations and communication. Chapter 2 presents a variety of concepts dealing with social cognition and information processing of relationships. Relational schemata, prototypes, and scripts are discussed. Research on the misconstrual of scripts is presented in the form of a date rape scenario in which the man's script for the date is different from the woman's.

Chapter 3 presents the concept of memory structures, distinguishing between recalled scenes and scripts in relationships. Relational memory structures help individuals interpret behavior that is observed in relationships. These structures provide a sense of trajectory about the direction in which relationships may develop, such as simply being a casual acquaintance or evolving into long-term friendship, platonic, romantic, or collegial relationships.

Chapter 4 discusses the relationship between emotion, communication, and cognition. Moods and emotions affect the way people process information. For example, people have prototypes for anger and jealousy. The sentiment-override hypothesis posits that current emotional states affect the way people perceive current behaviors. Thus, among unhappily married couples, the history of negative interaction affects the way that messages are interpreted so that messages that are designed to be happy or delivered with a neutral affect are often seen as negative by partners.

Chapter 5 reviews studies dealing with a part of daydreaming called *imagined interactions*. Individuals imagine talking with relational partners in a variety of situations, discussing a variety of topics. Sometimes people recall pleasant conversations with their partners, whereas other times they relive old arguments that energize them as they fantasize about the next time they encounter their partners and vigorously tell them how upset they are. Various functions are served by self-talk. A major function is keeping relationships alive in people's mind when their relational partner is not close by. "Absence makes the heart grow fonder." Yet individuals often rehearse imagined encounters with their partners, picking up a conflict where it left off. The themes of their conversations and relationships are manifested in people's self-talk with relational partners.

Chapter 6 reviews and critiques models of developmental relationships. For example, developmental models have been criticized for the arbitrariness of movement through the stage movement. Why do some individuals move rapidly or slowly through the stages? A cognitive approach to relational development addresses this criticism by assuming that expectations are a prime factor in determining the rate and direction of movement.

Chapters 7 and 8 present a series of studies dealing with expectations about the rise and demise of relationships, respectively. Chapter 7 examines studies of generating and processing behaviors that are expected to occur in a developing romance. Communication strategies for enhancing intimacy are discussed. Chapter 8 reports on individual differences in explaining the breakdown of relationships, as well as the content and ordering of behaviors that symbolize relational decay. The link between cognitive processing of relationship decay and emotions is explored.

Chapter 9 discusses gender differences in claims of commission (statements of what is happening in a relationship) and claims of omission (statements of what is not happening). These linguistic codes are revealed when men and women provide accounts of the decline of relationships. Women tend to use more commissions (the relationship breaking up because of what was happening) than omissions (topics for the relationship breaking up because of what was not happening).

Chapter 10 concludes and briefly discusses topics for further research using a cognitive approach to communication and relational development. These are Internet relationships, gender differences in rules for communication and conflict-resolution in relationships, the use of relational narratives, and the correspondence between attachment styles for relational bonding and the content of relational memory structures.

ACKNOWLEDGMENTS

We wish to acknowledge our students in our relational communication classes for their vibrant and energetic opinions on relationship development. We have had lively discussions about gender similarities and differences in attending to relationship processes. Indeed, it is an intriguing topic.

1

The Modern-Day Pursuit of Intimacy and Relational Memory Structures

Courtship can be thought of as a social ritual through which the development of romance manifests itself. At some point, it involves a sorting process for finding appropriate mates, a kind of filtering to determine basic compatibility (Duck, 1977). In this regard, the stimulus-value-role theory of Murstein (1987) suggested that courtship begins as a simple exchange of information involving initial impressions of physical attributes followed by an interpretation of individual values, attitudes, and beliefs about a variety of topics that are of interest to each. Once a similarity is noted, the individuals are categorized and assigned to potential roles such as business acquaintance, tennis partner, colleague who likes the history of Russian composers, or potential lover. Further communication and ritualized behavior provide additional information about the partners' abilities to function in additional roles in preparation for potential roles as mates or parents.

The concept of interpersonal intimacy in its current form began evolving in 19th century America and Europe, with the development of industrial society. More recently, in the computerized information society, the emphasis has been shifted more to the individual as a reaction to the impersonalization of factory and business life (Gadlin, 1977). This trend has continued and accelerated as

1

the world approaches the 21st century because the majority of people now live in urban environments. In urban society, individuals often gain their primary identity and psychosocial support from personal relationships rather than from their roles in the community.

More recently, individuals have developed relationships in cyberspace through the use of computer web groups for singles and divorcees, chat lines, and correspondence with others through e-mail. Because of the computer revolution, individuals can now work more easily at home via their computers. Working out of the home is a return to the pattern in colonial times when the business was the home, in the form of farms and shops attached to living quarters. The proliferation of computers decreases face-to-face interaction as websites are accessed to find individuals with similar interests. Only time will tell if courtship develops through computer contact, as it has evolved in face-to-face communication. It is certain, however, that such relationships are poor substitutes for having the ability to reach out and touch someone.

Courtship developed to promote successful mating. In earlier agrarian societies, a large family was essential to provide farm labor. Consequently, mates were chosen with great care for their potential as partners and parents, and were assessed and tested for their compatibility through the ritualized stages of courtship. According to evolutionary psychologists, these rituals of courtship are learned, defined, and expressed in the context of society and culture because of biological drives for procreation. For example, Fisher (1994) discussed how biochemical processes contribute to the development of romance. Human brain chemistry creates a heightened sense of excitement that people often describe as falling in love or infatuation. Fisher further suggested that the brain physiology and chemistry associated with bonding evolved as part of the human primordial mating system. Her research in various cultures reveals that in societies allowing divorce the most common length of marriage is 4 years. This length of time conforms to the traditional period between successive human births. Fisher proposed that this 4-year cycle is a pattern that evolved as a reproductive strategy to successfully raise a helpless infant.

In addition to human brain physiology, part of the reason for failed relationships is that the stability of contemporary relationships is contingent on positive emotions as the glue for relationship bonding and the reason for a relationship to continue. Commitment to a relationship depends on the ebb and flow of levels of intimacy. However, such has not always been the case in the United States. During the colonial period in the 18th century, intimacy was, at best, the result of the formal relationship rather than the cause of the romantic bond or marriage (Gadlin, 1977). Individuals were admonished to love their spouse even though physical assaults were common. Only later did affection became both the cause and cement of marriage.

In the 20th century, affection was eroticized, although seen as fleeting and unstable. Stephen (1994) discussed how people think of marriage as a status that symbolizes mutual affection. Affection is necessary for marriage, whereas its erosion is a sufficient reason for divorce. However, Lewis and Spanier (1982) explored temporary high-quality (i.e., high-affection), low-stability marriages that ended in divorce and cited examples of dual-career couples who, after having to relocate in different cities in order to pursue each partner's career, eventually terminated their relationships. Is something more than simple affection necessary here?

According to Stephen (1994), some other possible causes of divorce are living in a pluralistic society that is saturated with diverse information, lifestyle choices, political interests, and religious values. As a result of pluralism, people construct their realities from diverse sets of resources. An individual's sense of uniqueness comes from a wide selection and prioritization of informational sources because the information is so diverse and open to contradictory interpretation. For example, the qualities that attract two individuals sometimes become complaints if the relationship starts to sour (Felmlee, 1995). "At first, I thought he was carefree and laid-back. Now, he is indecisive and irresponsible." This process in which individuals change their evaluations of each other after a time, as opposed to persevering in their initial impressions, is known as cognitive accommodation. Box 1.1 contains sample cognitive beliefs about the qualities that first attract couples to each other that could be restructured later into negative attributions.

Today, each individual's sense of uniqueness permeates his or her views of the characteristics of an ideal relationship. Research by Wish, Deutsch, and Kaplan (1976) revealed that individuals distinguish communication behaviors (e. g., cooperative versus competitive) among relatively few dimensions that are used to distinguish almost all types of relationships (e.g., personal enemies, husband–wife). In addition, people make different distinctions in their own relationships than in typical or other people's relationships. For example, cooperation is more important for evaluating typical relationships than for evaluating their own relationships. In evaluating their own relationships, individuals mention fewer hostile relations (e.g., one's relationship with a lover is mentioned more often than one's relationship with a bitter enemy). Hostile relations (e.g., business rivals, political opponents, guard–prisoner, supervisor–employee, and interviewer–applicant) are perceived as characterizing other people's relationships. In essence, people select highly positive relational attributes to construct seemingly ideal life spaces in which they live, learn, and love.

People's constructions of reality are based on experiences, which also affect their beliefs about the development and decline of romantic relationships. Individuals vary in their expectations of how relationships should develop due to the variety of informational sources that form the foundation for their expectations. In this regard, Staines and Libby (1986) discussed predictive romantic expectations, which are beliefs about behaviors that are expected to occur in a romantic role regardless of one's desires. Thus, a person who has been spurned

---

Box 1.1
Cognitive Reframing: Sample Attractions in Couples That Later Evolved into Relationship Complaints

Initial Attribute of Attraction	*Evolved Complaint*
1. Direct; intelligent	Unfairly critical; given to outbursts
2. Easy going; laid-back	Self-absorbed and indulgent
3. Independent; strong	Has to have own way; selfish
4. Self-confident	Doesn't respect my wishes and withholds
5. Prudent, wise, and practical	Calm demeanor drives me nuts
6. Masculine; strong	Abusive; we fight
7. Feminine; warm	Hysterical; we fight
8. Good listener	Doesn't have own opinion
9. Exciting and likes to talk	Restless and doesn't let me relax
10. I am the center of his/her world	Despicably insecure
11. Open-minded and accepting	Doesn't give without being asked; no initiation
12. There's a mystery about him/her	No true intimacy; not completely there

---

before may be more likely to expect this to happen in future relationships than is someone who has not been rejected.

Staines and Libby (1986) also discussed idealistic romantic expectations. These are beliefs reflecting an individual's desires of what should ideally happen in the role of a lover or spouse. Perhaps not surprisingly, women report more discrepancies between prescriptive and predictive expectations than men do. A common complaint is that wives prefer their husbands to do more household cleaning even though they don't expect that it will happen. Consequently, women often report lower levels of marital happiness than their husbands (Gottman, 1994; Price & McKenry, 1988). Nonetheless, even in an age of too-often-failed expectations, women and men meet, fall in love, and some even live happily ever after. Why? Symbolic interdependence provides an answer to this question.

SYMBOLIC INTERDEPENDENCE IN RELATIONSHIPS

Long-term relationships provide continuity and confirmation for idiosyncratic beliefs and protection from doubt, loneliness, and ambiguity. Stephen (1994) discussed the idea of individuals sharing conceptions of relationships in terms of symbolic interdependence. This is a type of mental sharing in which individuals share similar beliefs about the world; relational partners react to events in similar ways and derive similar conclusions from information. In symbolic interdependence in couples, Stephen (1994) wrote,

> They come to appreciate their unique bond of shared knowledge, perhaps sensing that no alternative relationship can provide as much potential for confirmation and understanding. The process of relationship communication has gradually transformed both partners. It is not that ego has found an alter who can penetrate the self, but that both ego and alter have refashioned themselves (and indeed the rest of their world) through the dialogue of their relationship until they are possessed of a type of self consistent with the relationship world view. The couple creates an interpretive framework and at the same time reinterprets themselves within it. Needless to say, persistently deviant interpretations will be regarded as problematic and effort is likely to be expended in smoothing discrepancies. (p. 197)

These discrepancies can be seen as relational conflicts about behaviors, attitudes, and appropriate performance of romantic roles. If the smoothing does not resolve the discrepancies, the relationship may dissolve. More importantly, the smoothing strategies go into memory and act as a repository of information that may be opened for subsequent relationships. Thus, happy long-term relationships are enhanced when individuals have a shared social reality and relationship worldview. The partners share similar expectations about what constitutes relationship development and those qualities that characterize a satisfying relationship. The sharing of expectations reflects evolving stories that individuals construct as they communicate with each other.

So, it would seem as if the secret to relational bliss is pounded out on the familiar anvil of communication. Yet the mere sharing of expectations and predictions is not enough; the intimate conversations between romantic partners do not get lodged in memory in some pure form. Rather the discourse must become embedded in some form of preexisting mental structure that allows people to separate out irrelevant data, mill the appropriate associations between actions and intents, and forge a stable, shared relational worldview. Thus, relational schemata serve as memory structures that organize relevant information and, ultimately, test the tensile of any romance.

A BRIEF INTRODUCTION TO RELATIONAL
MEMORY STRUCTURES

Duck (1986) suggested that relationships should be regarded as changing mental and behavioral creations of individuals. The time spent alone analyzing future encounters reflects an individual's use of relational schemata to understand and differentiate among different types of relationships such as distinguishing a casual dating relationship from an exclusive romance. Baldwin (1992) reviewed studies indicating that people develop cognitive structures representing regular patterns of interaction. A relational schema includes an image in which people imagine seeing themselves with someone else.

Individuals have knowledge structures based on memory and experiences that create expectations about what is likely to occur during the course of their lives in different types of relationships. Relationship memory structures are hierarchically ordered on the basis of recall of particular scenes (e.g., meeting an individual for the first time at a specific place) and scripts for behavior embedded within various scenes. Even though relationships are in constant motion, relationship memory structures provide a perceptual anchor with which individuals can determine where they are in a relationship.

Memories about relationships may be functional or dysfunctional. For example, Swann (1987) reviewed research indicating that individuals chose relational partners who verified their self-concepts even if their self-concept at the time was negative. Individuals who had high self-esteem preferred their relational partners to view them favorably, whereas individuals with low self-esteem preferred their relational partners to view them in relatively unfavorable terms. An individual's preference for relational partners with either positive or negative views of the individual was associated with the actual appraisal of their friends. Hence, if an individual viewed him or herself somewhat negatively, a relational partner who perceived the individual similarly was liked more than a relational partner who did not. Swann (1987) suggested "that people translate their desire for congruent relationship partners into actual selection of partners" (p. 1040).

Relationships are constantly moving entities rather than static events. People tell stories or give accounts about their relationships that help provide order to events. Understanding is the result of an active, cooperative enterprise of the people in relationships. Problems in a relationship are understood as stories that individuals have agreed to tell.

Relationships represent the juxtaposition between individual needs and dyadic goals. A cognitive approach to the study of relationships examines how individuals mentally create their relationships. The behavioral study of relationships has a long, rich legacy. For example, communication patterns between happy and unhappy couples have been examined. However, an exclusive focus on the behavioral patterns of couples ignores the fusion between the individual and the relationship. The mental creation of a relationship may sustain or constrain individuals in everyday mundane living, depending on the content of relational expectations.

Relational expectations reflect people's past experiences in relationships. Cognitive researchers refer to expectations as knowledge structures. Various types of knowledge structures are discussed in chapter 2. For example, if an individual has experienced a lot of deception in prior relationships, then he or she could have a relationship-deception schema consisting of expectations that in intimate relationships, vows are often broken. He or she may believe that his or her partner's words may not be taken at face value and that caution is wise before venturing far into self-disclosure. The individual may even be wary of people who seem gregarious.

Cognitive researchers believe that people's complex personal memories (scripts) create the bias people read into one another's signals. Research indicates that the most influential scripts are those initially developed in early childhood through interaction with parents, particularly with the primary caregiver, which traditionally has been the mother (Ainsworth, 1989; Bowlby, 1982; Carnelley & Janoff-Bulman, 1992). Additional influences on people's relationship scripts develop from other life experiences and the media. And the role and influence of scripts plays out in everyday interaction in a relationship. For example, when partners interact, they often think about what they are going to say in the form of imagined interactions (IIs), mentally processing what has been said, and sorting through memory to compare and contrast new information with earlier experience (Honeycutt, 1995). As relationships develop, people's internal responses create not only their views of themselves, but their views of the partner and the ways in which they think about themselves in relation to the other person. In short, relationships are the combined products and producers of both cognitive activity and behavior.

SUMMARY

Individuals think about relationships based on experiences, observations, and cultural images. People experience relationships either through personal experience, vicarious experience, or a combination of direct and indirect encounters. As a consequence of these experiences, many people feel that they are experts on relationships. Yet, it can be argued that many people are experts at failed relationships. An analogy is the coaching profession, in which a coach with a losing record is not necessarily seen as an expert on coaching, but as an expert on defeat. The divorce rate is higher for remarried individuals than for individuals in their first marriages.

Memories of relational events create expectations for relationships that are hierarchically organized on the basis of scenes and recalled messages within those scenes. Thus, relationships exist in people's minds, as well as in the observable communication between any two individuals. The role of cognition in categorizing romantic relationships has been ignored in the scholarly literature, not receiving much empirical research attention, whereas behavioral studies for classifying relationships are more popular (cf. Duck, 1993). The cognition of romance is examined in this book in terms of relational memory structures derived from experience.

DISCUSSION QUESTIONS

1.1 Discuss the idea of individuals as experts at failed relationships. Define what is meant by a failed relationship. What lessons do people learn from failed relationships? People hear stories about individuals being in one bad relationship after another. How many individuals do you know who have gone through a series of failed relationships that seem to have similar characteristics? Did their expectations change after each relationship ended?

1.2 Discuss the proposition that successful relationships are more likely when individuals have a joint, relationship worldview and shared conceptions of relationships. How similar must the individuals' expectations for the development of relationships be in order to enhance the quality of the relationship?

APPLICATIONS

1.1 Think of couples you know who seem to be well matched and those who are not well matched at all. Interview the partners in these couples about how they met, what made the other person stand out, what hobbies or interests they share, the problems they deal with in the relationship, how they communicate, and what they expected from the relationship. Ask them their views about what characterizes a romantic relationship. You may interview them individually and contrast the partners' reports. Write a brief report in which you contrast the couples in terms of relationship happiness, compatibility of beliefs about relationship values, and anything that is especially memorable about these couples.

1.2 With a close friend, try an experiment in which each of you individually thinks of two couples whom you both know. One couple should be very happy and compatible; the other couple should be the opposite. Decide which couple is in each category individually; do both of you agree on the classifications? What made you classify the couples in the way you did? How similar or different are your perceptions of these couples compared to your friend's?

2

Schemata, Scenes, and Scripts for Romantic Relationships

One way of exploring the mental creation of relationships is to look at how individuals categorize information about behavior in their relationships. The model of relational expectations, presented at the end of chapter 1, reflects how such information about relationships is stored in and retrieved from memory. Integral to this process is the way in which people pigeon-hole what they observe in their daily lives. In this chapter, various types of categorization schemes, known to cognitive researchers as schemata, scenes, scripts, and prototypes, are represented.

As noted earlier, Duck (1986) believed that relationships should be regarded not as fixed states of being that are evaluated clinically, but as changing mental and behavioral expectations that involve a good deal of subjectivity. One teenage person, for example, may expect a developing romance to include instances of hugging or holding hands in public, whereas another, based on her or his experience, may not anticipate such public displays of affection. One way to think about the expectations encompassed in developing romance is to analyze the components of memory and its organization. Memory provides a frame of reference for experiences; it also creates expectations for relationships.

Memory components are called *knowledge structures*, which are defined as coherent and organized clusters of information that are based on experience

(Fletcher & Fitness, 1993). Knowledge structures are classified into two types; declarative and procedural knowledge. *Declarative knowledge* is open to conscious inspection, as when an individual chooses his or her words with great care so as not to, say, let a date know that he or she disapproves of a hair style (e.g., "That cut certainly accents your facial features!"). Baldwin (1992) defined *procedural knowledge* as descriptions about objects or people. Alternatively, procedural knowledge reflects the routines that people use to pursue personal goals, such as attracting a romantic partner or making sense out of what is being said. This knowledge is automatically activated and operates subconsciously (Simpson, Gangestad, & Lerma, 1990). For example, eyebrow flashes, smiling, body positioning, and canting the head are subconscious behaviors that indicate social engagement that are used by individuals to draw attention to themselves and present themselves as stimulating, competent, or socially skilled (Simpson et al., 1990).

Memory, stored in knowledge structures, assists in guiding people's beliefs and thoughts about, as well as their behavior in, relationships. Miller and Read (1991) discussed how knowledge structures reflect the ways in which the mind organizes memory as these structures emphasize various qualities of perception, kinds of content, and modes of mental processing. Regardless of kind or quality, knowledge structures categorize the behavior and observations people experience every day.

Researchers have developed classifications and models of memory, extrapolated from observed behavior, dialogue, and reports that appear to reflect the function and organization of the sense-making process. In their comprehensive review of the research on social cognition and interpersonal relationships, Fletcher and Fitness (1993) pointed to the interface between personal experience and socially shared knowledge structures. Stereotypes, social norms, and rules reflect culturally shared schemata, whereas beliefs about one's own marriage may be private and not shared by others. Furthermore, people's beliefs about themselves activate beliefs about others and relationships. Miller and Read (1991) provided a hypothetical scenario of John and Mary, who meet at a bar and have some drinks. John believes that others are untrustworthy and that he has to hurt others before they hurt him. Mary believes the opposite and feels she can depend on others. John has ambivalent feelings about being attached to someone else, whereas Mary finds security in such an attachment. In this scenario, imagine what would happen if Mary discloses something personal to John. Perhaps, John would not affirm her disclosures and would say very little.

A COMPARISON OF MEMORY WITH THE ORGANIZATION OF A COMPUTER

The primary function of a memory structure is to process new experiences and assign them to a particular type of structure or context necessary for understanding them (Schank, 1982). For example, a dating memory structure can include a number of typical dating scenes, such as going to a movie or restaurant. The existing memory structure serves as a reference that enables the individual to judge if a new dating experience is similar to or different from what happens on a typical date.

People's expectations about events in relationships can be compared to the organization of computer files. As in a computer system, human mental organization categorizes information about relational development in a hierarchical arrangement of nested subcategories. A directory, symbolized in computer terminology by a directory name, is comparable to a complex schema. Consider, for example, a directory entitled Escalating Relationship (c:\Escalat.Rlp). This directory reflects the memory structure for a developing romance; it consists of underlying scenes and scripts (in computer terminology, subdirectories and subfiles).

In the directory c:\Escalat.Rlp, there are subdirectories containing memory structures for various related topics. A primary subdirectory DATING, for example, contains a number of subfiles containing scenes and scripts for memories such as Dates Observed as a Child, Memorable Dates Seen in the Movies or on Television, Memorable Dates Read about in Novels or Stories, Interesting Dates Friends Have Described, and Memories of Dates Personally Experienced. To carry the metaphor further, in the subfile Memories of Dates Personally Experienced, there are specific memories or further subfiles of memorable dates, including MY FIRST DATE, MY MOST BIZARRE DATE, or MY MOST RECENT DATE. Research indicates that people tend to remember such specific memorable occasions rather than repetitious activities or routines, which are most often lodged in more general memory structures. The primary memory structure, or subdirectory, DATING might also contain the subfiles Good Dates, Bad Dates, Double-Dates, and so on, in which people tend to remember the most memorable examples and blend together or aggregate others into a general category for dating.

This process of aggregation is exemplified by the memory structures of those who are highly experienced at a specific task or skill, such as a sport. Because the experience is repetitive, its script has become automatic to some degree; consequently, specific occasions or instances may be more difficult to recall (Berger, 1993). In a dating memory structure, unless an unusual incident occurs, a person will not necessarily recall, say, small talk during a dinner date about what went on at work that day. The memory of the experience becomes aggregated, or clustered, in a broader Dating subfile—a process comparable to file compression in a computer.

Continuing in the computer metaphor, Dating subfiles (or scenes) include further subfiles (or scripts) for the routines of each of the recalled scenes. A first-date script, for example, is assimilated or accommodated into later first-date subfiles. Although different types of dates have different scripts consisting of underlying subscenes and subroutines, some scripts, such as the greeting ritual, are common to all dating scenes. These scripts, considered prototypical or the best example of the appropriate behavior, are adapted and replicated across all the subfiles in the DATING subdirectory. These prototypical scripts can then be accessed in order to provide step-by-step instructions for each new experience.

Honeycutt (1993) provided an example of a specific dating memory structure that may be accessed by recalling a first date at a movie. The memory structure will consist of a movie-date script (or subfile), which includes actions (or further subfiles) of waiting in line, ticket purchasing, buying refreshments, locating seats, watching the movie, and leaving the theater. If the couple decides to get something to eat after the movie, a restaurant-date subfile, containing further subfiles of waiting for a table, ordering the meal, small talk during dinner, paying the bill, and leaving the restaurant can then be accessed. Subfiles of both the theater and restaurant scenes will subsequently be replicated and adapted to compose the updated first-date dating memory structures. Memories of each physical setting can then be used (similar to computer icons) to access memories that will provide a frame of reference and create expectations for subsequent first dates.

Of course, the human mind is not a mass of networked computer chips and the analogy to computer processing breaks down at some point. In fact, the way in which people process information is even more complex than what occurs inside the most sophisticated computer. Thus, cognitive psychologists have developed a rubric of terms to specify the computer-like components of human cognition, based on what has been learned in tightly controlled experiments. The following sections provide definitions for the knowledge-structure terminology employed in the computer metaphor and review what researchers have learned about the influence of memory on the development of relationships. However, first the theoretical foundation that provides the basis for this discussion—constructivism—is discussed.

CONSTRUCTIVISM

Constructivism posits that each individual determines his or her reality and subsequently frames his or her social (and thus communicative) actions based on cognitive schemes. Whether these schemes are highly developed or rather simplistic is determined by how cognitively complex an individual is in a particular area. Cognitive complexity relates to the number, interrelationships, complexity, and variety of the schemes used when constructing messages. Cognitive complexity is an information-processing variable that indicates an individual's increased capacity to process information about personal relationships in a more highly adaptive way. In relationship to interpersonal skills, O'Keefe and Delia (1979) stated "in construing other persons, perceivers use a characteristic set of constructs relevant to interpersonal judgments" (p. 231). Martin (1991) emphasized the importance of distinguishing between cognitive complexity that relates to an understanding of individuals and the ability to conceptualize about a relationship. He wrote, "it is conceivable that an individual's 'relational cognition complexity' may be largely unrelated to the complexity of that same individual's understanding of other persons" (p. 468).

Burelson and Denton (1997) suggested that individuals demonstrating cognitive complexity in a particular area could be called experts (as opposed to novices; see later in this chapter for a discussion of novices and experts, and see chap. 7 for additional examples). He stated that the *expert* displays more differentiated, abstract, and integrative schemes. The *novice* has schemes that are global, undifferentiated, concrete, and diffuse. Martin suggested that those who display greater structural complexity in the relational domain are better able to finely tune their responses to experiences because of an increased ability to discriminate and differentiate. He reinforced the idea of a structural component when discussing this as a difference in an individual's "capacity" (p. 468) to respond to interpersonal experiences.

Wilson (1994) concurred with this view of more relationally complex individuals when he suggested that those who are better able to differentiate can make more appropriate responses to stimuli in the environment than those who display less differentiation. He wrote that "persons high in interpersonal construct differentiation spontaneously utilize a larger number of dimensions of judgment about people than do their less differentiated counterparts" (p. 7). He suggested that highly differentiated individuals have relational rules that are easily accessed, whereas less-differentiated individuals may have the same rules but the rules are only more difficult to access. He discovered that more highly differentiated people are able to attribute more supporting goals to target individuals who neglected to fulfill an obligation than those who displayed less differentiation.

Burleson and Denton (1997) cautioned, however, that it is important to recognize that factors other than relational cognitive complexity may influence behavior. They suggested that it is problematic to assume that responses to interpersonal situations are a result of cognitive complexity only, rather than being influenced by lack of motivation or the desire to communicate in a more simplistic or negative manner. They cited as examples studies that purported to demonstrate that distressed couples evidenced less constructive communication when problem solving than did nondistressed couples, and posited that other factors may come into play when individuals who are unhappy with their relationships are asked to solve problems.

Thus, constructivism and its related concept, cognitive complexity, appear to play a formidable role in interpersonal relationships. More cognitively complex individuals appear to have a greater repertoire of responses, which are more adaptive and differentiated. However, it is important to recognize that other factors, such as lack of motivation or deliberate attempts to obfuscate or to provide dysfunctional responses, can also significantly impact communication in relationships. However, even dysfunctional responses represent a type of schemata, developed, filtered, and refined through experiences.

SCHEMATA

The term *schemata* is frequently used in a global sense to indicate structures of memory or knowledge. Schemata are categorized according to the function and content of scenes, scripts, and prototypes. Andersen (1993) defined schemata as knowledge structures that stem from prior experience and organize the processing of information. Schemata also guide behavior in the form of expectations.

Schemata represent the mental organization of information— the storage of language and experience in memory. Each individual schema is a language-based grouping of ideas, such as shopping for groceries, preparing dinner, and cleaning the kitchen, in which the groupings reflect some commonality or similarity in the primary theme within a broader schema, such as "Routine responsibilities in the home." A schema may also consist of a series of ideas unexpectedly related to the single primary theme they have in common. The home responsibilities listed here, for example, may be interpreted as extremely pleasurable when making up a primary theme of "Quality time between two friends with a mutual interest in gourmet cooking."

Cognitive researchers point out that schemata are used to organize the processing of future tasks (Scott, Fuhrman, & Wyer, 1991). Andersen (1993) expanded the definition of schemata, indicating that schemata create expectations, anticipatory assumptions, and contingency rules to guide future behavior. In short, schemata is a broad term for knowledge structures—organized groupings of information in memory that summarize past experience and guide future behavior.

Relational Schemata

The study of social cognition focuses on schemata that store information about relationships and social interaction. The term *relational schemata* refers to units of organized information stored in memory, which act as repositories for fundamental beliefs and expectations regarding the development of relationships. Relational schemata provide the sources of people's most fundamental beliefs about the characteristics of relationships. People's beliefs about how relationships develop are derived from direct experience gained by participating in relationships or from indirect experience gained vicariously by watching others or reading about the experiences of others (Fig. 2.1).

FIG. 2.1   Relationship schemata are formed by what people read.

Fletcher and Fitness (1993) agreed that memories, beliefs, thoughts, expectations, and attributions reside in knowledge structures and remarked that people typically develop relatively elaborate theories, beliefs, and expectations about relationships. An example of an elaborated schema for marriage is presented in Box 2.1, in which a 27-year-old, engaged female student reports on her expectations for marriage and how these expectations were formed. She indicates that her expectations may be altered during the daily realities of married life. She mentions nine themes as part of her marriage schema. Each of the themes that the student mentions in her schema may be considered a schema subfile in the broader marriage schema file. For example, part of her religion subschema includes a belief in God and attending church. The young woman indicates that her schema for commitment includes subschemata, such as talking about problems and seeking marital counseling, if necessary, before splitting up. All of the subschemata reflect her values for marriage.

To summarize, schemata influence the search for information and its retrieval. Relational schemata, which contain information based on experience, are specific schemata for behavior in relationships (Scott et al., 1991). Relational schemata evolve as more information is gathered about the relationship between an individual and partner. Schemata can provide a basis for evaluating experiences, structuring information, anticipating the future, and setting goals or intentions for the relationship (Miell, 1987).

Box 2.1   Sample Marriage Schema of an Engaged Female Student

We as individuals all have some kinds of expectations, whether they are from work, a dating partner, marriage partner, or children. Unfortunately, some of us have expectations that others are incapable of fulfilling. I have expectations of my upcoming marriage and partner, including:

Finances.   There will be one checking account and savings account, which will include both of our names. In order to keep the records straight, I will have the only checkbook. I will be responsible for paying bills and for giving Kyle money or checks when needed.

Careers.   Kyle will continue to work and be the main provider during the marriage. I will work as a teacher and will be free to have designated weekends, holidays, and summers off. I will also continue to work during pregnancy, but will take off from work the appropriate amount of time allowed. The decision not to work will be mine alone, if financial matters allow it.

Children.   We agree to wait for at least two years or until we are mentally and financially ready for a baby. We also agree to have no more than two children. The sex of the children has no bearing, as long as they are healthy. Child rearing and responsibilities will be shared as much as possible.

Recreation.   We both agree that recreation is important. Therefore, we will try to set aside as many weekends as possible to devote to each other. We will also remember that we as individuals need time to ourselves. This time can be spent alone or in the company of friends.

Religion.   This subject has not yet been decided by either of us. I am Baptist and Kyle is a Catholic. Therefore, we will have to choose the religion in which our belief is the strongest and in which we will raise our children. We both agree that the main point is that a person believes in God and attends a church.

Housekeeping.   I will be responsible for the care of the inside of the house, while Kyle is responsible for the outside. Kyle will pick up his personal belongings (clothes, shoes, etc.) and put them in their proper place. I will be responsible for the meals during the week. Kyle likes to cook, so he will have the weekends to

	do so. The cleanup of the meals and table will be the responsibility of both.
In-Laws.	We will not live with either set of parents, unless there is no alternative. They can visit, within reason, anytime. We agree not to let them interfere or control our relationship. It is our marriage during good and bad times. We also agree to spend Thanksgiving and Christmas Day with my mother. We will on occasion go to New Orleans to spend one of these holidays with my father. We will go to Kyle's parents' house that afternoon and/or night during the time of the two holidays.
Commitment/ Faithfulness.	I promise to be faithful throughout the entire marriage and expect the same from him, because we love and have chosen each as a partner before God. If one partner does break this promise, we will try to find out what the problem is and correct it. After considerable trying, if the problem is not correctable, we will separate and then take legal steps for a divorce. If we have other marital problems and both wish for the marriage to continue, we agree to seek professional counseling.
Communication.	A marriage cannot last if partners cannot confide in one another. Therefore, I feel that it is very important to be able to communicate and be open about our feelings with each other. A spouse should be not only a partner, but a best friend as well.

I know that life or marriage can't and doesn't follow a set of rules or guidelines. I know that my expectations will be altered to a certain degree during the "everyday" of life. I can't say that one person or thing has helped me form these expectations. I have seen and learned a lot from my parents, friends, and school. Even though I have come to understand what's wrong and what's right through my experiences, that doesn't mean I will have the perfect marriage. Marriage is something I just have to try and then hope for the best.

SCENES

Scenes are memory structures often linked with information about a specific physical setting. Scenes can also refer to an entire complex episode: the setting, activities, and people involved. Schank (1982) defined a scene as a general description of a setting and activities in pursuit of a goal relevant to that setting. Scenes also may contain thought patterns of dialogue and action (or scripts) based on experiences that have occurred in that particular environment. They reflect imagery about a specific situation and provide a physical setting that serves as the basis for the reconstruction of memory. If an individual can remember the setting in which an event occurred (the scene), it is then easier to access specific dialogue and actions (the script).

Schank (1982) termed an ordered array of related scenes a *memory organization packet*. Collections of such memory structures constitute *metamemory organization packets*. Schank indicated that memory organization packets occur at the physical, societal, and personal levels. Physical scenes represent mental or visual images of particular surroundings at a specific time. A societal scene reflects a relationship between individuals who are pursuing a common goal at the same time, with a communication link between them. The actions and the interaction between the participants define the scene (Schank, 1982).

An example of one contemporary societal scene is the increasing use of the Internet to communicate with others having similar interests, described in chapters 1 and 10. For example, there are groups dealing with loneliness, finding a relationship partner, coping with divorce, and gender issues. Such Internet groups allow people to retain their individual identities and conceal their appearance. For those who regularly used this type of web-based venue for relationships, memory structures are created that order the various scenes contained therein.

Personal scenes are idiosyncratic and may be thought of in terms of repetitive private goals or strategies. For example, a dating memory structure may reflect an encounter at a specific movie theater (physical scene) or a disclosure in the environment of a restaurant (societal scene) that creates greater intimacy in an escalating relationship (personal scene).

Schank's physical scene is similar to the notion of a scene in the theatrical metaphors of Burke (1962). Burke's five-part model of communication (agent, act, scene, agency, and purpose) parallels the five key elements of journalism (who, what, where, when, and how). Schank's (1982) reference to societal scenes is analogous to Burke's notion of act (what transpired),whereas the personal scene is reflected in the notion of purpose (why something occurred). The physical scene corresponds to Burke's notion of scene (the context in which an action occurs). Boxes 2.2 and 2.3 demonstrate how these elements may be arrayed in terms of the types of questions people could ask themselves, either in general or in reference to an escalating romantic relationship.

SCRIPTS

A script comprises a set of sequential step-by-step instructions for accomplishing a specific task. The term *script* refers to the sequencing and categorization of behavior across time to accomplish a goal (Abelson, 1981; Bower, Black, & Turner, 1979; Schank & Abelson, 1977). Scripts are derived from interactions in one's family and culture and provide instructions for behavior in specific situations (Fiske & Taylor, 1984). Scripts are mindless in that they are well learned

---

Box 2.2   Fundamental Questions That Process Behavior in Scenes

Physical scene.   What physically happened? Where did it happen?

Societal scene.   What societal conventions or norms were used? What was
                     said? What effect did the behavior have on the individual's so-
                     cial position?

Box 2.3   Questions That Process Behavior in Developing Relationships

Physical scene.   What physically happened the first time my partner said,
                     "I love you"? Where were we?

Societal scene.   What was said? How was love communicated nonverbally?

---

and the behavior is somewhat habitual. People have innumerable scripts for relationship interactions, such as what to say when meeting a stranger, introducing a friend, requesting a favor, asking for a date, saying goodbye, making sexual
overtures, or offering an apology. Such scripts reflect social behaviors learned
through personal experience, observation of family and peers, and accessing information from the Internet and the media, including movies, music, and television shows.

Honeycutt (1996) investigated the popularity of reading various magazines
in order to learn about relationships. Respondents were asked to list any mag-
azine they read for information on romantic relationships. Fashion magazines
were the most popular (73%), followed at a dramatic distance by health magazines (13%) and news magazines (5%). Some of the fashion magazines were
Voque, Elle, Cosmopolitan, Mademoiselle, Glamour, Brides, Young Ms., and
Maxim. When asked to rank the sources of relational information from an extensive list, respondents listed friends, parents, siblings, magazines, and movies as the top five.

Scripts act as a type of automatic pilot and provide guidelines on how to act
when one encounters new situations. To access a script from memory, an individual first thinks of a general category of action (such as overcoming a crisis in a
relationship) and then recalls a scene. Once a scene is envisioned, the actions,
behaviors, or dialogue that occurred in that scene can be recalled. Scenes can
thus be considered as entryways to scripts and other memory structures. Recalling a specific scene allows the temporal ordering, or time sequencing, of specific scripted behaviors and actions to occur. Scenes, then, point to ordered and
sequential (scripted) activities.

As step-by-step instructions for any given behavior, scripts make it possible to plan and execute everyday activities and aid in the recognition of the familiar activities of others (Bower et al. 1979). For example, scripts provide instructions for greeting grandparents or significant others, or for what to say during a job interview or when arriving at a party. Alternatively, consider the various jokes people tell about opening lines or the ritual of meeting someone for the first time; these reflect cultural scripts of inept ways of saying hello or initiating interaction. Because scripts are sequential, they frequently reflect a logical order. Scripts are stereotypic representations of behavioral actions and reflect approaches acceptable in a given culture or subculture. A customary first-date script, for example, does not allow a young man to ask for a good-night kiss until he has come to know his date reasonably well.

Scripts range in specificity from metascripts that organize and specify what may be appropriate in other scripts to specific expectations in a given context. For example, a person may have the following script for attending a lecture: (a) entering the room, (b) finding a seat, (c) sitting down, (d) taking out a notebook, (e) listening to the speaker, (f) taking notes, (g) checking the time, (h) giving the pseudo-appearance of listening, and (i) leaving (Bower et al., 1979). Subscripts for entering the room (such as looking for friends, entering with a friend, or what to do when arriving late) may also exist. Scripts may also be situated in a variety of scenes. The scene of the lecture may be recalled as a function of time, of the specific physical environment, the size of the audience, or the specific lecture topic.

Mindlessness Versus Mindfulness

In many ways, ongoing relationships may be thought of as more-or-less scripted routines that, despite their apparent novelty, follow predictable patterns. Scripts allow people to be mindless. Mindlessness refers to situations in which individuals consider the available information rigidly with preconceptions, incompletely, and thoughtlessly.

Think of inane pick-up lines that men use on women. They use them over and over in the face of rejection and failure. Yet they keep using them because they are so ingrained in their language practices. They use them without thinking. Burgoon and Langer (1995) discussed how routine language encourages mindlessness, and how mindlessness also causes certain kinds of language use. Mindlessness entails limited information processing and the failure to process new information (Langer, 1989). Conversely, when mindful, individuals draw distinctions and create categories because they are sensitive to changes in context and are aware of creating new perspectives. People have expectations from each of the following roles: a pickup, committed dating partner, fiancée, and spouse. The script that is accessed to process what comes to mind for these roles is affected by a number of factors that precipitate mindlessness.

The first factor is certainty. Research by Langer (1989) shows how certainty results in mindlessness. Strong beliefs minimize the need to reflect on new or even contradictory information. For example, nice guys often complain that they are not noticed by women at bars where pickups are made. If the mindless script for being picked up includes that the man is aggressive, then nice guys are seen as unattractive or passive. Planalp and Honeycutt (1985) described situations in which uncertainty increases in long-term relationships. For example, a change in one's partner's personality, betraying confidences, or leaving with no explanation may increase uncertainty about what motivates the partner. For example, saying "I love you" during the development of romance may show one's partner that one really feels close intimacy, but over time saying this loses its uncertainty-reduction value. Consider the reaction to the following. A major expectation in intimate relationships is fidelity. In fact, the violation of this expectation may lead to the rapid termination of the relationship (Knapp & Vangelisti, 1996). Suppose a spouse tells his or her partner at the end of the day, "I was faithful to you today." Instead of the statement reducing uncertainty, it momentarily increases uncertainty because the other partner may question what heretofore was taken for granted—fidelity. The partner may immediately wonder, "Well, I assumed you were faithful, but now I wonder if you are implying that there were other times that you weren't faithful." At this moment, the partner is immediately mindful and desperately wants more information to further reduce uncertainty.

A second cause of mindlessness is dichotomization (Burgoon & Langer, 1995). In order to take action, clear choices are made. The need for action is based on well-defined alternatives that lead people to dichotomize. Antonyms such as attractive/unattractive, caring/uncaring, sensitive/insensitive, secure/insecure, and quiet/loud fail to note the nuances and gradations within these categories. Underlying ambiguities are conveniently ignored. "Love me or leave me" is a common demand that ignores the variety of factors affecting commitment.

A third cause of mindlessness is habitual responding. One can engage in repeated behavior in which each repetition is considered new by noticing different aspects of the situation, such as choosing a given response. Yet, ritualism in relationships is important in sustaining and maintaining the relationship, despite the mindless repetition. It is ritual to give an anniversary card on the date of one's anniversary. An example of violating a ritual would be for someone to forget to give the card.

A fourth cause of mindlessness is premature cognitive commitment (Chanowitz & Langer, 1981). When people are presented with information that they have no motivation to question, they cling to their initial impressions. Later, if additional or new information is supplied, people often do not reconsider the initial information in terms of the new information and change their impressions. For example, if people are shown a tape of a couple telling jokes about each other and told that they are happily married, then the jokes are seen as kidding around. Later, the serious moments tend to be ignored. If people are shown the same tape and told that the couple is unhappily married and having some problems in their relationship, then the jokes are seen as teasing, mockery, or put-downs. The serious moments are more easily recalled. This recall represents a confirmatory bias that is mindless because of the premature cognitive commitment that the couple is either happy or unhappy.

The rigid use of schemata for interpreting new information reflects mindlessness. People do this in the interests of cognitive efficiency because to process all the new information available would be too time consuming and mentally draining. People have language labels to describe others who are mindful, reflecting a range from positive to negative feelings (i.e., creative, imaginative, absorbed, analretentive).

According to Langer (1978), people are more mindful in five situations: when there are no scripts for a novel situation, when engaging in scripted behavior requires an effort because the new situation requires more behavior than was required by the original script, when enacting the scripted behavior is interrupted by external factors that disrupt its completion, when enacting the script results in a negative or positive consequence that is discrepant from the consequences of prior enactments of the same behavior, and finally, mindfulness is likely when the situation allows for sufficient involvement. Hence, mindlessness is more common when situations are familiar and uninvolving, when little effort is required, when behaviors are not interrupted, and when the consequences are similar to previous ones. Much of people's cognition about relationships is based on mindless scripts that are derived from communicating with significant others, from watching others, from the media (e.g., movies, books, and magazines), and, last but not least, from experience, even if the experience has been bad.

The following sections review the research on scripts that are accessed during various phases of a relationship. These scripts include initial interaction scripts, scripts for dating, sexual scripts, interactive scripts, memorable messages, and relational rules.

Initial Interaction Scripts

Although there is considerable research on script generation, there is much less information about the functions of scripts in terms of the conduct of personal relationships. According to Ginsberg (1988), scripts for particular scenes of interaction can be expected to reduce the effort of interaction because they function as a form of mental automatic pilot. Once a behavior is scripted and then called up, the individual proceeds automatically until a barrier to the script is encountered. Scripts also coordinate action and reduce the necessity of paying attention to the small details that tend to clutter everyday interaction.

Scripts appear to increase people's security in unfamiliar social situations by providing appropriate initial responses available for recall (Stafford & Daly, 1984). And although social situations vary in their degree of unfamiliarity, people encounter communication opportunities every day in which they are thankful that their minds can provide some tacit guidance. For example, Kellermann, Broetzmann, Lim, and Kitao (1989) analyzed how the topics people use in initial interactions with strangers are fairly common and accompanied by an appropriate order for discussion. The analysis revealed a progression of topics for initial encounters that is relatively consistent and can be adapted to situational needs. They found that initial interaction scripts contain verbal behaviors for obtaining, discussing, and evaluating facts; for providing explanations; and for discussing goals. On the other hand, it appears that when conversationalists know one another, the structure of the interaction is more flexible, allowing a greater flexibility in the ordering of topics, as long as the norms of interaction are followed. Such norms for conversations encourage turn taking, topic continuation, and topic-transition relevance (Goodwin, 1981) and seem to be associated with more generalized interaction scripts. It is interesting to note that the violations of these norms are tolerated more when individuals have specialized knowledge of each other or have special relationship rules for interaction, so that particular subjects may be pursued or avoided. As people come to know their partners, they understand what to say and what to avoid saying, as well as developing their own codes for communication.

One particular relationship script that has been researched involves statements used when meeting someone for the first time. Douglas (1984) examined initial interaction scripts that are reflected in language (greetings), topics (such as current events), and general conversational behavior (such as compliments). Stafford and Daly (1984) found that although participants' reports of specific conversations are sometimes inaccurate, their recall of recurrent conversations is generally on target. For example, a college student whose mother regularly asks her how she is doing in her course work will recall that she consistently responds, "Plugging away," in order to avoid giving a detailed account of her activities. And when interactions are purposeful, Stafford and Daly found that some participants are able to articulate their purpose consciously. For example, a woman interested in the possibility of a particular relationship may say, "I told him about my interest in classical music in order to see if we shared any common interests." However, many if not most simple interactions are found to be relatively automatic and performed without much strategic planning or forethought (Kellermann, 1992). For instance, when someone asks "What's up?" the usual reply is usually "Oh, not much" or the like, as opposed to "The sky, I suppose" or "Everything that's not down." It is as if people have adopted a series of little rituals that allow them to both process and produce communication without a second thought. And the same may hold true for even more extensive and complex interaction routines.

Scripts for Dating

People often think that the process of securing a date with someone is reason-ably conscious and uniquely suited to a particular situation. However, a variety of studies suggest that there may be a good deal less strategizing going on than one might expect.

For example, four studies were conducted by Pryor and Merluzzi (1985) to determine male and female scripts for Getting a Date and The First Date. In the first study, 30 male and 21 female undergraduate students were asked to gener-ate a list of 20 actions that typically occur when a man asks a woman for a date and when they go on a first date. The results of the study reveal that the partici-pants agreed on the contents and meaning of the Getting a Date and The First Date scripts. Typical actions reported in the Getting a Date script included the man observing the woman, eye contact and staring between them, smiling, other behaviors signaling interest, and information seeking about one another through friends. Other actions included potential partners manipulating events to create an accidental meeting or being introduced by a friend, the man initiat-ing conversation, the couple exploring interests through conversation to find compatibility, and the man asking woman for her phone number and then phoning her for a date. Yet the dating behaviors described in the study clearly implied a willingness on the part of the woman to be asked out. Of course, these actions could be perceived as negative if the woman did not desire them, but then how would an initiator know this before the fact? It is important to note that a number of the actions associated with male initiative in asking for a date could be perceived as a Sexual Harassment script.

In Pryor and Merluzzi's (1985) study of typical scripts for a first date, the re-ports of sequences of behavior were consistent, implying cultural consensus on expected, or typical, behaviors. The study attributed the following se-quence to the cultural consensus of a typical first date: the man goes to the woman's residence, the woman greets him, the man meets her family or room-mates, and they engage in small talk and decide where to go. If they decide, for example, to go to a movie, the typical script includes waiting in line, buying re-freshments, and getting something to eat after the movie. The man then takes the woman home and walks her to her door. The couple summarizes the eve-ning at the end of the date. The man may ask to call again; the woman may hope he asks to call again; they kiss, say good night, and thank each other for the evening; and the man departs. The stunning regularity of such verbal re-ports suggests that a script may be operating at a nonconscious level in most, if not all, of the first dates people experience.

Note that these scripts occur in context and reflect the customs and values of both the society and subculture in which they occur. There can be significant differences in the scripts for dating and courtship in urban, small-town, and ru-ral cultures. Differences, for example, would be observed between the dating customs in New Orleans and those of a village in France or in rural Malaysia. Subculture and socioeconomic status also influence scripts. There could be variations in the dating scripts for Hispanic, African-American, Asian, Native American, or white couples on a first date, even though they all lived in the same city. Yet most often the same physical, societal, and personal scenes are re-called and envisioned in order to access a variety of scripts.

Sequences of Dating Behavior.   The second study by Pryor and Merluzzi (1985) examined the underlying sequence of behaviors in the Getting a Date and The First Date scripts. The study participants were distinguished on the basis of their dating expertise. *Dating experts* were defined as those who re-ported having dated six or more different people in the past year. *Novices* were considered those having dated three or fewer different people in the past year. This criterion identified only a small number of women as experts. Conse-quently, the sample of participants with dating expertise was restricted to a group of 58 men. The participants were asked to create a sequential order for a stack of shuffled index cards, each card describing a typical example of behav-ior that occurs when asking for a date or going out on a first date. The behav-iors were selected from the lists of the 20 actions that typically occur when a male asks a female for a date and when going on a first date that were gener-ated in Pryor and Merluzzi's first study. The participants were instructed to read through the entire set of cards and arrange them into a logical order of events that might typically occur.

The results demonstrated that men with more dating experience were able to create logical sequences of dating behaviors with the cards more rapidly, compared to men who had little dating experience. Apparently, the dating ex-perts used their cognitive representations to create order from a random se-quence of events. The cohesion of their memory structures allowed them to recognize a sequence of random events rapidly and to categorize them into a so-cially acceptable logical order.

The third study by Pryor and Merluzzi (1985), was designed to distinguish necessary and typical behaviors that accompany dating scripts. They cited the work of Graesser, Gordon, and Sawyer (1979), who reported that behaviors in a script differ significantly in terms of how necessary or typical the various actions are. Some behaviors in a script are necessary in order for the script to continue. For example, ordering food is necessary for a restaurant script to be invoked. On the other hand, some behaviors may be quite typical in a script but not neces-sary. Ordering coffee at the end of a meal is typical, although not necessary for the script to proceed. Similarly, Abelson (1981) discussed that individuals peri-odically report that an action in a script is typical on seeing it, even though it is not frequently mentioned in a free recall. Examples of the behavior may be eas-ier to recall and available in memory due to a recognition of the activity.

Graesser et al. (1979) reported that when participants perceive actions as highly necessary, they are taken for granted and assumed to be inferred in scripts, even when not actually present.

Pryor and Merluzzi (1985) surveyed 30 men and 20 women, who were asked to rate how typical a given behavior was from the Getting a Date and The First Date scripts. Participants also reported how necessary or unnecessary the behavior was for the performance of other behaviors in the script. Most of the script components were considered more typical than necessary. In addition, behaviors reported as more frequent in the first study were described as more necessary in the third study. For example, smiling was mentioned by 20% of participants when they were freely generating lists of behaviors. Yet when a different group of individuals was asked to rate the typicality of smiling, they rated it as just as typical as other behaviors that actually had been mentioned more frequently in the script generation task. Actions considered as necessary in the Getting a Date script included the initial greeting by the woman, the man's initiation of conversation, and the man's initiation of requesting a date.

Sequence-Grouping in Dating Behavior. The fourth study by Pryor and Merluzzi (1985) revealed patterns that appear to indicate an underlying grouping of sequences in scripts. Students were asked to read two stories that corresponded to each script; the stories contained sentences that represented each sequence of the reported scripted behaviors. Participants were told that the story could be interpreted as consisting of several natural sections, or themes. They were asked to identify the distinct sections of the story by placing a slash mark, indicating a boundary, wherever they recognized a shift in theme. Boxes 2.4 and 2.5 contain the fictional stories the researchers used as scripts. The frequencies of slash marks or boundary notations identified by the participants are shown in parentheses.

Pryor and Merluzzi indicated that the participants were generally consistent in their agreement on the placement of boundary marks. The typical placement of the boundaries in the text demonstrated that the Getting a Date script had four basic sequence groupings or themes: (a) noticing each other, (b) trying to meet each other, (c) getting to know each other, and (d) making a date. The First Date script yielded five basic sequence groupings or themes: (a) meeting the date, (b) warm-up conversation, (c) main-event activity (such as going to a movie), (d) post-main-event activity (such as going to a restaurant), and (e) bringing the date to a close. Notably, each of these sequence groupings contains subgoals that are part of the hierarchical organization of the scripts.

The results of the story-reading procedure revealed that participants frequently agreed in their interpretation of actions. There was also a consensus on the grouping of sequences together according to themes. This agreement reflects culturally influenced schemata, implying that there are agreed-on scripts

within a society. The scripts spell out social behaviors, such as the unspoken rules that apply when asking for a date or the expected step-by-step routines of a first date. The influence of culture is apparent when researchers consider what the various schemata would be in such differing societies as Seattle, Bangkok, and Copenhagen. In addition, customs change rapidly in societies linked by media, perhaps as rapidly as every decade. For example, the script for answering the telephone has typically been for the person being called to say, "Hello," and wait for the caller to initiate the conversation. Now, with Caller ID, it is common for the person being called to initiate the conversations by saying, for example, "Hello, Jim. How are you doing today?"

Sexual Scripts

For some individuals, a part of their dating script may include expectations of sexual contact. Sexual scripts refer to the cultural norms for sexual relations (Gagnon & Simon, 1973), and may include such stereotypes as that men initiate sexual relations, and that these activities should occur in private. Yet, as Sprecher and McKinney (1994) indicated, the idea of sexual scripts implies that little sexual involvement is truly spontaneous, even though couples develop their own couple-specific scripts. At the broader cultural level, consider the scenario of a person being invited by a date to his or her apartment for some wine and music. This scenario may be intended as a prelude to making love.

Traditionally, formal courtship scripts reflected male prerogatives for sexual initiatives. Baumeister (2000) reviewed studies on the human sex drive. It is functional for women to deny sex to men because of evolutionary and biological processes; women cannot have as many offspring as men, and they are presumably more selective about their sex partners. When a couple begins having sex, it is mainly because the woman has changed her decision from no to yes. Research by Ard (1977) revealed that even in marriage husbands reported a significant gap between the amount of sex they wanted and how much they had. The wives' answers indicated that they felt less discrepancy between how often they wanted and how often they had sex.

A cross-cultural review of research on the human sex drive reveals that there is a standard script for sex between first-time partners that depends on the woman signaling sexual interest. Baumeister (2000) discussed how in nearly all known human societies, as well as in nonhuman primate societies, women constitute the restraining force on sex to the extent that they refuse offers or chances for sexual activity. Buss and Schmitt (1993) documented that in heterosexual attraction, men are typically ready for sex long before women are. Men are more willing to have sex with someone they have just met (e.g., Herold & Mewhinney, 1993).

Men also fall in love faster than women and hence are likely to feel loving affection and the accompanying sexual desire at an earlier point in the relationship (e.g., Baumeister, Wotman, & Stillwell, 1993; Hill, Rubin, & Peplau,

1976; Huston, Surra, Fitzgerald, & Cate, 1981). Evidence from direct communication was provided by Clark and Hatfield (1989). Men and women were approached by an opposite-gender research confederate who invited the participant to have sex that same evening. All the women refused this invitation, whereas most of the men accepted. By the same token, Mercern and Kohn (1979) found that both men and women rated all the communication strategies for avoiding sex as more typical of women than men, whereas all communication overtures for initiating and obtaining sex were rated as more typical of men than women. Clearly, the participants associated sex with masculinity and refusing sex with femininity.

Because sexual scripts embody socially appointed rituals and rules of social appropriateness, they are tricky to negotiate. Pepper and Weiss (1987) defined *proceptivity* as female behavior intended to initiate or maintain a sexual interaction, often through nonverbal cues. For example, a woman may give nonverbal signals or cues hoping that her potential partner will take the hint and assume the initiative. In the next phase of the interaction, the initiative passes to the man as he starts to stage direct their interaction toward intercourse. If the man does not respond to her overtures, the woman eventually ceases signaling. This indirect behavior on the part of the woman is the result of cultural taboos against too much female initiation of sexual scripts.

Sexual scripts exist in order to establish emotional and sexual rapport and to save face when one is confronted with unreciprocated desires or emotional needs. Unfortunately, a conflict arises when one person's dating script includes an expectation of intercourse and the other's does not. Such a miscommunication can result in the anguish of acquaintance or date rape. Although most cases of acquaintance rape do, indeed, constitute crimes of violence predicated on the exercise of power rooted in the psychopathology of lawlessness and disrespect, some cases appear to be grounded in the inappropriate use of cognitive scripts, leading to the misinterpretation of ambiguous behavioral cues. Box 2.6 reflects just such a scenario, in which a student shared her friend's experience in which different interpretations of behavioral cues lead to serious consequences.

Cultural Scripts and Performances for Sex

Both weddings and pornography are cultural performances. Each is filled with scripts that serve to illustrate what society terms legitimate and illegitimate sexual initiatives. Bell (1999) noted how cultural performances of sex, "both weddings and pornography depend on the efficacious enactment of conventions and scripts, performance consciousness of the performers, deliberate manipulation of time and space, and the imposition of frames of belief and play" (p. 175). Both hold consent and sexual intercourse as their *sine qua non*. Because they are as mirror doubles, not opposites, they are mutually dependent. Weddings and pornography hold similar constructions of culture, performance, and sex for

Box 2.6 How Miscommunication Can Result in Date Rape

Two of my friends went on a date in high school that turned out to be a tragedy as they misinterpreted certain behavioral cues. He had expectations of sexual intercourse in his dating script and she didn't.

Melissa and I grew up together. We became best friends in kindergarten and attended the same schools throughout high school. Toby and I met through our parents, who were good friends. He was the type of guy who would take me out when I needed a date. One night I introduced the two of them, thinking they would be a great match. That night at the party they hit it off. The next day, Melissa called, excited, saying that she had the best time last night talking and hanging out with Toby and that he had asked her out for Friday night. I later talked to Toby, who was also excited yet he tried to be calm and cool about the situation. Toby didn't talk much about their conversation the night before. All he could talk about was her body, how big her breasts were and how long her legs were.

I was actually having fun being the go-between. All week Melissa talked about what she was going to wear and asked nonstop if Toby had mentioned her. Toby on the other hand, wrestled with the question of what to do on the date. By Friday they had worn me out. I could have cared less about the date.

Friday evening Melissa called me again to ask what she should wear. "Should I go sexy or conservative?" she asked. I told her to go a little sexy, something I still regret. Saturday morning Melissa called me very early. I immediately knew something was wrong. My heart pounded as I tried to make sense of what she was saying. Her words were broken up with loud sobs as she told me about their date. She told me they went out to a movie and dinner. Melissa said that they were getting along great and that she felt really comfortable with him. She thought Toby was a complete gentleman, so she didn't worry about getting a little tipsy at dinner. Afterwards, Melissa said they parked on the levee and drank a bottle of wine. She said they continued to talk and he kissed her. By this point, Melissa was drunk and when Toby invited her back to his house she thought it was a good idea. Toby's parents were out of town, so they had the house to themselves. Melissa said things were blurry, but that she remembered telling Toby that she wanted to take a little nap. So she lay down on his bed and they made out for a while. She said that things got a little carried away, but that she knew all along that she didn't want to have intercourse. Melissa said she struggled and yelled, "NO!," but that she was too drunk and weak to do anything, so she gave in. By this point I felt guilty and really angry. When Melissa and I hung up, I called Toby to yell at him. He didn't answer the phone, so I decided to go to his house. When I saw Toby, I yelled at him for five minutes solid and I even threw a shoe at him.

After he calmed me down he told me his side of the story. Toby said that when he picked her up she was practically hanging out of her skirt. He said they had a good time during dinner and a movie afterwards. Then he said he kissed her and she didn't seem to mind his fondling her breasts. Toby told me that Melissa continued to ask, "What do you want to do now?" That's when he invited her back to his house. He said that going to his house was never in the plans and the only reason it came up was because Melissa wasn't ready to go home. When they got to his place, he offered her something to eat to sober up, but she declined. Melissa had crawled in bed to take a nap while he ate. Toby went into his room to find Melissa in his bed with only her T-shirt and panties on. He claims they started kissing and one thing led to another. He swears that he never thought that she would have sex on the first date, but that he wasn't about to turn it down. Toby did say that Melissa cried a little and said, "No," but that was after he was already in her. I asked if he felt Melissa struggle and he said that she wasn't struggling, she was just a little rough in bed.

After hearing both sides, I believe that they were both being honest. Toby acted on what he thought Melissa wanted and Melissa did not do a good job of communicating with Toby. Miscommunication and misinterpretation of behavioral cues can lead to horrible results.

their existence. If there were no legalized coupling through marriage, there would be no illegitimate coupling through pornography.

Weddings put their participants through ancient rituals to place society's stamp of approval on sex, which occurs out of view but which is often referred to as part of the ritual (e.g., consummating the marriage). In marriage, sex is the physical complement to the communication of action, "I do." Bell (1999) claimed that the centrality of sex to weddings is apparent in its universal acceptance as a cultural practice "until, of course, outsiders question its exclusivity, norms, and privileges" (p. 182). She also argued that sex is considered guilty until proven innocent. Married sex, created through consensual weddings, is the culture's sex "proven innocent," whereas pornography is the culture's "worst possible expression." Pornography carries societal condemnation. Here sex is public in the sense that it is available to be viewed by outsiders, even though the sex may not be real.

Bell (1999) concluded that weddings leave a cultural reminder that the ring must be worn in order to show fidelity, a major part of the marriage script. This reminder is always present when placing a pornographic videotape into a VCR, a reminder that the performance that is about to occur is not approved.

Interactive Scripts

Scripted routines for interaction include the opportunity for variations on the script, provided the variations are not so great as to destroy the identity of the scripted episode. Such interactive scripts may hinder rather than enhance smooth communication, particularly during episodes of conflict. Each partner's internal scripts are activated during conflict, typically echoing scripts from their families of origin. Thus, in a conflict situation, the tendency to replay old scripts in an automatic manner can be counterproductive. Hearing the internal script, rather than fully hearing the interaction in the moment, prevents partners from responding realistically to the situation at hand.

Interactive scripted routines offer a challenge to both participants. The initiator of the interaction may cue a partner by stating expectations, providing nonverbal signals, or modifying the environment in ways that provide cues. A candlelight dinner at an elegant restaurant, for example, may set the scene and cue the script for romance. Having tacitly agreed that a particular script is in the offing, there can still be violations that will not require a change in the script. For example, there is no violation if a restaurant is too chilly and the man goes to the car to get his date's sweater. Nonetheless, when an individual lacks sufficient information to understand a partner's script, misunderstanding often occurs. An example would be if a man asks a woman to see a movie with him, intending to pick up a video and watch it at her house, and she expects that they will be going to a movie theater; another example is provided in Box 2.7. Of course, either party may adopt other scripts once the misunderstanding is made clear. Sometimes, however, people remain oblivious to the problem because their scripts tell them that they know what is going on. Individuals who expect their partners to read their minds instead of expressing the script they want their partners to follow often find themselves involved in counterproductive interactive scripts. Gottman (1994) discussed how married couples often think they can read the minds of their partners by attributing emotions and feelings (generally without much accuracy) to one another while they are speaking.

To what degree do individuals negotiate interactive scripts, particularly in developing relationships? Because almost all behavior involves scripts in varying degrees, in a new relationship partners often compare scripts and expectations for every interaction. Who does the cooking, for example, and who does

---

Box 2.7   The Effect of Expectations on Interactive Scripts

A woman, stylishly dressed, expecting to be taken out for a gourmet meal, waits in her living room to be picked up for a first date with a business associate. Her date greets her at the door in cutoffs, with a carry-out pizza and a six-pack. The woman's script has been unexpectedly and negatively violated. In order to determine the script, she could have asked her date how formal the evening was going to be. In order to make his script clearer, he could have indicated that he planned to order take-out food. When expectations are unstated in relational encounters, miscommunication frequently results.

the clean up? What behavior is expected as an accompaniment to washing dishes? (Listening to rock and roll music? Classical music? Concentrating on getting the job done, or making small talk?) Do partners help one another, or is washing dishes considered to be women's work? Answers to such questions, and even the questions themselves, need not be voiced because people often consider nonverbal reactions as proxies for open communication.

When individuals perform an interactive activity, they often assume unconsciously that their partner in that activity knows what the script is. In reality, one of the tasks in every stage of a relationship is to determine scripts interactively. It is important that individuals communicate their expectations to one another. This interaction entails an enormous amount of negotiation and is often accomplished through trial and error as may be seen in Box 2.8.

Changes in Interactive Scripts. Changes in the status of a personal relationship are also likely to be occasioned by changes in the scripts that cue new behavior, as when a couple's relationship shifts from dating to engagement or from engagement to marriage. Ginsburg (1988) noted that alterations in the verbal content of scripts can be expected as a relationship evolves. Changes in a relationship are reflected in changes in the language used to discuss the relationship. When two people begin thinking of themselves as a couple, for example, they may begin using the first person plural pronouns (we, us) rather than the singular pronouns (I, me).

In summary, a significant problem in changing relationships is that individuals act out cognitive scripts and expectations. They may expect their partners to understand their expectations automatically, without even realizing they are doing so. In order for one's partner to get the script, it is important to

---

Box 2.8   Uncommunicated Interactive Scripts

Woman: "How did your day go?"

Man (sarcastically): "It went fine." His inner script: "It was a disaster; I don't really want to talk about it."

Woman: "You don't care about me. We don't communicate. If your day went so badly, why don't you just say it, instead of saying, 'fine.'" Her inner script: "Why doesn't he think enough of me to express his true feelings?"

The woman's script represents a desire for open communication. It may also reflect gender bias in that women seem to prefer talking about feelings and emotions more than men do.

communicate as clearly as possible. Indeed, communication difficulties are commonly cited as the primary reasons for relationships breaking up (Price & McKenry, 1988).

SUMMARY

Schemata influence how people perceive events in relationships. For example, going to college football games may mean spending quality time to one person in a relationship, whereas his or her partner may view it as a sacrifice in order to please the other. Expectations about relationship activities and the development of intimacy are based on the recall of scenes and scripts pertaining to particular activities; for instance, expectations for how one breaks bad news may be based on the recall of what was done the last time a similar situation was faced.

The use of schemata reflects mindlessness, in which people habitually do not process new information and use old stereotypes as guides to how to act in situations. People are often mindless when it comes to thinking about communication in their relationships because they do not think of alternative ways of thinking. Hence, some individuals are mindless and limited when it comes to communicating, "I love you."

People have sexual scripts derived from culture, socialization, and evolution. Cross-culturally, sexual initiatives are associated with masculinity, whereas refusing sex is associated with femininity. Women have become selective in choosing mates due to their limited ability to bear numerous children from different partners. Hence, part of the script for courtship involves women changing their desire for sex from no to yes (Baumeister, in press).

There are cultural scripts for legitimate and illegitimate sex that are seen in examining weddings and pornography. Consummation is legitimized when it is done in private. Pornography is illegitimate because it is viewed publicly by outsiders.

Scripts for initiating interaction, getting a date, what to do on a date, and communication about sexual arousal each contribute to what people typically think goes on in a relationship. Cultural relationship scripts involve jokes about opening lines, asking for a date, common behaviors on dates, proposing marriage, and communicating terms of endearment such as "I love you." Yet scripts may be personal and unique to the extent that people's experiences are not shared by others, and thus researchers always face the challenge of determining how two people can view themselves as an independent couple.

DISCUSSION QUESTIONS

2.1 Discuss the specificity of the sample marriage schema. What happens if one's expectations for marriage are rigid, versus remaining flexible?

What would you advise the woman to do concerning her expectations for her fiancée?

2.2 Discuss how men and women might interpret nonverbal communication cues differently on a first date. For example, how can a woman communicate, "No," to sexual overtures?

2.3 Discuss the differences between the male and female sex drives. What are examples of communication strategies designed to initiate sex? What are examples of strategies designed to refuse sex.

APPLICATIONS

2.1 Take a blank sheet of paper and number lines from 1 to 20. On each line, write down an important expectation that you have for what happens on a first date. Start the list with picking up your partner and end it anyway you desire. Choose a group of your friends and complete this survey with them. Compare and contrast your expectations with theirs.

2.2 Interview four people about the term "dating." What does it mean to them? Is dating now an obsolete term, given the informal sharing of time that many individuals do while studying, doing errands, and helping one another?

2.3 In the initial interaction script, what do you believe are appropriate lines of introduction other than "Hi" or "Hello"? Interview four friends and compare their responses.

3

Memorable Messages, Prototypes, and Relational Memory

This chapter reveals how people remember the content of messages from friends, parents, or other significant individuals in their lives. How this content affects the maintenance of these ongoing relationships and impacts the formation of new relationships are also discussed. Prototypes for love and changing relationships are discussed. Finally, a model of relationship memory is presented as a heuristic guide for categorizing expectations for the rise or demise of romance.

MEMORABLE MESSAGES AS A TYPE OF RELATIONSHIP SCRIPT

Research by Knapp, Stohl, and Reardon (1981) revealed that memorable messages are most often delivered by people who know the recipient intimately—parents, siblings, or significant others. The message is memorable because it is personally meaningful. For the individual receiving it, the memorable message may become scripted due to its enduring memory and theme. It is idiosyncratically directed, specifically and personally, to that individual and is highly relevant to the individual's needs at that particular time. The memorable message may be a cliché, but it provides profound insight for the recipient. Initially these messages function as triggers for recalling the enriched details of prior interactions. As they are recalled over time, however, they become internalized and schematized as part of a script. In the process, much of the specificity and detail of a particular encounter gets glossed over as the generalized script comes to the fore. A college student is told by his mother, "Blind romantic love is not enough for choosing a partner. You have to demonstrate self-interest and shop around." Given his mother's phrasing, the student recalls the lyrics of a 1960s song by Smokey Robinson, in Box 3.1. These lyrics, amplified by the memorable message from his mother, eventually become internalized into the student's dating scripts. Eventually, the sage advice "avoid blind love" is forgotten and the dictum "Date until you drop!" governs his general approach to romance.

Researchers examined the notion that recalled memorable messages offer guidance for behavior in current or future relationships (Knapp et al., 1981). The messages frequently reflect rules of what should or should not be done. Stohl (1986) considered these messages to be instructions, or *work scripts*, because they function as cognitive cues for appropriate or expected behavior. Examples of these messages are "Don't rush into relationships," "Be wary of moody people," and "If you look for the right one, the right one will find you." Memorable messages can thus shape and modify people's expectations for relationships. (Fig. 3.1)

Holladay and Coombs (1991) examined memorable messages that college students recalled from their adolescent years. The messages frequently reflected rules for dating etiquette. Typically, the recalled memorable messages were maxims that addressed topics such as criteria for selecting dating partners, managing impressions, evaluating a relationship, statements about sexual behavior, recovering from a breakup, and balancing life goals. A number of the messages reported were clichés, such as "Love is blind," "Birds of a feather flock together,"

Box 3.1   An Example of a Memorable Message

You've got to find yourself a bargain son.
Don't get sold on the very first one.
Pretty girls come a dime-a-dozen.
You got to find you one that's going to give you true lovin'.
My momma told me,
You better shop around.
Note.
Shop Around, From words and music by Berry Gordy
and William "Smokey" Robinson

FIG. 3.1   Memorable messages offer guidance for behavior and can shape expectations for relationships.

and "It takes one to know one." Yet these clichés held personal significance for the receivers. Some of the messages focused on the development of relationships, such as: "Don't date anyone you can't imagine yourself married to, because you never know how things will work out" and "Meet the family members before getting serious and see if you like them; if not, break it off." "I love you" was a memorable message that served as a major statement for evaluating the development of a relationship.

PROTOTYPES

Mental prototypes contain the images in memory of the most familiar and frequently used example of any behavior or dialogue for a given situation. Behavior or speech that is almost automatic, such as habitual patterns of speaking, gestures, and attitudes, is considered prototypical. In many ways, prototypes function similar to the default program on a computer. A prototype is characterized by a list of features common to a category. However, prototypes go beyond general categories in that they are unique to individuals and their experiences. Think of a prototype as the best example illustrating a category. For example, personal recollections of one's best date and worst date would be opposite prototypes of what typically happens on a date. Furthermore, prototypes contain individuals' unique definitions of life's fundamental elements. They may define, for example, what constitutes a mother or father, a home, or a partner. The image that flashes in an individual's mind at those times when he or she must define the sort of person she or he has encountered are the reflection of an individual's own personal prototype, based on accumulated life experiences that have been stored in memory. In memory, prototypes contain examples that are "complete with all their attributes" (Ginsburg, 1988, p. 33).

A prototype is thus a mental image of any subject that exists as an individual's own personal definition of a quintessential person, place, or concept, such as a best friend, vacation spot, or marriage relationship. The image consists of the most familiar example, rather than the most ideal. Prototypes may be formulated from observation of an individual family as well as from cultural stereotypes. For example, in thinking of the essence of Thanksgiving, what comes to mind? Turkey and all the trimmings? In this case, one's prototype may be based on the family Thanksgiving of one's childhood, as well as the cultural image of Thanksgiving reflected in the media. Of course, depending on people's childhood experiences, they might generate very different images, especially if their family structures were not typical.

Relational Prototypes

Prototypes for relationships exist as part of an individual's set of natural categories (Rosch, 1978). Researchers identified prototypes for friends and for romantic partners (Davis and Todd, 1982). These prototypes help distinguish among categories of relationships—whether, for example, individuals relate as acquaintances, casual friends, or best friend. As do other kinds of memory structures that organize information, prototypes facilitate the recall of experiences and influence expectations. Studies of the prototypes of friendship reveal that the expected characteristics of friends include intimacy, spontaneity, viability, stability, support, and enjoyment. Furthermore, these expectations provide benchmarks for distinguishing among best friends, close same-gender friends, opposite-gender friends, casual acquaintances, and former friends, as well as for distinguishing between satisfying and unsatisfying friendships (Davis and Todd, 1985).

Behaviors that are observed in romantic relationships may also be categorized on the basis of accessed prototypes. A prototype of the successful intimate relationship, for example, could be one that minimizes conflict between relational partners. By providing a kind of mental dictionary of social definitions, prototypes act as cognitive anchors by which people evaluate others and interpret behavior in changing environments. For example, if an individual's prototype for an ideal partner is characterized by helpfulness in day-to-day life, that individual would evaluate negatively a dating relationship with a partner who did not demonstrate this characteristic.

Smith (1997) examined the effect of expectations on the interpretation of behavior. Students were asked to interpret behaviors after being given distorted background information. After viewing a 2-minute video of a romantic couple interacting, some of the viewers were told that the couple was happily married, whereas others were told that the couple was meeting for the first time. Students who believed they were watching a married couple reported that the couples gazed at each other, nodded their heads, and touched, whereas viewers watching what they presumed to be new acquaintances reported gaze aversion, gesturing, and leg and arm movements reflecting nervousness. Hence, preinteraction expectations derived from prototypes affect what information individuals attend to and how that information is interpreted. For example, a shove might be seen as play in a couple perceived to be happy, but as reflecting dominance in a relationship perceived to be unhappy. Clearly, then, the ways in which people cast themselves and others into particular types of relationships, such as loving couples, are not wholly dependent on the actual behaviors that occur when people are together.

Prototypes of Love

Each person carries a multitude of prototypes in memory—including prototypes of love. Individuals compare what they are experiencing in their relationships with these prototypes of love they hold in memory. Couples in developing relationships typically compare the declarations and actions of their partner with their own inner prototypes of loving unions. Fehr (1993) discussed the extent to which individuals hold similar representations of what constitutes love. She documented prototypes of love by asking participants to recall important features of this state, based on the premise that the more frequently the values were mentioned, the more frequently they were retrieved from memory. The frequency with which values were accessed and reported was interpreted as an indication of their significance in the schemata of what constitutes love. Values recalled most frequently were considered the building blocks of a person's prototype for love.

The most common types of love reported were friendship, sexual, parental, brotherly, sibling, maternal, passionate, romantic, and familial love according to Fehr (1993) as cited. In analyzing the specific features of love, Fehr (1993) had university students recall characteristics reflecting the concept of love. The most common characteristics of love reported were caring, a sense of happiness, the desire to be together, friendship, and open communication. According to Fehr, romantic love reflected a perceptual bias in which only the partner's positive qualities were noticed. The partner was admired, respected, and thought about frequently when absent. Positive feelings found to be associated with romance were happiness, contentment, affection, excitement, and euphoria, as well as occasional uncertainty. Behavioral characteristics of romantic love included smiling, laughing, gazing, and helping one another. Physiological characteristics included increased heart rate, palpitations, sexual arousal, and butterflies in the stomach. Peripherally, participants described feelings of euphoria, dependency, uncertainty, and fear—both of emotional intimacy and excited anticipation.

In long-term relationships, companion or friendship features appeared to be central components of love. Fehr (1993) considered friendship to be more central to prototypes of love than passionate romantic features. She wrote, "Companionate kinds of love are at the core of what the term 'love' means to the layperson; passionate varieties are less likely to come to mind and are regarded as peripheral" (p. 92). Her research found that when describing love, individuals mentioned trust, caring, and respect more frequently than the romantic aspects of a relationship. The general prototype of love consisted of characteristics that describe friendship. Passionate attributes of love (e.g., physical attraction, thinking about the other person all the time, and sexual attraction) were secondary in describing both love in general and more specific types of love, such as romantic love.

Prototypes and Changing Relationships

Prototypes of love affect judgments about a relationship as well as changes in the level of commitment. In a study cited by Fehr (1993), individuals were given a description of a loving, committed relationship and asked to rate the effect of violations of trust in the hypothetical relationship. Violations of trust were viewed by participants as abrogations of the central values of a relationship. A loss of the prototypical features of love, such as caring, honesty, or respect, was seen as threatening to the extent the relationship was no longer perceived as loving.

Fehr (1993) concluded that prototypes of love influence beliefs about close relationships and suggests that individuals pay close attention to the characteristics of these prototypes when assessing the state of their relationships. She suggested in her 1988 study that individuals in developing relationships might use a prototype-matching exercise in which the characteristics of their actual relationships are compared with their prototypes of love (as cited in Fehr, 1993).

MEMORY AS A RECONSTRUCTIVE PROCESS

Martin, Hagestad, and Diedrick (1988) described the ways in which memories about events in family relationships are often recalled through the telling of stories of brief, memorable occurrences. These stories about relationships often focus on overcoming obstacles, hardship, or strife. When asked to recall the development of a current relationship, individuals also tell stories about brief but significant events that serve as milestones in the relationship, such as how they met their partners, an embarrassing moment, overcoming a crisis, or the recognition that the relationship was becoming intimate. The stories serve the purpose of consciously stating and reinforcing expectations about the quality and intimacy of the relationship, as well as imposing a sense of order on experience.

Of course, as a partnership unfolds, story telling about the relationship events also reflects the current moods of the individuals thus involved. Miell (1987) studied the responses of college students, who drew graphs to plot the strength of their relationships over a 10-week period. She had individuals report their retrospections each week about the previous week's feelings and predictions of future feelings. Past relationship events were reconstructed in light of current events, moods, and happiness with the relationship. In addition, the preceding 3 days of conversation between relational partners had more effect on partner's ratings of the future of the relationship than did previous months of relational history. It appears that the history of a relationship consists of the emotions associated with recall of an event (e.g., the first date) rather than the historical facts of what actually happened (Duck & Miell, 1986).

Duck, Pond, and Leatham (1991) argued that the literal recall of information is unimportant; recall is usually not factually accurate and it does not appear to be important that individuals remember the precise specifics of what went on before. Rather, the memory of events is filtered by the individual and mentally reframed. It is then described after it has been reshaped by the tone of present experience, personal values, and priorities. Hence, there is no one reality because everyone's reality is different due to different experiences and cognitive processing of behaviors.

This reinterpretive process of memory is at work throughout a relationship. Partners may reconstruct the account of their breakup and attribute different importance to elements of the story than they may have given before (Weber, Harvey, & Stanley, 1987). Duck (1991) described how recalling and reinterpreting events from a prior relationship is a process that often renders past events compatible with one's present feelings toward the relationship; the process of recall is a symbolic and integrative activity that helps individuals create new interpretations of the current relationship. Thus, the content of relational memory structures is subjective and open to interpretative and subjective distortions. Relationships constantly evolve and change through the interpretation of new experiences in light of old expectations. Memories are continually being reprocessed, reinterpreted, and reshaped, based on both new experiences and old scenes, scripts, and prototypes, and on their arrangement into various schemata. According to Miell (1987), memories about relational events determine appropriate behavior and can significantly influence the future development of a relationship.

IMPLICATIONS OF RELATIONAL MEMORY STRUCTURE THEORY

Relational memory structure theory provides a system that therapists can use to evaluate the development of a relationship and to convey fundamental paradigms about communication in relationships. Stable and rewarding relationships may be facilitated for partners who share similar conceptions about the development of romance and those properties that characterize a quality relationship. For example, Stephen (1987) demonstrated that individuals who share similar schemata for the value and conception of different gender roles facilitate the quality of interpersonal relationships. Further, Duck and Miell (1986) pointed out that people have internalized expectations for relationships that are part of their mental constitution and exist independently of their participation in a specific relationship. These values and expectations can be advantageously explored as part of the therapeutic process.

Individuals can use information about relational memory structures to better understand their own relationships and to determine where they are in a relationship. Even though relationships are in perpetual motion, with a dynamic, evolving psychological identity for each partner, relational memory structures provide a frame of reference for evaluation. Without relational memory structures, the development of relationships would seem random. The organization of the knowledge structures (schemata, scenes, scripts, and prototypes) provided by relational memory structure theory provides a mechanism for the evaluation and interpretation of isolated events in a wider relational context.

SUMMARY

Schemata influence how people perceive events in relationships. For example, going to college football games may mean spending quality time to one person in a relationship, whereas his or her partner may view it as a sacrifice in order to please the other. Expectations about relationship activities and the development of intimacy are based on the recall of scenes and scripts pertaining to particular activities; for instance, expectations for breaking bad news may be based on the recall of what was done the last time a similar situation was faced.

Scripts for initiating an interaction, getting a date, what to do on a date, and communication about sexual arousal each contribute to what we typically think goes on in a relationship. Cultural relationship scripts involve jokes about opening lines, asking for a date, common behaviors on dates, proposing marriage, and communicating terms of endearment such as "I love you." Yet, scripts may be personal and unique to the extent that our experiences are not shared by others, and thus we always face the challenge of determining how two people can view themselves as an independent couple.

Prototypes are defined as the best examples of a category. Research on prototypes of love reveals that the most common are friendship, sexual, romantic, and familial love. The common characteristics of love are caring, desire to be together, friendship, and self-disclosure of feelings. People access their memories and prototypes to decide if newly observed behavior reflects a category, such as an individual wondering what the first kiss signals when he or she is with a particular partner. Yet research also reveals that people's current emotions affect their memories and recall of relationship events. Past events that are told in relationship stories are reconstructed and reframed in reference to the current emotional state of the individual. Relational memory structure theory provides communication therapists with a mechanism to facilitate relationship quality. Individuals with similar expectations and who share similar values are more likely to be compatible.

DISCUSSION QUESTIONS

3.1 The way an individual currently feels about someone affects his or her recall of prior events in the relationship. Discuss your memory of the first time you met an important person in your life who is not a family member. What was the scene of the encounter? Do you have any recollection of what was said? How do you currently feel about this person?

3.2 Discuss positive and negative memorable messages given to you by individuals in your life? How did you react? Why do you remember the messages?

3.3 How valid is memory recall? Do you believe that recall is simply a reconstructed, fictional scenario of what previously happened in a relationship.

APPLICATIONS

3.1 Create a prototypical script, including specific lines of dialogue, for (a) initiating a date and (b) ending a close relationship. What scenes are associated with these situations? Compare your scripts with the scripts of some of your friends. To what extent have your personal experiences influenced your prototype?

3.2 Ask two or three friends to do the following. Recall a favorite story in a relationship in which you are or were a part of (e.g., parent–child, romantic, supervisor–subordinate, best friends, or competitors). What is the story plot? How long ago did the events take place? What is the theme of the story? Does your current level of satisfaction with the relationship affect your recall and interpretation of story events?

3.3 Ask three people to recall the most impressionable memorable message about dating given to them. Relate their messages to the following questions: Who said what? Using which channel (e.g., letter, face-to-face interaction, or telephone)? In a private or public setting? With what effect? How has this memorable message shaped or modified their expectations for relationships?

3.4 Interview a married couple who has a videotape of the couple's wedding. Ask the partners in the couple what they recall happening at the wedding ceremony, reception, or both. Compare the couple's recollections with what is on the videotape. How much discrepancy is there between the reports and what is on the videotape?

4

Emotion and Cognition About Relationships

When people are asked to describe the relationships that are the most meaning-ful in their lives, they often use emotional inferences to express how they feel about the relationship. Indeed, people find it difficult to be descriptive as op-posed to evaluative in describing their romantic partners. How they currently feel about a relational partner affects their recall about the events in the rela-tionship. For example, a married couple who has just had a heated argument will view their wedding video with more cynicism compared to how they felt on the day of the wedding. This chapter reviews research on the role of emotions in processing information about the development of relationships. People have emotion prototypes for anger and love that reveal an association with other types of emotion, such as despair or infatuation.

The role of emotions in the development of relationships is critical to under-standing how people differentiate different kinds of relationships. For example, friendships are distinguished from intimate relationships on the basis of arousal and feelings of passion. The role of emotions in interpersonal relationships is a frequent theme in popular music. Songs deal with love, finding the right part-ner, and how happiness is a consequence of being in a romantic bond.

CHARACTERISTICS OF HAPPINESS

Research suggests that there are six predictors of happiness, listed in Box 4.1. The most important predictor is being in a quality relationship.

Box 4.1   Components of Happiness

1. Being in a quality relationship.
2. Genes—as much as 50% of a person's happiness is due to a genetic tendency.
3. Internal locus of control, as opposed to being a victim or feeling helpless.
4. Belief in God.
5. Optimism—refusing to accept setbacks or hindrances.
6. Flow—feeling needed and use of one's training or experiences.

Source: Myers, D. G., & Diener, E. (1995). Who is happy? *Psychological science*, 6, pp. 10–19.

The genetic tendency for happiness has been demonstrated in cases of identical twins who were separated at birth and raised in different families in different states (Lykken & Tellegen, 1996). Later, the twins demonstrate similar levels of humor and reactions to events, even though they have not having shared family experiences. The genetic argument is strong in explaining happiness among individuals in countries where the standard of living is low and resources are scarce, and depression among individuals with more affluent lifestyles.

REPRESENTATION OF AFFECT ACCORDING TO COGNITIVE THEORIES OF EMOTION

The cognitive theories of emotion seek to explain how people experience emotion and the phenomenology of emotions (Zajonc & Markus, 1984). The cognitive theories of emotion assume that the representation of affect is imposed by individuals using contextual cues. According to Schacter and Singer (1962), individuals construe emotions by combining perceptions of their feelings with observations of external events. For example, individuals injected with adrenaline were friendly in a friendly context and hostile in a hostile environment. Yet, as Zajonc and Markus (1984) noted, the representation of people's internal feeling states, how they label their internal experiences as representing a given emotion, is rather abstract and is inferred by observing behavior and its antecedent conditions. By observing behavior and antecedent conditions, people often learn to habitually associate emotions with certain contexts. Emotion theorists have shown that by altering individuals' cognitive appraisals of a stimulus (e.g., viewing a disturbing movie of a surgical incision from the viewpoint of a surgeon or from the stance of an observer), it is possible to alter individuals' emotional responses (Mandler 1975).

People's expectations for relationships affect their emotional responses to events in relationships. Mandler (1975) argued that past experiences provide expectations about relationships. He suggested that an interruption of the expectations may result in positive or negative emotion, depending on the degree and intensity of the interruption. Low-level interruptions occur when people's expectations are more closely met, whereas high-level interruptions produce more arousal and more intense emotional reactions. An example of a low-level interruption would be an individual asking someone out after he or she has spoken with the other person, who is now involved in a conversation with others. Because it is now harder to isolate this person in order to pop the question, a low-level interruption in what was expected occurs.

Indeed, people have expectations for emotions in relationships and scripts for emotions in relationship. Planalp (1999) noted that many emotions are played out and negotiated through interpersonal scripts. Some emotions are only experienced internally and dissipate, whereas other emotions provoke a response from other people, such that there may be some mutual adjustment. A common example on a first date is avoiding any display of anger even if the dating partner has done something to offend one. The motivation for the emotional control is to foster the best possible impression of oneself, yet this may be part of individual's scripts for emotions in terms of appropriateness of display.

Following the idea of arousal labeling from contemporary theories of emotion (Lazarus, 1966; Mandler, 1975; Schacter & Singer, 1962), Gottman (1994) defined *affect* in terms of the nonverbal behaviors emitted by a speaker while delivering a message. Affect is the observable outcome of an emotion. For example, labeling a person "angry" is done by observing his or her facial expressions, tone of voice, or some combination of behaviors. Gottman coded affect on a continuum ranging from very negative to very positive. He found that nonverbal affect discriminates happily married couples from less happily married couples more than does the content of their speech. Unhappily married couples tend to match negative affect, whereas happily married couples tend to respond to negative affect with neutral or positive affect. Indeed, among less happily married couples, there is a vicious affective cycle in which the wife expresses negative feelings while the husband withdraws emotionally. She then responds with increasingly intense negative affect and the husband either withdraws or becomes exceedingly expressive as he loses control of his emotions (Fitness & Strongman, 1991; Gottman, 1979; 1994; Notarius & Johnson, 1982).

DIFFERENCES AMONG EMOTIONS, MOODS, AND AFFECT

Before discussing the affect of emotion on processing information about personal relationships, the terminology should be precisely defined. Emotion is a loosely used, vacuous term because it has multiple meanings to different people. Furthermore, what is emotional to one person may be unemotional to someone else. Although some emotion theorists believe that emotions are hardwired biological processes, Planalp (1999) discussed how emotions evolved not only in response to the physical environment but to the social environment as well. Andersen and Guerrero (1998) reviewed studies indicating how emotions arise more in social situations than in nonsocial ones. Examples of social emotions are guilt, love, contempt, jealousy, and embarrassment (Planalp, 1999). These emotions are commonly elicited in romance. Some emotions are even defined as being ways an individual feels about other people.

In this regard, Shields (1987) described research in which students were asked to think of the most emotional person they knew and explain why they chose the person. Emotional people were designated in terms of the magnitude of their responses such as the extremity of their reaction to an event. Negative emotions were cited more often than were positive ones. Participants were also asked to describe a particular situation in which the person that they were thinking about had been emotional. Sadness and depression were mentioned most (41%), followed by anger (37%). Shields (1987) reported that positive emotions such as love or happiness were mentioned in 13% of the cases.

Men were judged as hiding their emotions. The only emotion that men felt they could express without being labeled "girlish" was anger. Men also reported that the emotional women that they were thinking about expressed more healthy emotions than they did themselves. Shields (1987) wrote, "The emotional female is not the angry female. Anger or aggressiveness, in contrast to nearly all other specific emotions is considered a typically male response" (p. 235). The association between men and anger and between women and other common emotions such as sadness, fear, or happiness is learned by age 5 (Birnbaum, Nosanchuck, & Croll, 1980). Other studies have found that women experience just as much anger as men do, but that they may cry or feel hurt as a reaction to it.

Appraisal occurs when labeling the event. *Appraisals* are interpretations of the relationship between the individual and the environment in terms of how the individual's well-being is affected and his or her ability to cope with the event (Dillard, Kinney, & Cruz, 1996). Positive emotions emanate from a compatible fit between environmental events and an individual's motives, desires, or goals. Negative emotions occur when there is a mismatch between the environment and an individual's motives.

Appraisal theories distinguish between positive and negative emotions based on the relationship between events in the environment and individual motivations, needs, or desires at given times. Appraisal theories of emotion posit that emotions unfold in a sequence in which an event occurs in the environment that may or may not be noticed (Dillard et al., 1996; Frijda, 1986; Roseman, Spindel, & Jose, 1990; Smith & Lazarus, 1990). If the event is noticed, the individual appraises it by deciding if the event may harm or benefit him- or herself. Depending on the magnitude of the appraisal, an emotion arises.

Appraisal theorists claim that individuals compare what they observe in the environment to their goals, desires, or motives. When the observations are congruent with their desires, positive emotions follow. The perception of mismatch results in negative emotions. The intensity of emotion depends on the degree of congruence or mismatch.

Mandler (1975) also discussed how philosophers (e.g., Peters, 1969) and psychologists argued that emotions follow an initial appraisal of an object as good or bad. Yet it is important to note that there are instances in which an event generates some particular meaning regardless of whether arousal is associated with it and that the final emotional expression leads to a post hoc assessment of the event as bad or good (Mandler, 1975). In addition, behaviorists such as Bowlby (1982) argued that approach toward and avoidance of stimuli are not inherently positive or negative, respectively; rather approach and withdrawal tendencies with respect to a potential emotional stimulus are independent of linguistic labels "good" and "bad." People often approach bad stimuli, as well as the reverse. Indeed, Mandler (1975) argued that bad evaluations are often a consequence of invoking an expectation about some event and that the observed behavior cannot be assimilated into the expectation or the expectation cannot be accommodated to account for the unexpected behavior. An example is a person expecting an intimate partner to be supportive in times of need, only to find out that the intimate partner is busy coping with his or her own stress and is too busy to support the person. Negative evaluations of the intimate partner are likely to result. A relational expectation of support or comfort is violated.

This could be explained as the person's partner being too busy or under too much stress to help him or her. This is an example of the assimilation of the unsupportive behavior into the expectation that the intimate partner should be supportive in times of stress. On the other hand, accommodation occurs when the expectation is modified such that intimate partners are now conditionally expected to provide support only to the extent that intimate partners are not overwhelmed with stress.

A good working definition of emotion is provided by Clore, Schwartz, and Conway (1994). According to these researchers, *emotions* are defined as "internal mental states that are focused primarily on affect (where affect simply refers to the perceived goodness or badness of something)" (p. 325). Examples of emotion terms are "*adore*," "*aggravated*," "*anguished*," "*apprehensive*," and "*awe-struck*." These terms do not refer directly to events or to bodily reactions or behavior. Instead, they refer to mental events that integrate feelings. Common terms that do not constitute emotions refer to external events (e.g., abandoned) or bodily states (e.g., tired).

Clore et al. (1994) defined *affect* in terms of valence or the positive and negative aspects of things. Affect reflects the evaluative component of emotions. Indeed, Clore et al. (1994) stated that all emotions are affective, but that not all affective terms are emotions. They indicated that attitudes and preferences are affective, but are not emotions. Emotions are also seen as states, whereas preferences and attitudes are personality dispositions.

The distinction between moods and emotion is clear. Clore et al. (1994) cited the work of Batson, Shaw, and Oleson (1992), who stated that emotions are concerned with the present, whereas moods concern anticipation of the future. Emotions have a specific focus, whereas moods are nonspecific. Emotions have an object that moods may not have. Moods do not have to be caused by emotion. In essence, a working definition of *mood* is a feeling state, "which need not be about anything, whereas emotion refers to how one feels in combination with what the feeling is about" (Clore et al., 1994, p. 326).

An implication of these definitions is that cognition is essential for emotion, but not for mood (Clore, Ortony, Dienes, & Fujita, 1993). Hence, a person may be in a depressed mood on dreary morning because the absence of sunlight inhibits the release of a hormone, as opposed to simply appraising the day's opportunities as futile. In addition, Clore et al. (1994) argued that such changes may alter moods rather than emotions. In essence, emotions result from ongoing appraisals of situations regarding whether they are negative or positive for one's goals. Emotions serve as intrapersonal communication concerning the nature and urgency of the situation.

Given that emotion is concerned with feedback or information about the nature of a stimulus (Clore et al., 1994), the question arises about the characteristics that provide the prototypes for many human basic emotions such as love, hate, anger, and jealousy. Holmes (1991) noted that couples often have distinct and specific memories of past hurts. Furthermore, spouses may misremember or not remember specific emotions that are incongruent with their beliefs about the types of emotions that are commonly expected in marriage (Fitness, 1996).

SIMILARITIES AND DIFFERENCES AMONG LOVE, HATE, ANGER, AND JEALOUSY

Fitness and Fletcher (1993) examined the emotions of love, hate, anger, and jealousy in marriage. Both love and anger events, as opposed to hate or jealousy, had occurred in the preceding month. In addition, both anger and love scripts reflected the desire to communicate with the partner, whereas hate or jealousy scripts reflected the desire to withdraw from the partner (cf., Gottman, 1994).

A love, hate, anger, or jealousy survey was randomly assigned to 160 married individuals who were asked to remember the most recent time they had felt their assigned emotion in relation to their spouses. They answered a series of open-ended questions dealing with their mood before the event; details of the actual event including what they remembered thinking, saying, or feeling; whether they had any urges to do something; and how they actually behaved during the incident. They also reported about controlling their emotions, the duration of the emotion, their mood after the event, and their partners' reactions. Both love and anger events had occurred recently, whereas hate or jealousy events had occurred earlier.

As expected, love-eliciting events were evaluated as pleasant, involving little effort and few perceived obstacles. The cause of love was global ("She's such a beautiful woman") rather than being isolated to a context. Love was also associated with a feeling of security for some individuals. Recall from chapter 3 that in prototypes for romantic and companionate love trust, caring, and respect characterized both types of love. Characteristics of romantic love were contentment, euphoria, smiling, gazing, butterflies in one's stomach, and periods of uncertainty.

Passionate attributes such as "thinking about the partner all the time" were only secondary in describing love; however, they were primary qualities in describing emotions like hate. Indeed, people sometimes talk about the fine line between love and hate in a variety of co-dependent relationships involving chemical dependency, battery, or jealousy.

Not surprisingly, hate-eliciting events were seen as unpleasant and the opposite of love-eliciting events. Participants feeling hate reported lack of support by the partner and less control of the situation. Hate was elicited by being humiliated by the spouse in public. For wives, this often involved the husbands drinking too much at a social gathering and becoming aggressive. Husbands reported feeling humiliated and hating their wives when they made angry or jealous scenes in public. Both spouses reported wanting to withdraw and escape from the situation. There were feelings of being powerless and trapped.

Regarding jealousy-eliciting events, few of the spouses reported infidelity. The most common jealousy-eliciting event was a partner paying attention to or spending time with someone of the opposite sex (Fig. 4.1). The most intense jealousy occurred when the third party was the partner's ex-spouse. Jealousy was characterized by worrying, brooding, and less self-esteem. A common jealousy theme was that the partner was not necessarily responsible for the third party's overtures, but that the partner could have reacted more distantly.

These results reveal that people share socially constructed scripts or knowledge structures for basic emotions in close relationships like marriage. Fitness (1996) discussed how individuals share knowledge about emotions in general, as well as having more specific knowledge structures about the display of emotions in their own personal relationships. She provided an example of jealousy in which a spouse expresses jealousy to his or her partner because the expression of jealousy has positive outcomes such as loving reassurance from the partner, who perceives the jealousy as flattery. Guerrero and Andersen (1998) also reported that relational partners may respond to jealousy in order to maintain the existing relationship. However, in other instances, the negative sentiment endures and neutral or positive emotions are considered to be cynically motivated by a partner.

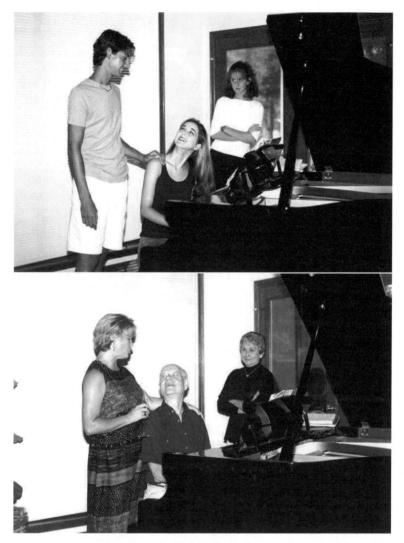

FIG. 4.1   Jealousy knows no limitations as to age.

Finally, the research by Fitness (1996) revealed that in contrasting anger with hate-eliciting events, anger was reported to be less demeaning and associated with less loss of self-esteem. The common elicitor of anger was the perception of having been treated unfairly, whereas hate was associated with humiliation and neglect. Anger events were viewed as more controllable and predictable than hate or jealousy events. Fitness (1996) and Fehr and

---

Box 4.2   Scripts for the Escalation of Anger Leading to Aggression.

Communication researchers Harris, Gergen and Lannamann (1986) discuss how anger and aggression may be sanctioned or even advisable after time has elapsed and the parties have not resolved the conflict. Aggression may be seen as a culturally sanctioned form of relationship governed by rules. Individuals were asked to predict, advise, and evaluate two scenarios in which two roommates came to blows and another scenario in which a husband criticized his wife's cooking after she had spent hours preparing the meal. Over time, as conflict escalates, individuals judge that the probability of aggressive actions increase, whereas the probability of conciliatory actions decrease. Individuals judge aggressive actions to be increasingly desirable, whereas conciliation becomes less desirable. Here is one scenario.

1.   Lee criticized Lisa's cooking.
2.   Her response could be any of the following: embrace or kiss Lee, apologize for the meal, laugh about the remark, defend her cooking, criticize Lee, curse sarcastically at Lee, throw the dinner on the floor, or slap Lee. How probable, advisable, and desirable is it that each of these responses be used at this time?
3.   Lee's reaction to Lisa's response was to defend his criticism. How probable, advisable, and desirable is this reaction?
4.   Lisa's reaction was to curse Lee.
5.   The conflict escalated until Lisa slapped Lee.

The study participants tended to increasingly recommend aggression as the scenario proceeded, and the recommended conciliation less and less. With increasing amounts of aggressive interchange over time, participants realize the name of the game and play accordingly. But how often does conflict escalate in an argument with a relational partner? What does it take to stop the argument from increasing to hostility?

Baldwin (1996) reported that the anger script is very common in and outside close relationships.

The role of communication in eliciting emotion is critical. Planalp (1999) and Andersen and Guerrero (1998) discussed that emotions are elicited by communication, manifested in communication, and socialized through interaction. For example, emotions in romance often serve interaction goals, such as embarrassing others to discredit or help them. An individual's inability to communicate effectively with partners can lead to anger, depression, and loneliness, just as effective communication may lead to happiness, joy, and contentment.

PROTOTYPES OF ANGER IN RELATIONSHIPS

There has been intriguing research on emotion prototypes of anger in personal relationships. Indeed, American culture has idioms indicating the prevalence of anger in people's closest relationships, such as "knowing which buttons to push." When individuals are asked to describe anger, 90% of the descriptions mostly involve another person as the target of anger (Fehr & Baldwin, 1996). Anger can be defined as a type of social relationship because the emotion so often emanates from frustration with another person.

Fehr and Baldwin (1996) described a series of studies of the conditions leading to anger and the reaction to it. Their research indicated that there are different types of anger, including hurt, rage, and contempt. There is a temporal sequencing of events for anger. Rage and hatred tend to precede feelings of contempt. Some individuals attempt to control the expression of anger until a saturation point is reached. There is a loss of control followed by verbal aggression, physical aggression, and leaving the scene.

Box 4.2 contains two scripts reflecting the escalation of anger that results in physical aggression. Violations that occur in the culturally endorsed rituals for compliments indicate that the rules for conflict resolution are not endorsed by both partners in a given interaction. Hence, individuals over time increasingly condone higher levels of coercive responses in the belief that the other person is being irrational and is unwilling to use constructive communication to reduce conflict.

Types of Anger

Fehr and Russell (1991) asked 317 individuals to list all the terms they believed to be synonymous with anger. A total of 635 terms were generated. Over one third of the participants listed terms such as "mad," "frustration," or "hate"; only 1 or 2% listed "exasperation" and "contempt." A subset of the terms was rated by a different group of participants on how representative the terms were of anger. The highest ratings were for "fury," "rage," and "mad." The lowest ratings were for "depression," "fear," and "sorrow." Intermediate ratings were given to "irritation," "bitterness," and "spite."

Anger often takes over other thoughts, so that when angered individuals often have difficulty focusing on anything else. Fehr and Baldwin (1996) reported that brooding and dwelling on the event are prototypical thoughts and that individuals formulate plans for revenge or imagine attacking the cause of their anger. In essence, anger results in intrusive thinking so that individuals often are obsessed with the emotion until it is lessened to intensity by time passage or other events.

A number of physiological reactions are associated with anger. Common features are headaches, increased heart rate, shaking hands or knees, tense muscles, and a tight or knotted stomach. The anger prototype also reflects behaviors such as using profanity, attacking something other than the cause (e.g., slamming doors), leaving the scene, crying, and attempting to resolve the situation. Fitness and Fletcher (1993) found that 75% of survey respondents reported that they tried to control their anger, whereas over 25% did not. Individuals who did not want to control their anger also reported that they wanted their partner to know they were angry or that the emotion was too intense to control. A minority (10%) of the respondents reported that they believed it was healthier to express anger rather than keep it bottled inside themselves.

Fehr and Baldwin (1996) indicated that the agreement about the anger prototype is widespread as shown by data gathered in different countries. People perceive different causes for anger, react in a variety of ways, and often think that their reactions will elicit a response by the target of their anger.

Scripts for Anger

Fehr and Baldwin (1992) examined gender differences in how an unfolding sequence of anger was interpreted. In one study, men and women rated how they would feel if their partner engaged in a number of anger-provoking behaviors. A second study was conducted to examine people's responses when feeling angry, and a third study determined the reactions that individual expected from their relationship partners in response to their expressions of anger.

The first study examined the causes of anger derived from earlier research. The causes of anger were being criticized, having one's trust betrayed (one's partner disclosed intimate confidential information about one to outsiders), and being rebuffed (one's partner repels one's plans for an evening together). Additional causes were negligence (such as forgetting one's birthday) and cumulative annoyance (when an irritating habit keeps recurring). Women were more angered by all of the events, especially by a betrayal of trust. Other research revealed that men were more likely to report feeling angered by their partners' moodiness, physical self-absorption, and withholding sex, whereas women reported feeling angered by their partners' neglect and remarks about their appearance (Buss, 1989).

The second study by Fehr and Baldwin (1992) revealed gender difference in responses to being angered. Women reported being more likely than men to express hurt feelings, use indirect aggression such as complaining to someone else or getting angry at someone else, and to use direct aggression such as trying to hurt the partner either verbally or physically. This flies in the face of long-standing evidence that men are more likely to behave with physical aggression (Stets & Straus, 1990). Several studies found that men would rather express anger to another man, whereas women were more comfortable expressing anger directly to their partners. In addition, when men used physical aggression, they were more likely to use intense forms such as hitting, whereas women used less intense forms such as slapping (Stets & Henderson, 1991).

A third study examined individuals' beliefs about their partners' reactions to the individuals' expressions of being angry. The actions considered were avoidance, responding with aggression, talking it over, responding with indirect aggression, being conciliatory, expressing hurt feelings, denying responsibility, rejecting the partner, and mocking the partner. Participants expected more positive reactions to positive expressions on their part and more negative reactions to negative expressions. In reaction to avoidance or withdrawal, men were more likely to talk and express hurt feelings. In reaction to indirect aggression, men were more likely to reject women and to express hurt feelings. When the men engaged in direct rather than indirect aggression, they expected their partners to avoid them, reject them, or express hurt feelings. Women were more likely to expect their partners to ridicule them or to deny responsibility. Individuals of both genders agreed that their partners would react positively if the individuals were to conciliate, talk without hostility, or express hurt feelings.

EMOTIONAL SCRIPTS FOR RELATIONSHIPS

Forgas (1991) examined the scripts for romantic heterosexual relationships and found that the scripts were based on affective and connotative characteristics rather than on objective and denotative features. Three dimensions characterize romance: love and commitment versus unlove and instability, mutual versus one-sided, and sexual or physical versus nonsexual or emotional. Having an affair with a married person was associated most with the sexuality dimension. This relationship was viewed as one-sided and reflected more of a transient, uncommitted, superficial, and unloving relationship. The most prototypical instance of commitment and mutuality was a marriage of 25 years. This marriage was modestly related to sexuality.

These dimensions are mostly affective and evaluative in nature, indicating the critical role of emotion in the cognitive representations of relationships. Only the sexuality dimension is descriptive. Forgas (1991) indicated that mutuality and love are more evaluative because they reflect how individuals feel about some relationships (e.g., a long-lasting platonic relationship) rather than the objective characteristics of the relationships themselves.

Individual differences were found among the relationship dimensions. Women tended to represent heterosexual relationships more in terms of their mutuality than did men. In addition, love and commitment were more important characteristics for those who were currently in a romance and who had idealistic attitudes about love in general. Individuals who were more extroverted tended to view relationships according to sexual appeal as opposed to mutuality (Forgas & Dobosz, 1980). These findings indicate that cognition about relationships is not based only on affect, but is related to an individual's personality, attitudes, and previous dating history.

COMMUNICATION AND THE SENTIMENT-OVERRIDE HYPOTHESIS

An important relationship attitude that has received considerable examination is the general sentiment that partners feel toward one another when they are asked to interpret the intentions behind their partner's statements. Weiss (1984) proposed the sentiment-override hypothesis, which links cognition in terms of the processing of current information with the history of interaction in long-term relationships such as marriage. The sentiment-override hypothesis proposes that the history of interaction with another person affects the interpretation of current behavior by the other person. For example, an unhappily married wife could interpret her husband's statements about being late for dinner as an irresponsible excuse indicating his lack of concern about her. This reflects the assimilation of his tardiness into the wife's overall sentiment that her husband is irresponsible. According to Piaget (1983), assimilation occurs when new information is made compatible with existing expectations or cognitive structures. Accommodation occurs when the expectation is changed or modified so that new events become part of the expectation. As Mandler (1975) noted, an individual's view of the world is changed by including the new event as a legitimate part of some new conceptual structure in terms of simply modifying the original expectation. Weiss (1984) suggested that many spouses are insensitive to the nonverbal intent behind partner's behaviors. Instead, their reactions to their partners' behaviors are determined by the general sentiments about the partner at a given time. Hence, assimilation is taking place as spouses with positive sentiments interpret their partners' behaviors in a positive light and respond positively toward their partners. Spouses with negative sentiments view their partners' intentions negatively and respond negatively. Research reviewed by Noller (1984) and Gottman (1994) confirm the hypothesis.

The implications of the sentiment-override hypothesis are clear. Spouses' cognitive and affective reactions to their partners' behaviors influence their own reactions "regardless of the communication quality of the partners' behaviors" (Floyd, 1988, p. 524). Still, the question persists as to why memories of past events are so powerful in biasing the cognition of current behaviors. In the following, some studies are reviewed that provide partial answers to this question.

Fitness (1996) cited examples of clinicians who comment that couples often have memories like elephants for past hurts. The gap-filling function of scripts indicates that using a script to process information is biased with the perception and recall of script-consistent features that, in fact, may not have occurred. Spouses may recall inaccurately emotions that are incongruent with their beliefs about the kinds of emotions that are permissible in marriage. Fitness cited the example of jealousy in a marriage in which jealousy is considered an unacceptable marital emotion. Therefore, the wife recalls her feelings about her husband's paying close attention to an attractive young woman as worry that he not look foolish or be exploited by another woman's flirtatious interests.

Forgas (1991) discussed how emotion affects the organization and storage of information events in the past. Emotions affect the recall of events from the immediate past as well as events in early childhood. Individuals who are feeling happy are more likely to remember interactions that are pleasant, whereas those who are in a bad mood are more likely to recall events that are sad or depressing.

Forgas, Bower, and Krantz (1984) examined the effect of emotion on how individuals interpret the behavior of others and their own behavior. Participants who were induced to feel sad or happy through hypnosis were asked to look at a video of a conversation they had had the previous day with a stranger. They were asked to identify positive and negative behaviors on the tape for themselves and for the interaction partner on the tape. Forgas et al. found a strong bias for interpreting the behaviors on the tape according to the temporary mood of the participants. Happy participants identified more positive behaviors than negative behavior, both in their partners and in themselves. Sad participants tended to be more critical of themselves than of their partners. Forgas (1991) attributed this to social norms that constrain negative evaluations of superficially known others, such as the Pollyanna Principle, the belief that initial encounters should be warm, polite, and cooperative as opposed to being unfriendly or competitive.

Forgas reviewed additional research supporting the sentiment-override hypothesis. Individuals were led to form impressions of others by reading about a variety of people on a computer screen and to evaluate the people along a number of social dimensions. The computer was programmed to record how long each individual took to read each piece of information and to evaluate the person. More time was spent reading and learning about information that matched the current mood of the individuals.

Other research revealed that positive thoughts generate other positive thoughts, regardless of any logical connection between the thoughts (Forgus, 1991). This is also observed in conversations in which individuals engage in a series of positive or negative statements during which they seem to be caught in a repetitive loop. Planalp (1999) argued that cognition and emotion often work hand in hand in conversations. She cited examples of talking to people about their fear or sadness and providing reasons for why they should feel differently. She speculated that communication is the principal mechanism for changing emotions.

In the absence of communication, individuals pay selective attention to mood-consistent rather than mood-inconsistent information. For example, happy participants spent more time focusing on the positive characteristics of another person, whereas sad participants noticed negative behaviors more. In addition, these studies support the concept of spreading activation, in which a dominant emotion (e.g., happy) enhances the availability of emotion-congruent perception. Noticing behaviors that are congruent with one's existing mood may enhance the intensity of the existing moods, motivating the individual to give such information more attention. Indeed, a number of studies in communication and psychology reveal that happy people make positive and lenient judgments of others' behavioral intentions, whereas sad people are more likely to be critical in their interpretation of others' behavioral intentions.

Forgas (1991) summarized the studies on the sentiment-override hypothesis in terms of adaptability. When a person is in a positive mood, he or she is open, constructive, and relatively mindless about the careful processing of information that is incongruent with positive feelings. In close relationships, a positive mood corresponds with easy-going and uncritical judgments that are associated with lenient and generous interpersonal evaluations. Being in a negative mood results in slow, detailed, and analytic processing of more available information and a focus on oneself. This reaction may result in conscious information-processing strategies that offset the greater availability of affect-consistent cognition and may lead to negative assessments of oneself without negative evaluations of others. Yet, in close relationships, the judgments of oneself and the judgments of one's partner are interdependent. In unhappy relationships, one's partner's behaviors are viewed with more cynicism.

Floyd (1988) provided qualified support for the sentiment-override hypothesis in which men in close relationships made judgments about their partners' communication behaviors that were affected by their previous sentiment. The women made judgments in accordance with their partners' current intent. Floyd had 40 dating couples discuss problems in their relationships for 10 to 15 minutes while being videotaped. Initially, the men and women individually completed surveys asking how satisfied or distressed they were with the relationship. During the discussion, couples used the communication box procedure developed by Markman and Floyd (1980) to evaluate the immediate impact of their partners' statements. The relational partners spoke one at a time and rated one another's statements after they finished on a 5-point scale ranging from "very negative" to "very positive."

Half of the couples completed a communication skills intervention program after the videotaping. The program consisted of lectures in small groups, homework assignments to practice the skills, feedback about their videotape, and individual practice sessions with a paraprofessional consultant. The intervention was designed to have couples focus on their expectations about marriage in general and their specific relationships in order to challenge any irrational beliefs or unrealistic expectations. Couples were encouraged to focus on specific communication behaviors (e.g., "He/she interrupts me when I state a problem.") rather than abstract negative personality traits (e.g., "He/she is a jerk.").

Two months after the videotaping, a second videotaping session was conducted for all the couples. The videotapes of the couples' pre- and post-interventions were rated by trained observers in terms of communication proficiency using a 5-point positive-to-negative scale.

The results revealed that the intervention did not improve communication proficiency. The men's ratings of the impact of the women's statements were consistent with the sentiment-override hypothesis in that their ratings at the second session were affected by their general satisfaction with the relationship. On the other hand, the women's ratings of the men's statements were not associated with the women's overall sentiment about the relationship. These results are consistent with the findings of other studies reviewed by Noller (1984) suggesting that men are inaccurate decoders of their partners' nonverbal affect. In the course of an interaction, men's interpretations of their partners' behaviors appear to be distorted by their own cognitive evaluations, which are incongruent with the communication quality of the behaviors. Men misinterpret their partners' communication behaviors and their own behavioral responses are a result of these misinterpretations (Floyd, 1988).

Despite relationship partners' shared knowledge of one another's experiences, similar behaviors or activities are understood and interpreted by the partners differently. In marriage counseling, there is often a situation in which partners have different feelings about the same conditions eliciting the underlying problems in the relationship. Forgas (1991) indicated that the effect of mood, cognition, and judgment is intensified in close relationships because close relationships provide a context in which the information base is so elaborate that selective processing is required.

SUMMARY

Cognition affects emotion and vice versa. Even though people's expectations about romance reflect emotions, the inferences represent the outcome of behaviors that occur in relationships. For example, if someone describes his or her best friend as caring, then the underlying behaviors may represent a script in which the friend is available in times of a crisis, the friend listens sensitively to the individual's concerns, the friend laughs at his or her jokes, or the friend calls at the right times. Caring is a constellation of many behaviors. Yet what is considered caring by an individual in a given context or time period may be labeled "intrusive" or "not minding one's own business" at a different time.

People have scripts for anger that reflect the intensity of the emotions. The sentiment-override hypothesis states that current emotions override objective judgments of a partner's behavior. If an individual is feeling comfortable and a partner interrupts him or her, the individual may overlook the interruption without comment. On the other hand, if the individual is feeling tense or agitated, then the interruption by his or her partner may be seized as an opportunity to escalate conflict.

DISCUSSION QUESTIONS

4.1 Discuss the sentiment-override hypothesis and think of two recent events involving yourself and a close friend in which you went into the interaction feeling (a) very elated about an event and wished to tell your partner and (b) you felt anger toward your partner for something he or she recently did that affected you. What happened in both scenarios? Did conflict escalate or did you both calmly resolve the issue in the second scenario?

4.2 Discuss how you often express anger. Does your expression of anger reflect the research findings on anger expression discussed in this chapter? How are your experiences similar to or different from the research findings presented here?

APPLICATIONS

4.1 Interview two people about the following situation and apply the sentiment-override hypothesis to their statements. Think about someone with whom you have been in an intimate relationship. It is a weekend and you want to go to a movie matinee to see a popular show that has received good reviews. You and your partner haven't done anything together for a number of weeks because of jobs and schoolwork. After asking your partner about going to the movie, you are told that he or she desires to read a novel at home for a few hours and then study some more. What is your reaction? Do you communicate your response to your partner or keep your feelings to yourself?

4.2 Think of the most emotional person you know. Describe him or her. What makes this individual emotional? Think of the frequency and amount of emotional displays. Are this person's emotions primarily positive, negative, or a combination?

4.3 Think of the most emotionless person you know. What makes him or her unemotional? What would make this individual more emotional? If possible, also interview this person and ask if he or she has ever had any difficulty expressing emotions.

5

Generating and Maintaining Relationships Through Imagined Interactions

From the book thus far, one might be tempted to conclude that people are somewhat obsessed with thoughts about their past, current, or anticipated romantic relationships. Certainly, private conversations with close associates may support the idea that people spend a great deal of time thinking about the state of their intimate relationships. However, an overlooked fact about the study of relationships is that, although people may intently consider their relationships, such may not be a very conscious or salient process. In fact, people may even discount their thoughts about romance as idle speculations having little to do with the real world. Yet, as Duck (1986) observes, something far more important may be going on:

> We can plan the relationship; we can think back over encounters and try to work out what went wrong with them or what we can learn from them (Duck, 1980). This out-of-interaction fantasy or thought work is important in building and destroying relationships. I believe that it has been overlooked because researchers haven't yet asked people how they spend their time. I'm sure that we spend a lot of our time thinking,

musing, and daydreaming. Maybe we can plan our relationships to make them work better. (pp. 95–97)

The sort of musings that litter everyone's days often take the form of imagined interactions (IIs). IIs serve as major wellsprings that create expectations for relationship development. In essence, they are internal dialogues with significant others that allow individuals to review relational encounters, and they also serve a rehearsal function for future relational encounters. IIs also create and sustain habitual scripts for various encounters (Honeycutt, 1993). In this regard, imagining what one will say on a first date, when proposing marriage, and when making a disclosure about some personal problem results in expectations regarding anticipated scenes of the interaction and the accompanying scripted lines of dialogue. The process of imagining conversations with relational partners keeps the relationship alive even when the individual is not in the physical presence of the partner; IIs are an integral part of the ongoing ebb and flow of romance.

In this chapter, IIs are discussed as a mechanism for mentally creating relationships, as well as for reliving old memories with ex-partners. The chapter also includes a discussion of the use of imagined dialogue for creating parasocial relationships in times of social isolation, for example, as when viewers fantasize about having a close relationship with a television star. The role of emotions in imagined conversations, in particular how individuals can reexperience prior emotions associated with relational events, are examined. The chapter concludes with a discussion of gender differences in imaging and offers the results of a study on topics of imagined dialogue in marriage.

IMAGINED INTERACTIONS
AND THE CREATION OF RELATIONSHIPS

Deeply ingrained schemas, prototypes, scripts, and personal constructs are reflected in everyday thought processes outside of conscious awareness (Singer, 1985). These may take the form of passing thoughts, fantasies, and daydreams. Daydreaming is one way people sustain interest and arousal while enduring boring situations, such as attending a committee meeting or listening to that well-intentioned professor drone on and on. Indeed, some jobs are particularly conducive to daydreaming. For example, Klinger (1987) reported that 100% of lifeguards and 79% of truck drivers admit to having vivid daydreams at times. According to Klinger, daydreaming serves the purposes of planning ahead and reviewing past events as people find relief from the monotony of doing the same thing again and again. Daydreaming appears to be a mechanism by which people often initiate proactive and retroactive imagined interactions (IIs) in order to rehearse anticipated interactions and relive previous encounters (Honeycutt, 1991). In addition to rehearsal and reliving of prior conversations,

IIs also serve such functions as catharsis, enhancing self-understanding, and keeping relationships alive in people's thoughts.

Relationships can be studied by tapping into the minds of individuals as well as by observing the communication and behaviors of two individuals. One way to tap into people's minds and examine the source of relational expectations in terms of IIs is to analyze individuals' journal entries and survey their accounts of recalled interactions. Another method is to induce IIs by asking subjects (e.g., college students) to imagine situations such as a conflict with a parent. These induced IIs have been behaviorally measured in terms of physiological responses.

The memory structure approach we advance in the previous chapters of this book assumes that individuals have particular expectations about what should happen in the progression of a romantic relationship and that the expectations can be used as an anchor for categorizing their own relationships and the relationships of others. Relationship expectations may be reinforced when observed behavior is assimilated into existing categories (e.g., self-disclosure may fit best into one's prototype for escalating intimacy). Occasionally, accommodation takes place, as when the expectations are modified to account for newly observed behavior (Planalp, 1985). For example, a faithful partner is no longer trustworthy if he or she has an affair and the other partner finds out about it. Regardless of whether assimilation or accommodation takes place, the person may play over in his or her mind images of conversations with his or her relational partner. These IIs may be of previous encounters, linking them to anticipated future conversations. The IIs may serve the purpose of keeping a relationship intact, rehearsing its ending, or initiating a new one (Berger & Bell, 1988).

Consider the following sequence of events. Two students talk in class a few times about projects and school. They establish a pattern of informal chatting at the beginning of the class period. Next, one of them decides that he or she wants to ask the other person if he or she would like to have lunch together on campus. The asked goes over in his or her mind what he or she will say and imagines the other person's response to the overture. The asker also may think of alternative responses in case the other person indicates that he or she is too busy to have lunch with the asker today. This imagining sequence is an example of a proactive II. *Proactive IIs* occur before an anticipated encounter and serve a rehearsal function (Honeycutt, 1989), ostensibly designed to enhance one's chances of competency in interaction (e.g., getting the commitment for a lunch date).

Now suppose that the person that the asker is interested in accepts his or her invitation. After lunch is over and the other person has left, the asker drives home or walks to class, and along the way, he or she might have a *retroactive II* in which the asker plays over in his or her mind parts of the conversation that occurred during the lunch date. The asker begins to imagine what he or she will say the next time he or she encounters the other person in class. If all went well, the asker probably would enjoy the retroactive II, but research has revealed that IIs are associated with negative and mixed emotions as well as positive ones (Zagacki, Edwards, & Honeycutt, 1992). Consider what the asker might recall or anticipate if, during the lunch date with someone he or she generally finds attractive, that person engaged in rather boorish behavior or unknowingly insulted the asker's best friend.

IIs have a number of characteristics that are similar to real conversations. Rosenblatt and Meyer (1986) noted that these internal dialogues may be fragmentary, extended, rambling, repetitive, or incoherent. Similarly, everyday discourse often exhibits the same sorts of patterns. And even in relatively formal or structured conversational encounters, interaction may be anything from disjointed to well-orchestrated and is often mirrored in the proactive and retroactive IIs that people initiate in their heads. For example, individuals even have IIs in counseling situations with their therapists (Honeycutt, 1995). In short, IIs occur every day, in a variety of situations, and may be taken as the cognitive representations of planning for interaction in a complex discursive environment.

Studies of relational partners indicate that IIs occur in all sorts of contexts, ranging from romantic partners (33%), to friends (16%), to family members (12%), to individuals in authority (9.4%), to work associates (8%), to ex-relational partners (6%), and to prospective partners (4%) (Edwards, Honeycutt, & Zagacki, 1988; Honeycutt, Zagacki, & Edwards, 1989; Zagacki et al., 1992). Depending on the differing values people place on their assorted relationships, some people have IIs with many different individuals, whereas others have recurring IIs with only certain individuals about a limited number of topics.

Additional functions of IIs include catharsis, self-understanding, and psychological-relationship maintenance. IIs can function to create catharsis for the individual by relieving tension and reducing uncertainty about another's actions. As with actual self-disclosure, IIs can enhance self-understanding by helping one to clarify his or her thoughts. For example, Caughey (1984) discussed how inner dialogue may help individuals to retain a sense of values and purpose. IIs can also help a person psychologically maintain relationships by concentrating his or her thoughts on relational scenes and partners. The II relationship-maintenance function enhances an awareness of the relationship and helps galvanize one's attention to details that may otherwise be overlooked. Acitelli (1993) discussed relationship awareness in terms of a person's thoughts about interaction patterns, that is, comparisons and contrasts between oneself and a relational partner. Individuals may use IIs to maintain imaginative contact with partners who are living far away and long-distance or commuter relationships can even be strengthened through frequent recourse to IIs featuring the absent partner. Herein lies the arbitration between two seemingly contradictory maxims: "Absence makes the heart grow fonder" only insofar as the IIs auger against the sense of "Out of sight, out of mind."

Positive emotions may be attributed to the excitement that accompanies relational initiation and growth (Honeycutt, Zagacki, et al. 1989). Individuals may imagine pleasant activities with their relational partners, such as engaging in small talk, planning dates, and discussing shared interests. For instance, the journal entry in Box 5.1 was written by a 25-year-old woman who imagines seeing a lover who has been away on a trip. Note how the II serves cathartic, rehearsal, and relational-maintenance functions within the same coherent episode.

Imagined Interactions With Ex-Partners

IIs sometimes feature ex-partners. For example, a woman in one study (Honeycutt, Zagacki, et al. 1989) reported an II with an ex-lover who had terminated the relationship. In the II he apologized for the hurt he had caused her and confessed that he was wrong to let her go. She responded that she hated him and that she was better off with her new boyfriend. This is an example of an II occurring in what might be referred to as the post-termination awareness of an ex-partner. This phase occurs when a romantic relationship has ended, but the individual still thinks about the ex-partner and reconstructs previous encounters or imagines future encounters (Edwards et al., 1988).

IIs after a romance has soured can create valued psychological contact with the ex-partner. This is a type of reminiscence that often occurs during the process of de-escalating relationships when people remember the good times. It may be that individuals are likely to have these retroactive IIs and be in this post-termination phase until an alternative relationship develops or the individual diverts attention to other endeavors such as hobbies, friends, or work. The journal entry in Box 5.2, written by a 33-year-old man, supports this thesis.

Imagined Interactions and Social Isolation: Parasocial Relationships

While IIs may help people to think about their relationships with friends, romantic partners, or family members, they also may be used dysfunctionally to imagine a relationship with someone with whom a person has never communicated in face-to-face interaction. Caughey (1984) discussed cases in which individuals fantasized that they were involved with a celebrity. A well-publicized and unfortunate case of this type of dysfunctional behavior became public in April 1981, when John Hinckley attempted to assassinate President Ronald Reagan. Hinckley had seen the movie *Taxi Driver* and had become infatuated with the actress Jodie Foster, who was one of the film's stars. Hinckley wrote love letters to her and began to imagine that he had a personal relationship with her. He eventually began to believe that he could win her love by killing the president. It is interesting to speculate about the types of IIs Hinckley may have had with Foster in the time leading up to the assassination attempt.

Box 5.1   Imagined Interaction Journal Entry About Seeing a Long-Distance Lover

Andy and I both have had numerous imagined interactions concerning our relationship. An imagined interaction is a process that helps people in the construction of social reality. A person may develop visual or verbal scripts in her head to help them deal with certain situations. Imagined interactions serve specific functions: rehearsal for actual upcoming communication situations, evaluation after an important encounter, obtaining a greater sense of our own feelings, and improving our own self-knowledge. Perhaps the best example of imagined interactions being used in Andy's and my relationship occurred during our separation last summer.

It was a very difficult time for both of us because we missed each other so much. The thing that helped each of us deal with the pain was the use of imagined interactions. I was amazed to discover that we both had imagined interactions over the same thing, the moment that we would be reunited at the end of the summer. Whenever I was feeling lonely or especially missing Andy, I would think about the moment we would be able to see each other again. I would imagine the inevitable embrace, kiss, and words of love that we would give to each other. I would rehearse over and over again in my head the things that I would tell Andy at that moment. Things like "I love you more than anything else in the world." At the actual moment, we did hug, kiss, and give romantic proclamations of love to one another, but then there was an awkward moment of silence for two reasons.

First, we had each gone over in our head that moment so many times that we neglected to think about what would come next. Second, we were still in shock that we had finally been reunited. Now, we both laugh when we think of that moment because we realize how rehearsed the whole thing was on both of our parts. Nevertheless, imagining conversations with each other and being together again helped us survive the separation. Through the process we learned a lot about how we felt about each other also.

One-sided imagined relationships, such as Hinckley's, reflect extreme cases of parasocial relationships. More common are parasocial relationships in which individuals imagine talking to television characters portrayed by celebrities. However, in some cases, the individuals are infatuated by the celebrity him- or herself, rather than the character that he or she plays. Individuals in parasocial relationships are often lonely and isolated from real-life interactors (Caughey, 1984). Edwards et al. (1988) found that loneliness is negatively correlated with having IIs; lonely individuals are less likely to experience such mental conversations. Loneliness is also negatively correlated with how well IIs prepare a person to talk about feelings or problems in later actual conversations ($r = -0.40$), and

---

Box 5.2   Imagined Interaction Journal Entry About an Ex-Girlfriend

I had a relationship in high school with a girl that was serious as far as high school relationships go. We dated for almost a year and then broke up. Even though I was the one who terminated the relationship, I was also the one who was the most lonely afterwards. I can remember keeping up with the girl through our mutual friends. I wanted to know who she was dating, what they were doing, and whether or not she still liked me. I would have imagined interactions with this girl where I would tell her the things that bothered me about her. She would change the behaviors that I did not like and then we would get back together.

For whatever reasons, I was not able to come straight out and talk to her about the problems I was having with her. Instead I just terminated the relationship. I often still imagined being with this girl years afterwards and would go over in my mind things we had said and what could have been said different. Sort of a cross between fantasizing and imagined interaction. A couple of years after high school and probably four years since we had dated, we met in a college town and had a few dates. Within a very short time, maybe two weeks, our relationship was right back to where it was before I terminated it with her in high school.

Again she showed behavior that was close to that which I had not been able to accept in high school and again I terminated the relationship. This time, however, we both sort of broke contact and did not make an effort to reach one another. Although I still think about this person on occasion, it is only because she was a big part of my past and I tend to reflect on my past experiences and relationships at times.

---

with their being able to make a person feel more confident ($r = -0.30$). There is also a weak but positive correlation between loneliness and the discrepancy between IIs and real encounters. Greater loneliness is associated with a greater difference between actual and imagined interactions.

Lonely individuals experience less satisfaction and more negative emotions in IIs than do nonlonely individuals (Honeycutt, Zagacki, et al., 1989). These results suggest that the tendency to have IIs is affected by various personality characteristics, such as locus of control, sensitivity to conversations, and communication competence (Honeycutt, Edwards, & Zagacki, 1989–1990; Honeycutt et al., 1992–1993). One reason that lonely individuals may have fewer IIs is that they have fewer actual conversations to review and rehearse. The low number of actual interactions leaves lonely individuals with few real resources for constructing (or reviewing) later IIs. However, one resource available to a lonely individual is to engage in an imagined dialogue with a celebrity, thereby creating a parasocial relationship that is fostered through IIs.

Not all imaginary relationships are associated with loneliness or dysfunctional cognitions. Related to the idea of parasocial relationships are what have been referred to as imaginary-playmate relationships among children. Imaginary playmates (IPs) are the partners in children's imagined relationships in which they talk with a chimerical significant other, such as a make-believe friend, companion, or mentor (Connolly, 1991). There is also research on adults who report about the IPs they had while growing up. For example, Connolly interviewed 69 community college students and discovered that 24 (34%) admitted to having had an IP. Those students who had had IPs had higher grades in school than those who had not had them. Connolly summarized studies that reveal positive profiles for children reporting IPs, suggesting that they are more self-reliant, are more socially cooperative, are less bored, are less impulsive, smile more frequently, watch less TV, and do not have greater or fewer emotional and behavioral problems than children without IPs. In addition, Singer (1979) found that children as young as 3 and 4 who have IPs are happier, have more advanced linguistic skills, and exhibit more ability to concentrate than children without IPs. Thus, as with most aspects of human cognition, the IIs that accompany IPs should be viewed as processes that are neither good nor bad and whose value can only be seen in the social context that surrounds interpersonal communication.

AFFECT AND IMAGINED INTERACTIONS

IIs can help to maintain relationships by allowing people to think about previous encounters and reexperience the positive emotions associated with them. People become closer to those they care about through mental rehearsal and anticipation. Furthermore, pleasant emotions are associated with having more IIs that are similar to actual encounters rather than being different from actual interactions (Honeycutt et al., 1989–90). Data collected using thought-sampling research, in which individuals were given beepers and told to write down in a small diary what they were feeling at the time they were beeped, reveal that subjects' thoughts are concerned with present-life concerns 67% of the time and with the past or future concerns 24% of the time. Thoughts about the past tend to involve reviewing previous events and using critical evaluation (Klinger, 1987). Thoughts about the future tend to be in the form of rehearsals and setting up alternative scenarios for anticipated events. According to Singer (1987), this process "helps us to maximize the lessons we draw from past experiences and to plan better ways of dealing with upcoming contingencies" (p. 8).

Support for Klinger's (1987) notion that emotion is concerned with current concerns is provided in the findings of additional research. For example, Zagacki et al. (1992) had subjects evaluate the level of emotional intensity (1 = low intensity, 2 = medium, 3 = strong) in a recently recalled II, the level of emotional feeling associated with the II (1 = positive, 2 = neutral, 3 = mixed feelings, 4 = negative), and the level of communication satisfaction they felt with the II. Analysis indicated that highly intense IIs featured romantic partners and family members, whereas less-intense IIs featured work partners. High intensity was also associated with II topics that had to do with relational conflict. Medium intensity was associated with topics related to school, work, and small talk. So it seems that the most prominent IIs are associated with intimate relationships, even though they may attend a wider range of potential interaction contexts.

Negative affect in IIs may be linked with Sherman and Corty's (1984) simulation heuristic. According to this heuristic, individuals who narrowly fail to achieve certain goals may find it easier to construct counterfactual scenarios that would have led to their success. To the extent that retroactive IIs can simulate earlier unsuccessful experiences, the individual may imagine the same events with more successful outcomes. It should be noted, however, that the construction or reconstruction of scenarios that avoid failure may evoke strong negative affect because of the importance of the issue (Zagacki et al., 1992). People often wonder, "If only I had said.... " and find that such wishful thinking results in them mentally kicking themselves for not having the foresight of hindsight.

An intriguing study by Klos and Singer (1981) revealed that various induced IIs elicited different kinds of emotions on the subject of parental conflict. The researchers studied the determinants of adolescents' ongoing thoughts following simulated parental confrontations. They examined the effect of resolved versus unresolved situations with parents, as well as nonconflict interaction with parents versus conflict interaction. The researchers also investigated interactions in which the parents' attitudes were coercive or collaborative. They proposed that exposure through a simulated interaction to these conditions affected later recurrence of simulation-relevant thoughts about the parent.

The subjects' induced IIs were in one of six conditions: (a) collaborative decision making with the parent that was resolved, (b) collaborative decision making with the parent that was unresolved, (c) collaborative confrontation with the parent that was resolved, (d) collaborative confrontation with the parent that was unresolved, (e) coercive confrontation with the parent that was resolved, and (f) coercive confrontation with the parent that was unresolved. Subjects engaged in simulated interactions with one of their parents, with a research assistant reading the parent's part in a predeveloped script appropriate to each situation.

Coercive confrontation involved the parent trying to win the argument and not listening to the subject's viewpoint. In collaborative confrontation, the parent expressed his or her own view while trying to understand the subject's view and remaining open to a mutually acceptable compromise. In collaborative decision making, the parent and the subject worked together to find a solution to an interpersonal problem that they shared but that was external to their relationship. The resolution and nonresolution of problems were operationalized by having subjects either reach a solution or leave the dialogue unresolved at the end of three imagined interactions.

After these IIs, subjects were taken to another room and over a period of 20 minutes thought samples were elicited. A buzzer was sounded 20 times at random, and each time the subjects reported what they were thinking, feeling, or imagining. The thoughts were coded as simulation-related if they included direct references to or associations with the simulation conditions. Affect was measured before and after the simulations using Likert scales (1 = absence of emotion; 5 = strong emotion) reflecting interest, anger, distress, joy, disgust, and contempt. How much stress the subjects felt regarding their parents was measured using items that assessed the extent of interpersonal conflict and the satisfaction of needs such as acceptance, recognition, and support.

The results revealed that after the simulations were over, anger was higher in the coercive conditions than in the collaborative conditions. The thought-sample intervals revealed that once exposed to a simulated parental conflict, students with a history of parental stress devoted as much as 50% of their later thoughts to things associated with the simulations. Klos and Singer (1981) surmised that the reawakening of unpleasant past experiences is enough to sustain arousal and recurrent thought, even if the conflict is resolved. It could be that the thoughts of adolescents who have a history of parental stress are frequently unpleasant because many environmental cues (e.g., television and film plots) trigger recurrent conflict thoughts. Perhaps it is reasonable to surmise that the same could be true of adults and their romantic liaisons.

USE OF IMAGINED INTERACTIONS IN LINKING TOGETHER PRIOR CONVERSATIONS

Repetitive, stimulus-relevant cognitions may be related to linked IIs in which multiple functions are served. In the case of long-standing conflict between parents and children or between romantic partners, conflict may be kept alive and maintained in the absence of the other person by having retroactive and proactive IIs. Even though a retroactive II is experienced, it may be immediately linked with a proactive II (e.g., "Last time, I bit my lip. Next time I see him, I am going to say exactly how I feel."). Given that IIs tend to occur with significant others, it may be that many of them are linked and occur between encounters as a means of reviewing and previewing conversations. Box 5.3 contains a sample protocol from a 21-year-old wife in which she described a recent II. She felt positive while imagining it, although the II was a reconstruction of a prior conversation with her husband in which she felt ignored.

The linking of a series of actual interactions through IIs helps explain why it is often difficult to counsel people in conflict-habituated marriages. Conflict

---

**Box 5.3   Sample II Protocol Linking a Prior
Conversation to an Anticipated One**

Gender: Female
Age: 21
Relationship of other participant: Husband
Length of conversation: 10 minutes
Scene of II: home
Topic(s) discussed: My expectations and his attitude toward me
Self-reported emotions about the II: Felt better because I had an idea about
what I was going to say.
Me: You know, you really hurt my feelings by your comments a few minutes
ago.
Husband: Why? That's stupid! They had nothing to do with you. You should-
n't be so sensitive.
Me: They had everything to do with me. When you snap at me like that, when
I'm just being concerned, it hurts my feelings. It makes me feel like you have
something to hide. I mean, I just asked you a simple question and you get all
sarcastic. I don't understand why you have to react that way.

---

may be kept alive through IIs in such a way that a conflict theme emerges within
the relationship. For example, out of the presence of a spouse, one partner may
keep conflict alive by reliving the conflict scenes and rehearsing what he or she
wants to say at the next encounter. Thus, conflict may pick up where it left off.
At the next encounter, couples in such marriages need to be instructed about
how to produce more positive images of interactions with their spouse and en-
act the positive, imagined messages in an actual encounter.

Acitelli (1993) speculated that married couples in conflict are less likely to
remain in conflict if their actual conversations shift from individual blaming to
discussion that is more relationally oriented. One way to do this is to welcome
positive IIs and to practice talking in the plural, using we, for example, and saying, "We've got a problem," instead of "You've got a problem." In doing so, romantic combatants might be better able to focus on the interdependent nature
of relational conflict while avoiding the personalization of problems that are
typically rooted in the dynamic between the two parties. Given the perceptual
basis for IIs, however, this might be easier said than done.

Research has revealed that the self talks more during IIs (Edwards,
Honeycutt, & Zagacki, 1989). In IIs, people have easier access to their own
thoughts and know our own attitudes better. It is easier to think about their own
attitudes than to accurately predict another's speech or action. In this regard,
there is evidence that married couples often reenvision egocentric attributions
as to who is responsible for various behaviors in marriage. For example, individuals tend to assume more responsibility for giving compliments and trying to re-

solve problems in their relationships compared to how much credit they give their partners. Thompson and Kelley (1981) found that individuals reported remembering more information about themselves than they recalled instances of their partners providing similar information. After having gone through the divorce process, individuals often take more credit for positive events because this serves the function of enhancing their self-image and presenting themselves in a favorable light. These attributions have been explained in terms of Tversky and Kahneman's (1974) availability heuristic, according to which it is easier for individuals to retrieve from memory instances of themselves doing positive behaviors precisely because those thoughts are more likely to have been dwelt on at the time of enactment.

The domination of the self in IIs is consistent with findings in attribution theory. Attribution theorists (Kelly & Michella, 1980; Nisbett & Ross, 1980; Ross, 1977) examined the fundamental attribution error, in which there are actor–observer differences in accounting for the cause of behavior. Attributional studies reveal that information about an individual is more available to him- or herself than is information about others, and that the individual is relatively unable to take the perspective of others. Therefore, individuals process primarily their own roles and thoughts when imagining actions and dialogue with others.

As noted earlier, in addition to psychologically maintaining relationships and linking a series of interactions, IIs serve the functions of catharsis and enhancing self-understanding (Honeycutt, 1991). Catharsis relieves tension and reduces uncertainty about another's actions during the imaging process. Individuals imagine interacting with others in such a way that messages are explored and tested for their effect on others. Individuals may feel better while imagining. The account in Box 5.4 provided by a 22-year-old male who kept a journal on IIs for a 7-day period, illustrates this point. The account also reveals the discrepancy between an II and a real interaction.

GENDER DIFFERENCES IN IMAGINED
INTERACTIONS AND MEMORY

There are a number of gender differences in the use of IIs. Edwards et al. (1989), found that women have more frequent and pleasant IIs than do men. Women also talk more in these imagined dialogues than do men. Both genders tend to recall both the lines of dialogue and the visual scenes of IIs, rather than only the imagined dialogue. However, women reported that they were able to see the surroundings in their IIs and recall the scene in which the II took place much more often than men did. Men were twice as likely to have IIs with female partners rather than with other men. Yet, due to the increased frequency of IIs among women, women still were three times more likely than men to have opposite-gender partners in their IIs.

**Box 5.4   Imagined Interaction Journal Accounts of a Man
Encountering a Woman After a Long Absence**

Last summer I met a girl in Florida and we wrote each other for quite some time.
We both kept saying we wanted to see each other, but our plans never material-
ized. Finally, in September she was going to fly to New Orleans to see me. From
the moment she told she was coming to visit, I began imagining what it would be
like when we saw each other. I figured we would embrace passionately at the air-
port and have a million things to say to each other. I figured we would go out Friday night to the French Quarter and go to bars. She had never been to a bar
before. At the time the drinking age was 18 in New Orleans and 21 in Alabama
(her home state). Saturday I planned for us to go to the Riverwalk all day and then
go out again that night. Sunday morning I was supposed to bring her to Biloxi,
where she had a ride home to Alabama.

Well, welcome to reality. When she got off the plane, we kind of half-hugged each
other and really didn't know what to say to each other. Most of our conversation
was small talk. After we got to my house and showered, we went to the French
Quarter. We probably didn't stay there any longer than an hour before we decided
that we were exhausted and ready to get some sleep. Surprisingly, Saturday was
pretty much like I had planned. We spent the whole day at the Riverwalk and really enjoyed ourselves. However, Saturday night was a different story. We began
the night as I had planned by going to bars. Then the real excitement began. At
about one o'clock in the morning she told me she had to make a phone call. After
she got off the phone, I was informed that she had to leave for Biloxi right then.
Instead of spending a nice evening out with her, I spent most of the night going to
Mississippi. This was definitely a good example of an imagined interaction being
quite different than the actual experience.

Fortunately, all of my imagined interactions were not this disappointing. Because
my present girlfriend is living in New Orleans this semester, I often have imagined
interactions about the two of us. For instance, I often imagine us embracing and
kissing when we see each other on Fridays. These imagined interactions are often
fulfilled and then some. I also imagine things we are going to say to each other and
these dialogues are also fulfilled. We often tell each other how much we thought
about each other and how much we missed each other.

Of course, the vividness and specificity of women's IIs are largely consistent
with other studies revealing that women think more often than men do about
relationship processes. Women are more aware of problems in a relationship, are
less surprised when a relationship is terminated, and have more vivid memories
of relational events (Hill et al., 1976; Ross & Holmberg, 1992). Edwards et al.

(1989) surmised that women are more socialized to think about the socioemotional aspects of relationships than are men. This is reflected in II topics about dating that are pleasant. Edwards et al. found in their sample that the primary II topic for both genders was dating. They decided that one cause of gender differences in relationship awareness may be that messages for interactions are derived by observing the actual conversations of others, after which the messages are incorporated into IIs. Another possibility is that men and women approach communication about relationships differently, and that these different approaches are reflected in thoughts about communication, whether in IIs or in actual encounters.

Acitelli (1993) examined relationship awareness in terms of how couples perceive the effects of talking about their relationships on their feelings of contentment. Married couples read stories about couples in which the partners either talked or did not talk about their relationship in pleasant and unpleasant situations. After reading each story, real spouses rated the fictional spouses' feelings. Acitelli's results revealed that fictional spouses who talked about their relationship made real spouses feel better, regardless of the tone of the conversation. However, relationship talk during pleasant situations had more of a positive impact on wives than on husbands. Men felt better about relational talk in unpleasant situations than in pleasant ones. Scott et al. (1991) speculated that women may be likely to view their conversations as relationship-relevant and to store the conversation as a relationship memory, whereas men see the conversations in terms of the issue discussed. If this is correct, this hypothesis might account for the robustness of women's IIs, because presumably, people have imagined conversations with a person in a relationship about an issue rather than with an issue itself, and it is those interpersonal dimensions that women tend to focus on.

Acitelli (1992) interviewed married couples about their lives, an analytic device known as collecting an oral history of the marriage (Gottman, 1979). One of the benefits of this kind of interview is that even unhappily married couples often relive pleasant events that occurred in the early stages of their marriage. Couples were asked to tell the story of their relationship from the time they first met to what they thought their future will be like. The spontaneous expression of feelings or needs while telling a story was considered to be an expression of the couples' important concerns. Acitelli coded the partners' responses for relationship talk. Wives' marital and life satisfaction was positively associated with their husbands' relational talk and less with their own relational talk. Wives tended to talk more about their marital relationships than did their husbands. They also reported thinking more about their marriages than did their husbands.

Acitelli (1992) reported that relationship talk in the first year of marriage is related to relationship quality in the third year of marriage. Statements reflecting of relationship awareness (e.g., "We were very much in love at that point.

We wanted to get along better.") correlated positively with marital stability and happiness in the third year of marriage. In addition, the husband's ease, reflected in lack of tension, resentment, and positive adjustment to marriage, was a mediating factor between the spouses' perspective at the end of the first year together and their opinions of marital quality in their third year. A direct effect between relationship talk in the first year of marriage and marital well-being in the third year remained for wives, in addition to the effects the husband's ease variable had for both partners. Hence, Acitelli concluded that relationship awareness influences marital quality only if it leads to the husbands' ease of adjustment. For wives, this relational awareness happens, but need not occur for the relationship perspective to influence her marital quality. Men value relationship talk if it is instrumental in solving a problem, whereas women value relationship talk in pleasant and unpleasant situations.

There are also gender differences in using imagined interactions to maintain roommate relationships. Honeycutt and Patterson (1997) surveyed college roommates about how they maintained smooth relations in which they liked their roommates and the role of IIs in maintaining the relations. They found that women liked their roommates more than did men and that liking their roommates was associated with having more IIs that were pleasant and specific, as opposed to being filled with abstract images. Women also imagined more positive outcomes in their internal dialogues than did men. Liking one's roommate was associated with including the roommate in social activities and occasionally disclosing personal information about one's feelings, fears, or insecurities. Women who imagined conversations with their roommates tended to report acting in warm, caring, and empathic ways. Honeycutt and Patterson (1997) also noted that women's roommate relationships are not as likely to be seen as expendable commodities, compared to men's roommate relationships; and that male roommates are more distant with one another. The finding that women think about conversations with their roommates than do men is consistent with other research that women monitor their personal relationships more compared to men and think about relational events or problems (Harvey, Flannery, & Morgan, 1986 ; Honeycutt, 1993; 1995).

IMAGINED INTERACTION TOPICS WITHIN MARRIAGE

Additional gender differences in IIs and memory in marriage have begun to accumulate. Box 5.5 lists the 10 most frequent II topics from a recently conducted survey, as well as the number of responses and the rank orders for the topics, which were coded using a list of categories that commonly have been identified in marital research as problematic issues in marriage (Spanier, 1976). The results are based on surveys issued to 136 couples. Interestingly, the topic discussed most often by the wives was how the couple communicated. The topics

Box 5.5   Rank Order of Spousal Imagined Interaction Topics Combined

Topics	Rank Order*	Husband	Wife
Future plans and goals	1	1(12)	2 (7)
Sex life	2*	2 (8)	4 (5)
How we communicate	2*	6 (4)	1 (9)
Financial management	4	3 (6)	4 (5)
Our social life	5*	6 (4)	3 (6)
Our relationship	5*	3 (6)	6 (4)
Children	7*	6 (4)	8 (3)
My job	7*	5 (5)	10 (2)
Feelings and emotions	7*	9 (3)	6 (4)
Fantasies	10	9 (3)	8 (3)

Note. Numbers in paretheses reflect raw frequencies

*Asterisk (*) denotes ties.

most discussed by both partners were future plans and goals. The next topic most discussed by husbands and wives was sexual relations, followed by how they communicate.

Imagined Interactions Among Engaged and Married Couples

Giles and Wiemann (1987) in discussing the relationship between language and cognition, indicated that "our very mouths influence our own cognitions" (Giles & Wiemann, 1987, p. 364). Cognition about talk also influences language and message production. Honeycutt and Wiemann (1999) conducted a study among engaged and married couples who were distinguished on the basis of Fitzpatrick's (1988) types of marriage.

Fitzpatrick (1988) developed a polythetic classification scheme of marriage in which individuals are categorized according to their ideologies about marriage, degree of sharing, and engagement in conflict. There are three marital: traditionals, independents, and separates. *Traditionals* have conventional beliefs about marriage, such as emphasizing stability, sharing a lot of activities, and arguing over serious topics. *Independents* have a moderate amount of sharing, willingly engage in conflict over numerous topics, and endorse more contemporary ideologies about marriage, such as believing that marriage should not hinder an individual's autonomy in any way. *Separates* are ambivalent about family values, share few activities, and tend to avoid conflict. The separates have been described as emotionally divorced due to the lack of sharing.

Little research has been conducted examining how the functions of talk are associated with characteristics of imagined interactions among engaged and married couples. Many individuals report spending from 85% to 100% of their time thinking about their partner (Fisher, 1994). Intrusive thinking involves IIs with the partner. Given the strategic functions of communication, such as providing information, interpersonal influence, and impression management, IIs may be used to rehearse message strategies or replay prior messages in order to prepare for future encounters.

Honeycutt and Wiemann (1999) found that there was an association between enjoying serious discussion, talking about the events of the day, equality of talk, and having frequent and pleasant IIs that followed expectations with the relational partner. In his marital interaction research program, Gottman (1994) discussed how talking about the events of the day reveals differences between couple types. The discussion of daily events was related to metatalk or talk about communication and talk about love. Furthermore, the importance of intrapersonal communication is demonstrated through these findings because the functions of talk are linked with specific characteristics of IIs.

Honeycutt and Wiemann (1999) also found that relational satisfaction was associated with being engaged and having pleasant IIs. Thus, internal cognition in which an engaged individual imagines talking with his or her partner predicts happiness in this type of relationship. This finding is important in terms of social cognition because it reveals that a common outcome of close relationships, relationship happiness, is reflected in the minds of individuals internally in the form of intrapersonal communication in which individuals imagine pleasant interactions with relational partners. Hence, communication occurs internally as well as dyadically.

It was found that engaged partners had more IIs, IIs that were pleasant, and IIs that were used to compensate for the lack of real interaction than did marital partners. These findings can be interpreted in terms of the old maxim, "absence makes the heart grow fonder." There may be less rehearsal among the engaged partners due to less conflict in the honeymoon phase of their relational development.

Honeycutt (1995) discussed how one function of IIs is conflict linkage, which explains why conflict is kept alive in the absence of actual interaction. (This theory is discussed in more detail in chap. 10.) Individuals rehearse for the next episode which may reflect a self-fulfilling prophecy insofar as an episode of conflict is imagined and conflict-escalating statements are uttered with the outcome being that the conflict picks up where it left off in a prior encounter. The conflict is kept alive outside of real encounters through imagined dialogue.

Honeycutt and Wiemann (1999) also found that traditionals reported that more-discrepant IIs were used less for rehearsing messages for anticipated encounters than did independents. Because little rehearsing is taking place, there could be more discrepancies in conversational outcomes from what was expected in an II. The research of Sillars and his associates (1987) revealed that traditionals have more communal or sharing themes that are reflected in their conversations compared to independents. However, traditionals and independents also differ in intrapersonal communication processes insofar as the characteristics of IIs are concerned. Other research found that individuals who are sensitive to conversations also see themselves as having a great deal of communication competence (Honeycutt et al., 1992–1993). In turn, communication competence is negatively associated with having a lot of discrepant IIs, whereas conversational sensitivity is associated with a variety of IIs that are specific and occur after real encounters.

Recall that in a discrepant II, a message that is imagined is not communicated during an actual encounter. Traditionals may imagine encounters with their partners to rehearse messages that also inhibit misinterpretation, misunderstanding, or confusion that result in active conflict. Traditionals engage in arguing and conflictual encounters less than independents. Fitzpatrick (1988) reviewed research indicating that traditionals tend to avoid conflict except over serious issues, whereas independents are more likely to disagree about a variety of topics.

Honeycutt and Brown (1998) also investigated the use of IIs to rehearse the telling of jokes in marriage. They found that traditionals used IIs to rehearse jokes and that traditionals reported a greater sense of humor compared to independents and separates. Furthermore, traditional wives laughed at their husbands' jokes more than did the other marital types. Perhaps, amateur comedians in marriage may not feel a strong need to rehearse jokes. In this regard,

Crawford (1989) showed that wives tend to laugh at their husbands' jokes in order to signal affiliation. Yet in order to allow a joke to realize its full impact, the joke-teller must rehearse the joke. This joke rehearsal must take the joke and move it from the unconscious realm of "Oh, that is a funny joke" to the more conscious realm of "How did that punchline work so I can tell my husband?" Imagined interactions are a form of operant thought, not respondent thought. Moving joke rehearsal from the level of unconscious thought to actively, mindfully rehearsing jokes may increase one's sense of humor.

Husbands imagined more joke telling than did their wives. The husbands' jokes are laughed at by their wives, which encourages more jokes. Men use humor more for self-presentation and women use humor to enhance intimacy (Crawford, 1989). Zippin (1966) described women's humor as being at odds with common cultural definitions of femininity, including quietness, nonprovocativeness, and self-consciousness.

SUMMARY

Imagined interactions (IIs) help create relational expectations and thereby contribute to people's memories about romantic pairings. Expectations regarding relationships can be envisioned as the knowledge or memory structures for relationships. Memory structures for relationships help people make sense of behaviors that they observe in other people's and in their own relationships, and they provide a sense of the trajectory relationships are taking. IIs, consequently, provide an important bridge between romantic behavior and the way in which those statements and actions function in the sense-making of the mind.

A romance can be kept alive when the partners in a couple are away from each other by their thinking about it. Individuals in long-distance or commuter relationships report that they often think about their partners. Individuals also have IIs concerning romantic partners they see every day. People imagine conversations with relational partners in which they rehearse anticipated encounters, replay prior encounters, and even keep interpersonal conflict alive. IIs can bring up a variety of emotions that depend on the outcome of the imagined conversation. In addition to rehearsing events and keeping conflict or relationships alive, IIs serve a number of other functions including enhancing self-understanding, catharsis, and compensating for a lack in the actual time spent with one's significant other. In some cases, individuals have parasocial relationships in which they imagine talking with a celebrity or fabricated associate. However, most IIs occur with significant others, including relational partners, family members, and friends. Finally, women seem to produce more stalwart IIs than do men, suggesting that their imagined interactions may exert a stronger influence on the type of communication that occurs in romantic relationships.

IIs help engaged couples maintain the relationship in terms of intrusive thinking. Having positive intrapersonal communication in the form of IIs helps couples maintain their marriages, particularly the traditional marital types. Joke telling also is done by traditionals; husbands use imagined interactions to rehearse jokes while their wives laugh at the jokes even if they are not that funny. Humor helps to maintain people's relationships in the face of adversity.

DISCUSSION QUESTIONS

5.1 Recall the most recent imagined interaction (II) you have had with an individual who is very important in your life. When was it? What was said? How did you feel about the II? What purpose did it serve (e.g., rehearsal for an ensuing encounter, catharsis, enhancing your own understanding, keeping conflict alive, or keeping the relationship alive in your mind)? If the II was before an anticipated encounter, what happened in the encounter? Was the II different from or similar to the actual encounter?

5.2 Discuss any recurring IIs you have with long-lost loves of the past. How often do these occur? Why do you believe you reminisce about these people?

APPLICATIONS

5.1 Keep a daily journal of IIs for a 3-day period. Note the time of day the II occurred, where you were when you had the II, your relationship with the dialogue partner, the topic of the imaged conversations, and how you felt about it.

5.2 Interview three couples about their IIs with each other. How often do they imagine talking with their partners? Do they enjoy the IIs? What purpose did the IIs serve (e.g., keeping conflict alive, replaying love scenes, or reliving pleasant memories)? Are there differences between partners on the topics of the IIs and the vividness of memory about the IIs? If the IIs were used to rehearse for anticipated encounters with partners, are the IIs similar to or different from later interaction scenes?

5.3 Interview three men and three women about imaginary playmates they recall having had as children. Who were these playmates? How old were they when they imagined the playmates? What purposes or functions did the imaginary playmates serve (e.g., companionship, rehearse messages for real-life others, or escapism)? How did the relationship end (e.g., did the person stop imagining the playmate at a certain age or time period)? Did the imaginary playmate teach them anything about human relationships?

6

Development
of Relationships: Stage
Theories Versus Relational
Memory Theory

Scholars studying personal relationships have maintained that relationships develop through a series of phases or stages that reflect an individual's different levels of intimacy with another, ranging from impersonal interactions to intimate relations. Kelley et al. (1983) indicated that "when a relationship changes markedly in a property, it is reasonable to say that it has moved to a new stage or level" (p. 38). The stages reflect different expectations for behavior in any period in a relationship. For example, an initiation stage occurs at an initial meeting and may consist of greeting rituals, small talk about innocuous topics such as the weather, and the discovery of shared interests. The individuals may see one another again and become acquaintances, develop friendship, or become romantically involved.

A common element of these models involves an assumption that there is systematic movement through stages of interaction, even though there is difficulty in accounting for alternating periods of growth and decline over the life history of relationships (Surra, 1990). Movement may occur forward, backward, and laterally. This assumption has been ignored by critics of stage models, who claim that the models posit linear movement in which individuals proceed from one phase to another in a regular sequence. However, stage models allow individuals to enhance intimacy and decrease intimacy at various times and in a variety of contexts. For example, opposing dialectic needs can be used to calibrate the intimacy that is seen as comfortable in a relationship at any time. If one person feels another is coming on too strong or being impulsive, the person may distant him- or herself hoping to set the intimacy at a lower level. *Filters* and *phases* are terms in the literature that are synonymous with developmental stages.

This chapter reviews a number of stage models of relationship development, discussing their contributions and limitations, and how the models have been revised. The chapter concludes with a brief discussion of the role of cognition in reflecting stages in the minds of individuals, followed by sample male and female expectations about intimate relationships.

DEVELOPMENTAL MODELS OF RELATIONSHIPS

Many of the labels that people use to describe relationships (e.g., strangers, acquaintances, friends, best friends, lovers, fighting couple, separated couple, and ex-partners) reflect stages of intimacy. In an examination of 166 cultures, Jankowiak (1995) found evidence of romantic love in 88% of them. Moreover, there are also systematic stages of romance in these cultures. Following are two developmental models based on physiology and communication behavior, respectively.

Physiological Model

Chapter 1 mentions the biochemical work of Fisher (1994), in which she argued that brain physiology drives romantic stages. In this regard, she discussed three stages of romantic love that occur cross-culturally and that are based on brain physiology associated with infatuation, attachment, and detachment that has evolved as part of a primordial mating system. The first stage, infatuation, begins the moment another individual takes on special meaning. This person may be an old friend viewed in a new light or a stranger. The characteristics of this stage include intrusive thinking in which many individuals report spending from 85% to 100% of their time thinking about their partners. Negative traits of the beloved are overlooked, whereas positive traits are aggrandized. Many emotions are felt at this stage, including elation, hope, apprehension, uncertainty, shyness, fear of rejection, helplessness, irrationality, uncontrollability, and longing for reciprocity.

Tennov (1980) measured the distance from the moment that infatuation started to the moment of feeling of neutrality. She found that this stage typically lasts from 18 months to 3 years. The end of infatuation may be linked to brain physiology because the nerve endings in the brain become habituated to the natural stimulants or the levels of these amphetamine-like substances begin to drop.

As infatuation declines, the second stage of romantic love, attachment, begins. The end of infatuation may be linked to changes in brain physiology because the nerve endings become habituated to the level of neurotransmitters in the brain. Fisher (1994) cited researchers who hypothesized that endorphins give partners feelings of safety, peace, and stability. Contentment characterizes this stage. The duration of attachment is not known.

Detachment is the third stage of romance. The physiology that accompanies detachment has not been analyzed. However, Fisher (1994) suggested that the brain's receptor sites for the endorphins or other neurochemicals become further desensitized or overloaded after the decline of attachment. This decline sets up the mind for separation from the partner. As noted in chapter 1, Fisher (1994) proposed that there is a tendency for men and women to pair and remain together for about 4 years, which reflects an ancestral reproductive strategy to cooperatively raise a single helpless infant.

Fisher noted that in many cultures divorce occurs regularly during and around the fourth year of marriage. Men and women tend to divorce in their 20s, the height of their reproductive years. Men and women are more likely to abandon relationships that have produced no children or one dependent child. In addition, many divorced individuals of reproductive age remarry. According to Fisher (1994), the longer a marriage lasts, the older spouses get, and the more children they have, the more likely they are to remain together. Although there are obvious exceptions, these characteristics persist across cultures regardless of the standard of living.

The brain physiology for stages of romance may have evolved to fuel the human primordial mating system. Fisher (1994) discussed the emergence of serial monogamy more than 4 million years ago, when male hominids were unable to obtain enough food to sustain a harem, but could provide food and protection for a single female hominid. This pair-bonding during the infancy of a child was critical for human women and practical for men, and monogamy evolved.

Fisher (1994) posited that as a couple aged, as the length of their pair-bond increased, or as a couple bore successive young, the flexible neural circuits in the brain helped to sustain the pair-bond. With the expansion of the human cerebral cortex over 1 million years ago, humans began to build on the core of primal cyclic emotions by adding other feelings; cultural rituals; and beliefs about attraction, attachment, and detachment.

Fisher (1994) also discussed how culture plays an important role in infatuation. By the teenage years, people carry with them an unconscious mental template or love map that consists of physical, psychological, and behavioral traits that an individual finds attractive in a mate. Mental templates for relationships are discussed in detail in the chapter 7, in terms of relationship schemata.

A Communication Model

Other models of relational development concentrate on the communication behaviors of the individuals. In this regard, Knapp and Vangelisti (1996) defined relationship stages in terms of the amount of repetitive communicative behaviors over time. For example, physical affection, self-disclosure, and dating occurring within a time period reflects the intensification of a relationship. Their model contains five stages of communication growth.

1. Initiating. Two individuals meet and communication is stylized to allow the individuals to talk with little knowledge of one another.
2. Experimenting. There is the use of small talk and interaction rituals in order to discover similarities with one another. Norms of politeness characterize these interactions and individuals present a desired image of themselves.
3. Intensifying. A close friendship develops, intimate disclosure increases, and private symbols are used to identify the couple as a unique dyad.
4. Integrating. Personalties fuse, social networks merge, and the couple is seen as a couple by outsiders. A jointly constructed view of the world emerges and plans are made with one another in mind.
5. Bonding. There is a serious discussion about commitment. There are public rituals that announce that the commitments are formally contracted, such as exclusively seeing one another, becoming engaged, or getting married.

Knapp and Vangelisti also discussed five stages of decay in which communication progressively becomes restricted and eventually, ceases to exist.

1. Differentiating. Partners begin to remind one another of how different they are. There may be a repetitive cycle of breaking up and making up, as partners move from bonding to differentiating, back to integrating, and so on.
2. Circumscribing. There is less communication, both in terms of the number of interactions and the depth of the topics discussed. Familiar phrases are "Let's not talk about this anymore," and "I have nothing to say."
3. Stagnating. Communication is at a standstill. As a result, there may be imagined interactions (IIs) about topics because they feel they know how the encounters will go. It is useless to communicate because the encounters are perceived to be unproductive. Knapp and Vangelisti (1996) indi-

cated that communication becomes more stylized, difficult, rigid, hesitant, awkward, and narrow.

4. Avoiding. There is a physical separation of the partners. The other person is seen less, and reasons may be given about why one individual cannot see his or her partner.
5. Termination. Relationships can terminate immediately, after a greeting, or over many years. There may be a summary statement reviewing the relationship's history and providing the reasons for the ending of the relationship.

An additional stage of decay could be called post-termination awareness of the ex-partner. This stage happens when the individual thinks about the ex-partner or the relationship and recalls events in the relationship. Individuals are likely to be in this stage to the extent they have not found alternative interests, diversions, behaviors, or partners that allow them to focus externally on other stimuli. Even remarried individuals with children from a prior marriage are aware of their ex-partner through visitation encounters and reports from their children about the ex-partner.

Movement is basically sequential in the stage models, as individuals tend to progress through adjacent stages rather than skipping stages. Knapp and Vangelisti (1996) indicated that "(1) each stage contains important presuppositions for the following stage; (2) sequencing makes forecasting adjacent stages easier, and (3) skipping stages is a gamble on the uncertainties presented by the lack of information that could have been learned in the skipped step. Some social norms even help to inhibit skipping steps" (p. 53). For example, even though sexual intercourse may occur as an isolated event for individuals getting to know each other, it is often associated with couples in an intensifying stage, due to its repetition.

Although movement tends to be orderly, it may occur at various speeds in various directions with a variety of results (Altman, Vinsel, & Brown, 1981; Baxter, 1985; Knapp & Vangelisti, 1996; Taylor & Altman, 1987). In addition, there are many paths on the road of relational escalation and deescalation that may lead to the continual recalibration of the relationship or to its ending. Consider couples who argue a great deal compared to couples who argue only intermittently. Repetitive arguing reflects the differentiating stage, in which the relational partners are distancing themselves and stressing individual needs (Knapp & Vangelisti, 1996). Intermittent arguing could be subsumed under another stage label, depending on what preeminent behaviors characterize the communication of the relational partners.

Contributions of Developmental Models

The developmental models represent a relational life cycle symbolizing the evolution of different kinds of relationships, from initial meeting to final encounter in some cases. Different types of relationships are the result of the progression toward or away from intimacy. Developmental models have helped researchers to understand relationship dynamics by describing the role of communication (e.g., self-disclosure, reading one's partner's nonverbal cues, sending clear nonverbal cues, resolving conflict in constructive manners) in defining the current state or stage of a relationship (Knapp & Vangelisti, 1996). The amount of self-disclosure in a relationship reflects the importance and intimacy of the relationship as well as reducing the uncertainty about attitudes and roles (Baxter & Wilmot, 1984; Berger & Bradac, 1982).

The developmental theories are helpful in generating questions about stage identification. For example, when does one stage end and another begin? What is the transition period between stages? How long does each stage last? What is the theoretical justification for the concept, other than the passage of time? These questions have led stage researchers to revise the assumptions in their models to allow a recycling through stages (Altman et al., 1981).

The developmental theories have been helpful in marking the passage of time in relationships. For example, family researchers have used the notion of the family life cycle for the past 40 years to describe temporal order in families. The family life cycle has assumed the existence of an intact marriage. Other family forms, such as those with remarried individuals, single parents, or older couples with additional children who are younger than their grandchildren, have not been captured well by the stages of the family life cycle. For example, older couples are in multiple stages of the cycle.

The developmental models have great appeal because they help people to reduce uncertainty about the type of personal relationships people may find themselves in. Duck (1986) noted that these theories "draw our partner's personality in finer and finer detail as the relationship deepens and develops" (p. 83). Yet the models have been criticized for emphasizing thinking about relationships and observing oneself and one's partner's actions or reactions. On the other hand, college students exposed to these models often report that they are able to recognize behaviors and make sense of what is happening in their current relationships or to attribute meaning to behaviors in their previous relationships. The recognition of behaviors involves memory recall of events in relationships. Relational schemata are activated in order to make sense of the progression of events, behaviors, or activities in personal relationships, and one way this is done is by conceptualizing relational development in terms of stages.

Stage theories of relationship development have been useful in helping individuals in relationships bring order to what otherwise may be seen as a series of unrelated events. Hinde (1979) noted that relationships are constantly developing and that it becomes a matter for developmental theorists to partition the concept of personal relationships into smaller meaningful categories that provide an understanding of the properties and life cycle of relationships. Thus, the stage concept has been used to reflect relational properties in terms of the occurrence of repetitive behaviors (Honeycutt, 1993).

The identification of recurring behaviors and the categorization of these behaviors into categories reflecting developmental stages provides individuals with a vocabulary to assist in their understanding the movement and dynamics of relational development. For example, increased dating may be categorized as the intensification of a relationship if one wonders about reciprocal intimate feelings from one's partner. Relationships may also intensify after partners overcome some type of relationship crisis, such as feeling insecure or jealous about one another's activities (Planalp & Honeycutt, 1985). Hence, developmental models serve a critical function in symbolizing motion in relationships. Movement is based on need, exchange of rewards, social background, and shared relational memory structures based on similar experiences.

Duck (1990) discussed how motion is the fundamental property of relationships, rather than a steady state. However, couples often present an image to others of orderly, routine, or predictable patterns of communication in order to stabilize that perpetual motion. In addition, individuals often tell stories about relationship events to provide order for time-ordered events (Askham, 1982). The provision of order reflects a desire for structure and predictability. The ordering of relational events often reflects underlying stages that reflect the passage of time.

People's memories of relational events often reflect stage-like qualities because individuals tell stories about meeting for the first time, developing intimacy, getting married, dealing with conflicts in the relationship, and ending prior relationships. Yet if someone is asked to tell the story about his or her marriage, the person will look bewildered and may reply, "Well, what do you want to know about my marriage; the story of how we met, the wedding, the time we went to Cancun, or the time we were both in the hospital?" Stories about events bring order to the passage of time and punctuate the relationship into a series of identifiable events that often can be viewed as reflecting stages of intimacy. In essence, the developmental models have advanced people's understanding of the temporal organization of relationships.

Limitations of Developmental Models

Critics of stage models have argued that the stages are hard to identify, may be skipped, are arbitrarily defined, and simply represent the passage of time in relationships. It is argued the stages do not really exist because movement through them is capricious and depends on the individual relationship. Despite the problems of precisely identifying stages, as well as the direction and rate of movement through the stages, a variety of models have been proposed. In fact, a saturation point seems to have been reached with the diversity of models (e.g., Altman & Taylor, 1973; Baxter, 1985; Coleman, 1977; Duck, 1982; Knapp & Vangelisti, 1996; Lee, 1984; Levinger, 1974; Murstein, 1974, 1986).

Early models of relational development were simple. Levinger (1974) proposed a three-stage awareness model. In unilateral awareness, the individuals are not aware of each other in a reciprocal fashion; A may be aware of B, but B is unaware of A. Bilateral awareness involves small talk; relationships between acquaintances represent this type of awareness. Mutual awareness is more intimate and involves a shared dependency between the people. Additional three-stage models have been proposed. For example, Duck (1986) described a physical appearance stage followed by an assessment of the other person's attitudes and one's compatibility with the other person's personality.

Levinger (1980, 1983) revised the three-stage awareness model and proposed a five-stage model that includes: (a) initiation and awareness of the other person, (b) building the relationship, (c) continued interaction that may lead to marriage, (d) deterioration or decline of the bond, and (e) ending of the relationship through death or some type of separation. These five stages correspond to three states of growth, maintenance, and termination.

A three-stage model that has received a great deal of attention and criticism over the years is the stimulus-value-role (SVR) model. The assumptions of this model were debated in research journals (e.g., Leigh, Holman, & Burr, 1987; Murstein, 1974, 1986, 1987; Rubin & Levinger, 1974; Stephen, 1987). Murstein (1987) proposed that individuals who initially encounter another are in the stimulus (S) stage in which an individual evaluates an encountered person in terms of physical qualities and nonverbal inferences based on voice or clothing. The second stage, value (V), is presumed to exist when the individuals share basic attitudes regarding a variety of opinions or beliefs on issues such as religious beliefs, politics, abortion, euthanasia, and so on. The final stage is the role compatibility (R) stage in which the partners evaluate the functions of roles that have evolved in relation to each other. For example, individuals may perceive themselves as co-equal decision makers, supporters, lovers, guardians, and so on relative to one another.

SVR theory has received continued attention even though the basic premises of the theory have been questioned. Individuals may require information about stimulus, values, and roles continuously. It appears that the rate of acceleration in which information is acquired defines each stage. Stephen (1987) argued that a model that proposes that values and attitudes are created through communication is a problem for stage theorists because communication theories assume individuals can value different kinds of information unequally. Some individuals value stimulus information above all else (physical appearance) whereas others may examine role information first.

The SVR sequence is not the same from individual to individual. Further, what happens if two individuals who meet have different sequences? Does that relationship end, do the individuals negotiate sequences, or does one person follow the sequence preferences of the other? These questions are important because they define what happens in the development of a relationship in which the participants have different expectations about the occurrence or timing of behaviors that may be indicative of various stages. Individuals are likely to be more compatible when they have similar expectations about relationship development.

Another problem with the SVR model is role classification. What roles are partners assigned to, friend, lover, best friend, and so on? Leigh et al. (1987) had difficulty classifying individuals in the value and role stages using Murstein's (1986) model. The recognition of this difficulty in classification has resulted in an attempt to set more precise standards for categorization. Murstein (1987) indicated that "information on all classes of variables accrues continuously, with the rate of acceleration determining the three stages ... Information about values accumulates during the R stage, but not to the extent it did during the V stage" (p. 931).

The problems associated with the SVR model apply to other developmental models. Lewis (1973) posited a stage sequence in which individuals initially notice similarities to one another, develop rapport and begin to self-disclose, and cast themselves into roles vis-à-vis one another. Finally, the bond between the partners is crystallized or cemented. Yet the movement may not be sequential because individuals can develop rapport and then notice dissimilarities from one another.

In addition to these problems associated with the SVR model, the developmental models present a view of relationships as being relatively predictable, orderly, and rational to the extent that individuals progress through stages. This view of relationships has been referred to as the *linear assumption* of the development of relationships. The linear assumption has been criticized by a number of researchers on the basis that individuals seemingly skip some stages, do not progress through all the stages or have different rates of movement through the stages.

King and Christensen (1983) modeled relationships using a Guttman scale—an additive scale in which the endorsement of certain items is necessary before other items can be endorsed. That is, a Guttman scale presumes that an individual will endorse the item "We have spent a whole day with just each other" and "I like you" before reporting "I love you," and that a discussion about becoming engaged or getting married will occur before a discussion about living together.

King and Christensen's scale has six stages of relational growth: (a) expression of mutual attraction in terms of the amount and variety of interaction increasing, (b) identification by the social network of the individuals as a couple, (c) increase of emotional investment as the participants identify their feelings as love and avoid rival romantic involvements, (d) projection of their relationship into the future while considering commitment and maximum levels of interdependence, (e) coordination of time, money, and activities for the benefit of joint interests, and (f) commitment to the permanence and exclusiveness of the relationship through engagement, living together, or marriage. Some of these stages are similar to the social-penetration escalating-stages model discussed by Altman and Taylor (1973) and Knapp and Vangelisti (1996).

There are a number of examples in the literature of nonsequential move-ment through the stages of decaying relationships, the stages of breaking up or relational disillusionment. Lee (1984) proposed a five-stage dissolution model: (a) discovery of dissatisfaction, in which a problem, conflict, or dissatisfaction threatens the continuance of the relationship, (b) exposure, in which dissatis-faction is discussed with friends or the partner, (c) negotiation, which begins when serious discussion occurs concerning issues of dissatisfaction, (d) resolu-tion, which takes place when one or both partners reach a decision about the re-lationship and any action to be taken, and (e) final transformation, in which a change actually takes place.

Other researchers have found support for the omission of stages, calling the linear assumption into question. For example, Lee (1984) analyzed subjects' memories about 112 relational breakups and found that only 17% of disengag-ing relationships went through all of the stages. Complex scenarios or mixed for-mats involving stage recycling included 31% of the cases. Other scenarios involved omission of the discussion of dissatisfaction (26.8% of cases). Lee con-cluded that although the ending of relationships may be messy or uncontrolled, the individual's retrospective memory recall suggested that the dissolution pro-cess occurs in regularities. These regularities include a high association between the dimensions of termination (length of the ending, and the conclusiveness or finality of the ending) and the lack of intimacy in the couple.

Termination characteristics were also associated with negative affect dur-ing a breakup, such as confusion and fear, as well as in post-breakup behaviors when encountering the ex-partner. Lee (1984) also found that individuals re-porting little or no communication about issues of dissatisfaction had shorter, less intense relationships that also had less commitment and were more super-ficial. Little or no communication during a breakup represents the omission of the exposure and negotiation stages in his model of disengaging relationships. The omission of stages highlights the difficulty in identifying transitions be-tween adjacent stages.

Problems in Identifying Stage Transitions. The boundary points between stages have been called into question. Duck (1988) indicated that although some sequencing of stages has been demonstrated in a number of models, "no precision or specificity as to their exact operation has been advanced" (p. 73). He viewed process as the essential state of all relationships and apparent stabil-ity as only a temporary equalization of opposing forces.

Conville (1991) argued that developmental models have not provided an adequate view of relationship transitions because they fail to give priority to re-lational partners' personal narratives. On the other hand, Conville believed that the models seem to grant priority to relationship dissolution when relation-ships are placed in the arenas of intrapersonal, interpersonal, and social interaction. Further, there is no precision or specificity as to the exact operation of the transition between the stages.

The lack of precision about stage transitions is revealed in a study by Hays (1984) in which he examined the development of friendship over a 3-month period among male and female college students. Students were given a series of self-report behavior checklists as the year progressed asking their ratings of individuals whom they believed might become good friends. Dyads that developed into close relationships showed more intimacy of disclosure and more talking about a variety of topics. In the successfully progressing friendships, the number of superficial and casual behaviors engaged in slightly increased from time 1 to time 2 and then decreased until time 4 was assessed. The number of affection behaviors, as revealed in the expression of positive or negative sentiment toward the partner, remained relatively stable as the months passed. However, there was a gender difference: women engaged in more affection and casual communication behaviors with their friends than did men. Finally, behaviors such as providing goods, services, or support were the best predictors of the intensity of the friendship at the end of the 3-month time period.

Hays (1984) concluded that some of his findings supported the social penetration model of relational development. The initial interaction of friends was found to correspond to a Guttman-like progression from superficial talk to increasingly intimate levels of behavior. Yet the emergence of intimate behaviors was not gradual. After only 6 weeks, the dyads reached their peak in the reported number of intimate behaviors performed, a pattern no different from that of their nonintimate exchange of behaviors. It was interesting that after 3 weeks of acquaintance, the activity of doing things together was more related to friendship ratings than assessments of how intimate the communication was in the dyad. However, as time passed, the intimacy levels of the dyads' interactions emerged as equally and, in some cases, more associated with ratings of friendship compared to the variety of topics that were discussed. These findings suggest that as friendships develop, individual expectations about and standards for evaluating friendship may change.

RELATIONAL DIALECTIC MODELS

The criticisms about linearity and stage definition have resulted in contemporary developmental theorists revising the models. Their goal was to reflect the dialectic view that relationships never really achieve a particular stage or a steady state because there is continual negotiation and recalibration. Altman et al. (1981) argued for a dialectic model in which the formation of relationships is characterized by cyclicity in that relationships have elements of stability and change that are cyclical. Thus, sequential movement is insufficient to explain the development or decline of relationships (Altman et al., 1981; Baxter, 1985; Taylor & Altman, 1987).

There is continual recalibration of relationship roles. Relationship recalibration may be passive or active. For example, spouses who achieve a certain level of intimacy may give little thought to intensifying the relationship except after arguments or squabbles. On the other hand, a person who wishes to maintain a dating relationship at an existing stage of intimacy, although his or her partner wants to intensify the intimacy, may withdraw from relationship activities and inform his or her partner of the person's hesitancy in escalating the intimacy in the relationship.

VanLear (1987) found support for dialectic behaviors in the development of college friendships. He audiotaped 15 dyads that initially had no history of interaction. The dyads met once a week for 30 minutes over a 6-week period. They were given no instructions on what to talk about in order to create an environment for naturally occurring conversation. Over time, VanLear found that private personal disclosures tended to increase, whereas public (small talk and demographics) and semiprivate disclosures (attitudes and opinions) revealed no systematic trend, reflecting an increase or decrease in these disclosure areas. Reciprocity of disclosure at the same level of intimacy was the rule rather than the exception from period to period. Reciprocity of semiprivate disclosure was more frequent and stronger than reciprocity of public or private disclosure. Self-disclosure occurred in concurrent cycles of reciprocal small talk and semiprivate disclosures. Thus, relational development was not a strict linear process regarding the amount and type of disclosures.

Research has revealed that dialectic behaviors (e.g., one partner discloses, but the other withdraws from the interaction) often reveal systematic patterns of interaction. This was referred to as the *punctuation problem* in communicative encounters by Watzlawick, Beavin, and Jackson (1967). Current behaviors (e.g., He's withdrawn.) are the result of preceding behaviors by a relational partner (e.g., He's nagging because she was asking him personal questions about an issue he did not want to discuss. From her perspective, she asked him questions because he was nagging); the cause of a given response is the effect of a preceding message. Hence, messages are linked, and cause and effect are arbitrary labels applied at particular times. In terms of relational dialectics, John may be trying to escalate intimacy in a relationship because he believes that Mary is withdrawing. On the other hand, Mary is withdrawing because she sees John as moving too fast. At one level, these behaviors may seem to be uncoordinated actions and random movement in different stages of a relationship, with one person escalating and the other de-escalating. Yet the dialectics are inherent in relationships because individual needs may be contrasted with relational obligations or desires.

Dialectic behaviors in relationships reflect changing interpersonal needs. Indeed, Schutz's (1958) classical interpersonal needs theory stressed that individuals have needs for inclusion, control, and affection in a variety of circumstances. Given individual needs at specific times, movement may occur within stages, such as an individual increasing physical affection but the partner reducing the level of affection in order to stabilize the relationship at a particular level of intimacy. Although movement seems to be random, there is the assumption of movement generally occurring through adjacent stages. Yet if relationships are dynamic organisms, then how are one-night stands, holiday romances, and life-long platonic friendships classified in terms of sequential movement? Researchers may be dealing with apples and oranges and referring to them as relational fruit. The varying movements through stages makes the stage (or filter or phase) concept difficult to apply with complete confidence. How does one account for movement backward to earlier stages? Due to the repository of memory and experiences, one can never go back to "The Way We Were," despite the title of the movie.

It is impossible to go back to earlier stages of intimacy after reaching a more intimate stage because memory of prior intimate scenes affects how new information is processed. Conville (1991) argued that because of memories the same event cannot occur. Human experience is presented as a spiral. Due to memory, whenever one repeats an experience and recognizes that one has returned to the experience, the fact of recognition proves that one has not returned to the same experience. In essence, memory is the element that individuals bring back to the same place to acknowledge that it is not the same place. Repeated events are not the same event; rather, repeated events are events of the same type (Conville, 1991).

Although acknowledging that movement may be dialectic and nonsequential, some theorists argued that the decline of relationships often follows a reversal of stages that the partners progressed through while developing the intimate bond (Knapp & Vangelisti, 1996). Yet there is compelling evidence against this reversal hypothesis for declining relationships (Baxter, 1985; Duck & Lea, 1983). On the one hand, Baxter and Montgomery (1996) review research that found support for declining disclosure for individuals reporting on the disengagement of a recent relationship. However, she did not find support for the reversal hypothesis on communication characteristics regarding social knowledge of one's partner.

Other research revealed that the diversity of strategies for relationship growth is greater than the number of disengaging strategies (Baxter & Montgomery, 1996). The beginning of a relationship requires the agreement of both partners in order to succeed, whereas disengagement may be accomplished by one party. Baxter (1985) argued that the reversal hypothesis is less useful as one shifts away from emotion-based features of communication to more cognition-based features. Stages of disengagement such as discovery of dissatisfaction, seeing one another less often, and spending less time together (e.g., Knapp & Vangelisti, 1996; Lee, 1984) do not mirror stages of relational growth. Instead, love and distance are continually being negotiated in relationships. Individuals need varying amounts of love or independence, depending on needs and circumstances.

Communication provides a mechanism for labeling feelings of love and detachment. Yet, the early stage models have been criticized not only for ignoring dialectic needs but for following what Stephen (1987) referred to as a lock-and-key view of development that ignores communication as an ongoing, dynamic process in which roles emerge through interaction and negotiation. Researchers have typically chosen to treat matching characteristics among individuals as traits rather than as being relationally defined through social interaction.

Criticisms of Relational Dialectic Models

Criticisms of dialectic models have also surfaced. First, they have been criticized for overstating the sequential argument at the expense of ignoring an assumption of developmental models that allows for nonsequential movement. Second, the models have been criticized for misrepresenting the social construction of reality by assuming that this only occurs through the negotiation of meanings at a dyadic level and not within the individual.

Berger (1993) disagreed with dialectical theorists who argue that developmental models do not adequately represent process and change and that dialectical approaches are better able to explain nonsequential movement in relationships, as contrasted with smooth trajectories of growth and decay.

Berger (1993) also criticized the belief of dialectical theorists that developmental models focus on the individual and thus are not capable of explaining relationship-level phenomena as the negotiation of meaning and mutual understanding. From a dialectic view, the negotiation of mutual understanding is a dyadic and not an individual phenomenon. Individuals negotiate meanings to determine their appropriate roles in their relationships and the level of affect that is preferred. Recall from chapter 1 that Stephen (1994) discussed happy couples sharing a relationship worldview; he was not clear if this sharing is incidental or negotiated. He indicated that people's conceptions of relationships are transformed by what is brought into the relationship and exposure to one another's constructions of reality. In contrast, Berger (1993) argued that what people commonly call mutual understanding may arise from the joining of individual systems of knowledge. Hence, there is no negotiation, but instead a meeting point or juncture of experiences.

This argument applies to happy couples sharing expectations for the development and maintenance of their relationships, which is an assumption of the relational memory-structure approach, discussed in the next section and in chapter 8. Berger (1993) claimed that "what appear to be 'negotiated meanings' for relationships may in fact simply be the result of overlap of knowledge representation systems that persons bring with them to relationships" (p. 54).

These systems of knowledge include memories about relationships and corresponding expectations for how relationships develop, can be maintained, or die; and they vary in complexity depending on one's experiences or exposure to informational sources. Recall from chapter 1 that much of this knowledge is knowledge of failed relationships (e.g., soap opera viewers may expect romance to be whimsical with infidelity a rule, not an exception).

SOCIAL COGNITION:
THE MEMORY-STRUCTURE APPROACH

As noted in chapter 2, it is important to examine people's expectations about the rise and demise of romance as part of how they interpret events and communication in close relationships. Relationships are states of mind derived from prior experience, which organizes the processing of information. Andersen (1993) wrote, "We collaboratively can think relationships into and out of existence. Because these relational cognitions exist for both partners and rarely match exactly, relationships are tricky, dynamic, and sometimes frustrating" (p. 29). Indeed, the study of communication and human relationships is intriguing because it takes two people to form one, whereas one person alone can dissolve the relationship.

Duck (1986) argued that relationships should be regarded as changing mental and behavioral creations of participants, which play a crucial role in creating and sustaining relationships. Similarly, Berger and Roloff (1982) discussed that the development of relationships can best be understood in terms of individuals' existing or emergent scripts that enable the anticipation of what is likely to happen in a relationship. For example, one individual may have a script for opening lines to introduce oneself to the opposite gender (Kellermann et al., 1989). Expectations for romantic relationships could include behaviors such as walking in a park, periods of touching, intimate communication, and an endless array of actions.

The concept of stage has utility from a cognitive perspective. People have memory structures that consist of prototypical behaviors that they expect to occur in escalating and de-escalating relationships (Honeycutt, 1993). The order of the behaviors reflect stages for relationships; thus, the concept of stage may be useful for examining individuals' perceptions or beliefs about what should occur during the course of relationships.

Marriage therapists often contend that a major factor in the decay of marriages is the erroneous expectations that never-married people bring to their marriages. High expectations before marriage may result in unsatisfactory outcomes (Sabatelli, 1988). For example, never-married individuals tend to expect higher levels of sexual activity, interest in sex, discussion of sexual issues, companionship, and affection from their partners. There are similar expectations when comparing married and never-married individuals about dealing with conflict over daily decisions, recreation, and friends; regarding the amount of arguing over petty issues, agreement on lifestyle, the freedom to pursue friendships, jealousy expressed by partner, and the degree of privacy. Sabatelli (1988) suggested that a reevaluation of expectations should take place after marriage if couples are to continue to be satisfied with their relationships. The reevaluation reflects an accommodation of expectations in order to adjust to new experiences in the marriage.

The memory structure approach places importance on the mental creations of relationships based on memory, talk, and expectations that sustain individuals in everyday living. In addition, current relational experiences affect the reconstruction of prior events in relationships. Recall from chapter 3 that reconstructive memory is longitudinal—current feelings affect how events are recalled in a relationship. A person who is currently angry is unlikely to recall many positive events from his or her relationship.

The developmental models serve as a heuristic anchor for processing relationship behaviors (Honeycutt, 1993). They help people interpret prior events in relationships and prescribe subsequent events. Other research also revealed that prior expectations may influence how people view current behaviors (Nisbett & Ross, 1980). Prior expectations are important in deciding what behaviors are likely to co-occur together. For example, if an older couple is observed eating lunch, holding hands, and kissing in a park, they may be initially seen as married by a stranger. Yet the couple may be having an affair! The observed behaviors may be associated more with a quality marriage than with a romantic affair because the behaviors of demonstrating physical affection are part of the observer's script for marriage.

GENDER DIFFERENCES
IN INTIMATE RELATIONSHIP SCRIPTS

There are gender differences in the complexity of relationship scripts. Consider the excerpts in Box 6.1. The first is provided by a 24-year-old woman who indicated her expectations for an intimate relationship in a journal entry; the second is a journal account from a 28-year-old married man. These two students were enrolled in an interpersonal communication course and kept communication journals for a 2-month period. These excerpts were in response to a question concerning personal expectations for intimate relationships. The students were not exposed to the idea of schemata or scripts at the time of their journal keeping, and the excerpts represent the students' thoughts before being exposed to any theory of relational development. Their expectations reflect reconstructions of memory about previous relationships. For example, the woman writes about how her expectation about a partner's honesty has been changed by memories about relationship activities from a prior relationship.

The italicized words in the journal extracts in Box 6.1 represent keywords that reveal a portion of the woman's and man's scripts or expectations for an intimate relationship. Her expectations include commitment, willingness to invest in the relationship, mutual respect, and equal division of labor. These

Box 6.1 Sample Men's and Women's Expectations for Intimacy and Relationships

Woman's Expectations

I have many expectations for intimacy. These expectations have been developed throughout my lifetime and have been derived from my own relationships, the influence of other's relationships, and my basic morals and beliefs. Basically, an intimate relationship should establish a *commitment* from two people to continue to develop a deep, emotional tie which will stimulate and bring happiness to the couple. Another expectation of intimacy I have is the *willingness to try, or give and take*. I learned this the hard way. My boyfriend would always say, "You're only happy when things go your way." I was willing to try, but only enough to satisfy my own needs. Two people are not going to agree on every issue. Therefore, sometimes one person must accept what he doesn't agree with and go on with matters. Disagreements shouldn't always be a battle with one opponent emerging as the "winner" and the other as the "loser." Another expectation which ties into the idea of trying is *mutual respect*. If there is mutual respect in a relationship, each person can understand the other's beliefs and ideas without necessarily agreeing with them.

The following expectation I hold, may have been influenced by the fact that I live in a small town where this is often seen. The old-fashioned stereotypical roles of the man as the "leader" and the woman as "passive" is an idea which I totally disagree with. I believe in *roles being equal*. The following is an example of this notion. One day a married friend and I went shopping. She repeatedly said she had to be home at a certain time to fix her husband's supper. This is only one example of people still conforming to stereotypical roles. I also feel that my friend probably would think she was not being a "good wife" if she did not conform to these behaviors. My belief on housekeeping is that all duties should be divided equally if both partners are employed.

I would be willing to invest whatever it took (time, patience, emotional support, etc.) to make a relationship work, to the extent that my own identity was not lost in the process. Also, my efforts would be greatly affected by the honesty and sincerity of the other person. Including this idea as well as others I hold have been changed by various memories about relationship activities while being involved in a six-year relationship. Although I may not know exactly what to expect of a relationship such as marriage, I do have a more firm grip on what not to expect.

Man's Expectations

I have a number of expectations for relationships. With the divorce rate so high, it is evident that very severe problems exist between men and women and society today. Those engaged couples are constantly being reminded of the divorce rate as they prepare to embark on a life-long encounter of their own. At this phase in my life, I thought, "We're different. We're older and more mature than most couples. *We share a lot of common interests* and we really love each other." My wife and I have been married for 2 years and we have experienced few arguments in that time. Most people would say that constitutes a good marriage. I feel like my wife and I have a good marriage; however, I think that many relationships exist where there are conflicts and there is still happiness because *they can communicate with each other without being defensive*.

Attitudes are important in determining the quality of a relationship. You must learn to recognize strengths and weaknesses in yourself and your partner. The most important point for any two people to realize is that *conflict is inevitable*. No matter how well you think you know a person, you will always be surprised by something that is said or by some behavior that they engage in from time to time. Two people are going to have opposing ideas on certain issues. I think the key to success is to know your partner and be *sympathetic* to their needs. I look at relationships optimistically. My parents have a good marriage and this is probably the reason I feel the way I do about the institution. My views on life in general today are very similar to those of my parents. I can also see resemblances between my wife's behavior and the behavior of her parents. Nevertheless, I think that *understanding* is the key to a successful marriage and this can only be achieved through *effective communication*.

appear to be key ingredients of a satisfying marital relationship for this woman. The man's expectations include sharing common interests, communicating effectively, expecting conflict, being sympathetic, and believing that one understands his or her partner.

The woman's expectations seem to be more detailed than the man's expectations. This is consistent with research indicating that women monitor their personal relationships more closely than do men and are more aware of events occurring during the life cycle of relationships (Rubin, Peplau, & Hill, 1981). The woman mentions learning about relationships from a wide variety of sources, whereas the man mentions only his parents. This is consistent with previously reported gender differences in reported sources of information about relationships. Although both genders report learning about relationships from parents as a major source, women have reported learning more about relationships from siblings than do men (Honeycutt, Cantrill, & Greene, 1989). This has resulted in some social-learning theorists arguing that modeling same-gender behavior is easier for women than for men due to the lesser availability of fathers (Arliss, 1991; Lynn, 1969). Other theorists have speculated that men may use their mothers as counter-role models once they realize their mothers belong to the opposite gender at between 24 and 36 months after birth.

The themes in the journal entries in Box 6.1 reflect the components of the various developmental theories discussed in this chapter. The woman in the journal entry is in a premarital-engaged stage, whereas the man is in a stage of the family life cycle referred to as young, childless, married couples (Olson et al., 1983). Social-exchange profits and resources are reflected in the woman's journal entry. The woman refers to her boyfriend's believing that she was only happy when her needs were satisfied. In addition, the woman refers to equal division of housekeeping duties, as well as making references to investing time and emotional support in the relationship. The woman refers to the satisfaction of her own needs. This statement reflects interpersonal needs theory in which there is an emphasis on the satisfaction of interpersonal needs, which may include desires for affection, control, and being recognized as a unique individual with self-worth (Schutz, 1958).

The journal entries are compatible with existing research on gender differences in recall about relational events. Women have more vivid memories of relationships events than do men (Harvey, Flannery, et al., 1986). Women are socialized to be more concerned with relationships and to be more aware of the feelings of others than are men (Deaux, 1976), which suggests that they think about relationships differently or have different expectations about them. The woman notes that she learned about giving and taking "the hard way" and cites a specific message.

Traditionally, the two genders have been socialized differently in terms of gender-role orientation in ways that affect perceptions of relationships. For example, women have been socialized to be cooperative, nurturant, and supportive, and to seek self-identity in terms of their relationships with others, whereas men have been socialized to be competitive, independent, aggressive, and less expressive of emotions (Pearson, Turner, & Todd-Manchillas, 1991). Memories and expectations about relationships as a function of gender are likely to reflect differences in gender-role socialization by parents, peers, and the media.

SUMMARY

There is a long legacy of research in developmental communication based on the idea of relationships developing through a series of stages. Developmental models have been criticized for problems in stage identification; specifying the direction, speed, and rate of movement; and using a researcher's imposed view of what the stages are. A fact that has been ignored by critics is that early assumptions in these models allowed for nonsequential movement. As a result of these criticisms, developmental models were modified and expanded.

A cognitive approach addresses some of these problems by looking at the role of expectations for the development of romance. Relationships are initially created in people's minds, even though it is communication and observable behavior that constitute the relationship (Duck, 1993). There is evidence of gender differences in relational expectations. Women have a greater recall of relational events and more detailed expectations for relational development than do men.

Despite their limitations, developmental models have extended researchers' understanding of communication across the lifespan of romantic relationships. Communication varies over the course of relationships and serves different functions, such as bonding, increasing intimacy, decreasing intimacy, and reinforcing the relationship. Individuals often ask themselves, "Where is this relationship headed?" The models have provided a framework in which to understand where relationships may be headed in terms of a trajectory.

DISCUSSION QUESTIONS

6.1 Discuss your expectations about the following relationships: dating, same-gender best friend, mentor, parent–child, and marriage. (a) How complex are these expectations? (b) Have your relationship expectations changed or been relatively stable over the years?

6.2 How is motion the fundamental property of relationships? Why can't couples just walk off into the sunset and live happily ever after?

6.3 How can high levels of expectations for close personal relationships affect satisfaction with the relationship? Would you counsel individuals to have high or low levels of relational expectations, or no expectations at all, when entering into new relationships?

APPLICATIONS

6.1 Interview three men and three women. Ask them about their expectations for a romantic and for a platonic relationship. Compare the men's responses with the women's responses. Does one group have more or less articulated expectations?

6.2 Discuss Fisher's (1994) physiological love stages of infatuation, attachment, and detachment with a group containing men and women. Ask a mixed-gender group what they think about the idea of love being hardwired in the brain's neurotransmitters.

7

Memory Structures for Developing Relationships

Studies of memory structures for escalating romances have unearthed an interesting array of behaviors that characterize their development. This chapter reports on the results of a series of studies that reveal the variety in the amount of repetitiveness found in generating lists of expectations for relational growth. First, that some individuals restate actions, whereas others mention only unique behaviors, is discussed. This redundancy may be associated with having simple expectations for evolving relationships. Individuals cite recurring behavior such as sharing time together and ignore a variety of other behaviors that may have been infrequently or only once, such as meeting parents for the first time. Second, the results of a study concerning the content of escalating metamemory structures as a function of the number of personal relationships an individual reports having had and his or her general beliefs that relationships follow a set pattern are reported. Third, the correspondence between the likelihood of a subject's mentioning certain behavioral expectations and the number of intimate relationships the person has been in is examined. Thus, serial lovers can be unmasked by knowing what expectations predict multiple relationships. Following this discussion, there is an examination of differences in the typicality and necessity of expected behaviors. Some behaviors may be more or less typical and necessary in order for a relationship to develop. For example, engaging in sexual intercourse before marriage may be typical but not necessary for intimacy to develop. Typicality and necessity ratings of relational behaviors are also examined for their ability to predict individual beliefs that relationships follow a set pattern. Next, the temporal ordering of behaviors is analyzed to assess the degree of agreement about their sequencing and determine if the temporal order of the behaviors reflects the stages of relational growth discussed in chapter 6. The additional results of a story segmentation study are reported as an alternative method of discovering where individuals separate clusters of relational actions. Finally, gender differences in these studies are reported.

REDUNDANCY AND THE COMPLEXITY OF ESCALATING MEMORY STRUCTURES

Early studies of script generation made the assumption, in terms of information theory, that the stating of actions is relevant and nonredundant. For example, subjects were told to write a list of expected actions for a given situation with each line representing one action. There were individual differences in the number of generated actions, with some subjects writing more actions. The differences were interpreted as the degree of experience in the contextual area. However, counting the number of action lines may not be a good representation of the complexity of the memory-structure actions. Individuals may repeat actions in a number of lines and this repetition of actions may reflect the recycling of actions throughout a relationship and the enduring pervasiveness of the actions. For example, arguing may occur throughout the history of a relationship. Yet subsequent arguments will be influenced by the memory of previous arguments; therefore, the same exact event does not occur because of this memory.

Because of memory, whenever individuals go around in a circle of events (e.g., recurrent conversations about the same topic) and seem to wind up where they started, the fact they recognize that they have returned indicates that they have not really returned to the same place. This type of recollection is reflected in statements like, "We've discussed this many times before." Conville (1991) added, "The 'place' is now grown over with memories. Memory is the one thing that we bring back to the 'same' place that keeps it from being the same place" (p. 65).

Even though people may recycle expectations for the development of relationships, the recycling also may reflect an inability to generate a diversity of actions. This lack of diversity could be interpreted as reflecting simplistic expectations. Burnett (1990) believed that individuals are not very mindful or bright about what is going on in their relationships; people often do not pause to reflect on their relationships. Burnett asked subjects to think about relationships they recently had thought a lot about. Negative life events such as like illness and periods of transition were events that stimulated relational thought. The accounts revealed that personal relationships are thought about frequently but superficially; they were in the form of summary statements and lacked detail. Burnett even wondered about the extent to which participants were biased by the study to the extent they felt they had to come up with something for the experimenter. Additional data revealed that subjects reported the difficulty of thinking of a reply to a question about writing to a friend about "what your relationship with X is like?" Thus, recycling may reveal the inability to cite a variety of distinct actions and inattention to relational events.

Box 7.1 contains samples men's and women's escalating memory structures that highlight differences in redundancy. Noted that these memory structures are different in terms of their structure and content from the sample marriage schema in chapter 6. Relational schemata do not reflect behaviors in a time-ordered sequence, as does the memory structure. The relational memory structure is a type of schema that reflects time-ordered behaviors in the development of a relationship. At first glance, the man appears to mention 20 actions, whereas his partner, the woman, refers to 14 actions. Research reveals that women mention more unique actions than do men in terms of their expectations for developing relationships (Honeycutt, Cantrill, et al., 1989). However, in the sample male memory structure, note that some of his actions are redundant, such as calling (action lines 3, 10, and 11). Action lines 4, 5, and 7 concern going out. There is a difference in specificity; simply going out (line 4) is more vague than going to a bar (line 5). The woman's memory structure reveals less redundancy (action lines 4 and 5).

The man's expectations in Box 7.1 refer to cyclical patterns of arguing and getting back together. On the other hand, both memory structures refer to initial meeting, sharing time together, the exclusivity of the developing relationship, overcoming crisis (e.g., arguments, parental interference, and breaking up), and ending the relationship or getting married. These actions reflect common events that a number of individuals mention in their memory structures. These samples highlight the dialectics of escalation in terms of conflict about relational problems. Although there is a progression toward intimacy, there is also the dialectic of the relationship possibly ending (see action lines 20 and 14 in the two memory structures). Further, although arguing is a commonly mentioned behavior for de-escalating memory structures, it is part of relational development.

The metamemory-generation instructions assume Grice's (1975) maxims of relevance and nonredundancy, in which individuals write or speak in order to be informative without being too redundant. A problem with these assumptions, discussed by Rosch, Mervis, Gray, Johnson, and Graem (1976), is that individuals use action-summary terms (e.g., "He kissed her," to indicate physical affection) rather than discrete, microscopic terms that segment actions (e.g., "He approached her with his eyes fixated on her lips. He touched his lips to her lips. He opened his mouth and extended his tongue to her tongue. The interface between lips and tongue continued for a few seconds."). The action-summary terms are more likely to be redundant, whereas discrete terms are more specific and less likely to repeat. As noted previously, this is apparent in actions four and five of the man's expectations in Box 7.1, in which action 4 (going out) is more abstract than action 5 (going to a bar).

Box 7.1   Sample Escalating Memory Structures Illustrating Redundant Actions

Man's Escalating Expectations

Participant:

18-year-old man, been in three to five relationships, talked about relationships with friends and parents

1. Party—meet at friends
2. Get their phone number
3. Call the next day <u>C</u>
4. Go out that night <u>G</u>
5. Go to a bar <u>G</u>
6. Don't talk about anything important
7. Go to a park, etc. <u>G</u>
8. Mess around (a little)
9. Go home
10. Call the next day <u>C</u>
11. This goes on for a while <u>C</u>
12. Until one day, they find they're committed.
13. Forget about their friends
14. See each other every day
15. Break-up and make-up patterns
16. Argue greatly but always seem to go back to each other
17. By now they have gotten into heavier things
18. Parents are annoyed
19. Want to finally break them up
20. Eventually they do & it's over

Woman's Escalating Expectations

Participant:

18-year-old woman, been in one to two relationships, talked about relationships with friends

1. Meet each other—at a party, in class, or some sort of social gathering
2. Become infatuated or fascinated with each other
3. Begin to talk regularly/semi-regularly
4. Go to a party or social event together <u>G</u>
5. Go out in one-on-one situations <u>G</u>
6. Start to become emotionally involved with other's feelings and thoughts
7. Some form of intimate contact
8. Decide to have a relationship
9. Relationship intensifies/enjoy each other's company
10. Reach a plateau—sort of a boring time in relationship
11. Stumble on a problem in relationship/occasionally breakup but not permanently
12. Back on track
13. Know each other very well
14. Eventually breakup or marriage depending upon which way the relationship goes

Note. Redundant actions are indicated by the underlined abbreviations: <u>C</u>, calling, <u>G</u>, going out.

The memory-structure generation procedure also assumes that Grice's (1975) maxim of nonredundancy leads individuals to describe activities at approximately the same level and that the nature of the generating task motivates them to revealing "normally boring details within a script" (Bower et al., 1979, p. 183). The calculation of a redundancy coefficient reveals that this assumption is not totally supported (Honeycutt, Cantrill, et al., 1989). The coefficient is calculated in such a way that higher values reflect less redundancy; the ratio of the number of unique actions divided by the total number of action lines a person records in the generation task. The mean redundancy for escalating metamemory structures is 0.70, which indicates a slight degree of repetitiveness (Honeycutt, Cantrill, et al., 1989). The correlation coefficient may range from −1.0 to 1.0 and represents the degree of association between two variables, in this case redundancy and the number of total actions. A score of 1.0 would be perfect nonredundancy, in which the number of nonrepeated actions equals the total number of listed actions. As the number of action lines increases, so does the probability of redundancy. The correlation (r) or association between the length of an escalating memory structure and redundancy is significant ($r = -0.54$, $p < .001$; Honeycutt, Cantrill, et al., 1989).

A problem with the redundancy measure is that number of actions that a person lists is not revealed in the ratio. For example, a person listing only one statement would have no redundancy ($1/1 = 1.00$) whereas a person listing four and five unique total statements would have more redundancy ($4/5 = 0.80$). A person mentioning 20 actions, in which 15 are unique, would have the lowest score of the three (0.75). These are isolated examples. People mention an average of 11.53 actions (range: 3–20 actions, standard deviation = 3.93). The measure is valid because a person mentioning only one action is not redundant, but is simplistic. Redundancy is not meant to reflect the length of a person's memory structure. However, a person listing more actions with low redundancy has a more complex set of expectations than a person listing one action. The data presented in this chapter and in chapter 8 on the number of relational actions generated by men and women take the amount of redundancy for each individual into account in computing the number of generated actions. Following are the results of a content analysis of escalating memory structures.

CONTENT OF ESCALATING MEMORY STRUCTURES

There are differences between individuals who have never been in an intimate romance and those who have been in at least one, in terms of believing that relationships follow a consistent pattern. Individuals who have never been in a previous intimate relationships report fewer expectations about what should occur in the development of a relationship compared to individuals who have been involved in relationships (Honeycutt, Cantrill, et al., 1989). On the other hand, the two groups generate approximately the same number of actions that are perceived to characterize a developing relationship.

A sample of 102 men and 120 women from introductory speech communication classes at the University of Illinois were asked to write a list of up to 20 actions that were typical in developing an intimate relationship and put them in the order in which they occur (Honeycutt, Cantrill, et al., 1989). The students ranged in age from 17 to 25, with an average age of 18.24. They had not been exposed to the academic literature associated with relational development and communication. Previous studies used a form with 20 blank lines in order not to make the task cumbersome (Bower, et al., 1979; Pryor & Merluzzi, 1985). In addition, pilot studies in which no limit was specified revealed that no individual generated more than 20 actions. From the sample of 217 individuals, the average number of actions listed was 12 and the range was from 3 to 20 actions. However, only five individuals used all 20 lines.

Box 7.2 presents the list of actions and underlying phases that characterize a developing romance, coded from the students' lists. The students were asked to begin the list with two individuals meeting for the first time and end the list with the individuals expressing a long-term, serious commitment to each other. They were instructed to report behaviors (e.g., saying hello) and avoid inferences (e.g., reporting feeling or emotions). The reason for distinguishing between behavioral activities and inferences is that inferences often are an outcome of a series of underlying behaviors. For example, a person listing as an action "Feeling inseparable, more intimate" is reporting on feelings that may be associated with several underlying behaviors such as self-disclosure, displays of physical affection, and sharing activities together.

As revealed in Box 7.2, the most frequently listed activities were meeting, calling, small talk, showing physical affection, dating, engaging in informal activities, self-disclosure, meeting parents, giving gifts (bonding ritual), making a commitment, sexual intercourse, making other-oriented statements, and getting married. Each of these actions were mentioned by 25% or more of the participants.

Box 7.2 also reveals actions mentioned less often. Overcoming a relational crisis (jealousy, uncertainty, arguing) was listed by 13% of the sample. Talking about the future in terms of a couple or "we" orientation was mentioned by 16% of the participants. In this regard, Knapp and Vangelisti (1996) discussed that individuals use the plural pronoun "we" in referring to future activities. The verbal expression of love was mentioned by 18% of the sample, whereas 7% reported living together (cohabitation) as an expectancy for relational development.

Bower et al. (1979) used a decision rule of 25% of subjects mentioning an action for its inclusion into a prototypical metamemory structure. This rule was based on examining the distribution of the frequency of responses and determining where a distinct gap existed. Using the 25% decision rule, a distinct gap was evident in this study between two behaviors mentioned by 26% of the subjects and the next most frequently mentioned behavior at 18%. On this basis, 13 actions constitute the prototypical memory structure.

Some of the escalating memory-structure actions have been reported as turning points in developing romantic relationships. Baxter and Bullis (1986) defined a *turning point* in a relationship as any event that is associated with change in the relationship. They surveyed romantic college couples and asked them to identify all of the turning points in their relationships since their first meeting. Fourteen turning points were identified, several of which appear in the study presented in Box 7.2. "Getting to know the other" occurs in many of the memory-structure activities, such as initial meeting, small talk, dating, sharing time together, self-disclosure, and overcoming crisis. "Quality time," which included meeting the family and special occasions, is another of the identified memory-structure actions. "Passion," which referred to events involving physical or emotional affection between the partners; and intercourse, kissing, and saying "I love you" reflect the memory-structure actions of physical affection and verbal expression of love. "Exclusivity," which consisted of a joint decision to be romantically involved with only one another as well as breaking any romantic liaisons with others except one's partner is reflected in the "verbal commitment" memory-structure expectancy. "Serious commitment," which reflected living together or getting engaged, appears as cohabitation, another of the escalating memory-structure actions. "Sacrifice," which involved offering assistance to one's partner when he or she is experiencing personal problems as well as giving gifts or favors, mirrors the bonding-ritual expectancy in which relational partners exchange mementos and gifts.

It is interesting that direct talk about the relationship was involved in the turning points of exclusivity, passion, and serious commitment. Thus, disclosure about status of the relationship was important in turning points. This is reflected in the escalating memory-structure expectations in the separate actions of self-disclosure and verbal commitment. A number of the other memory-structure actions also reflect direct talk about relationship status, such as the use of partner-oriented statements reflecting interest in the other person's goals and talking about future plans as a couple. Obviously, the statement "I love you" reflects the memory structure expectation of verbal expressions of love.

Baxter and Bullis (1986) indicated that relationship development can be seen as a series of discrete events accompanied by positive or negative indications of commitment. Such events may be self-contained packages of important behaviors that are easier to recall than subtle, incremental changes in relationships. These events may be salient because they provide useful story lines to reminisce or present a couple's relationship to others. The specific turning points identified by Baxter and Bullis provide some insights into individual's implicit theories about relationship development. For example, the quantity of time may be an important early indicator of romance, whereas quality time becomes more critical for intimacy to develop. Further, the turning point event exclusivity shows the salience of loyalty and fidelity in implicit theories of romantic relationships.

Box 7.2	Behavioral Expectations for Escalating Metamemory Structure	

Behavioral Expectation*	Percentage of Subjects Mentioning Action	Social-penetration Stage/Phase
1. Meet for first time* (party, class, office, etc.)	97%	Initiating
2. Ask for other's phone number and call later*	57%	
3. Small talk* (discuss weather, school, etc.)	69%	
4. Formal Date* (dinner, movie, concert, etc.)	92%	Experimenting
5. Show physical affection* (kiss, hug, touch, etc.)	43%	
6. Engage in joint activities* (informal time spent together)	64%	
7. Self-disclosure of intimate information*	52%	Intensifying
8. Sexual intercourse*	26%	Integrating
9. Meet parents or in-laws*	26%	
10. Bonding ritual* (giving flowers, gifts, jewelry, mementos, sentimental objects)	30%	
11. Other-oriented statements* (communicate interest in each other's orientations, goals, etc.)	54%	
12. Verbal commitment* (both partners talk about a long-term relationship)	49%	
13. Marriage*	28%	Bonding
14. Cohabitation	7%	
15. Overcome crisis (jealousy, uncertainty, arguing)	13%	
16. Talk about future plans	16%	
17. Verbal expression of love	18%	
18. Miscellaneous behaviors	21%	

*Asterick (*) indicates prototypical memory-structure actions in which 25% or more of participants mentioned the expectation.

Each action in the escalating metamemory structure represents a discrete memory-structure expectation in and of itself. Some of these actions may be recalled as turning points in the development of a relationship. Thus, a memory structure for relational escalation could include scenes of meeting at a party, class, video dating service, office, and so on. In the accessed scenes, there may be scripted lines of dialogue (e.g., "Hi, my name is John. Do you think you will like this course in family communication? I am taking it as an elective."). Recall from chapter 3 that individuals tend to have conversational expectations for initial encounters regarding the content and ordering of statements. Casual speech such as the initial encounters contains speech acts of getting and discussing information, evaluating it, providing explanations, and possibly discussing intentions (Kellermann et al., 1989).

There is more flexibility in the structure and ordering of topics for individuals who know each other from prior encounters. For example, there may be a wide variety of ways to communicate commitment, including verbal statements and nonverbal actions. Baxter and Wilmot (1984) discovered that individuals use a variety of techniques designed to test the intimacy of a relationship. Many of the tests are unstated actions, such as testing commitment by creating a situation in which an individual has to drive a long ways over a holiday in order to be with the partner. Although some of the actions, such as stating a verbal commitment, may be seen as a characteristic of developing romances, it is interesting that the percentage of participants mentioning such actions was low. Indeed, commitment is often signaled through actions and behaviors, not simple statements.

PREDICTING MULTIPLE RELATIONSHIPS: THE UNMASKING OF DON JUAN OR CASANOVA, AND ROMEO

The frequency with which actions such as stating a commitment are mentioned in the growth of a relationship is important because expectations of various behaviors could be related to some previous outcome, such as having been in many or few relationships. It is possible that individuals who have been in few relationships mention different expectations than to those who have been in more relationships. To put it another way, do the expectations of a Romeo differ from the expectations of a Don Juan or Casanova?

Recall the legendary characters of Don Juan and Romeo. Don Juan was a Spanish nobleman who was known for his abilities to charm numerous lovers. On the other hand, the Shakespearian character of Romeo was the fervent and exclusive lover of Juliet. These characters reflect prototypes of multiple and exclusive lovers, respectively. Individuals may lean toward one of these prototypes as shown by the number of intimate relationships in which they have been involved.

Honeycutt and Cantrill (1991) examined the number of relationships that individuals report having been in and how this is affected by the complexity of their memory structures for the development of personal relationships. Individuals who have never been in a relationship have fewer expectations of what should occur in the development of a relationship than do individuals who have been involved in a relationship (Honeycutt, Cantrill, et al., 1989). However, it is of interest to determine if specific expectations are related to a person's having been in relationships. If certain expectations of behaviors are found to predict a person's having been in zero or few relationships, then therapists may be in a better position to counsel individuals who have these expectations in the advancement of more helpful and realistic expectations for relational development.

The statistical technique logistic regression allowed the prediction of the number of relationships a person had been in, based on his or her mentioning or not mentioning the various memory structure activities listed in Box 7.2 (Honeycutt & Cantrill, 1991). A series of three logistic regression models were tested comparing individuals with zero with one to two, zero with three to five, and one to two with three to five relationships.

An intriguing profile appeared for individuals generating expectations of relational actions in light of relational histories. When comparing individuals who had never been in a close relationship with individuals who reported having been in one or more relationships, the nonexperienced individuals had few expectations of what should happen in a developing relationship, mentioned the use of small talk, and expected that marriage was the criterion of a close relationship. Nonexperienced individuals did not mention talking about future plans, did not mention the display of physical affection to their partners, and did not mention a verbal statement of love, compared to more experienced relational partners. No memory-structure actions distinguished individuals reporting one to two relationships from those reporting three to five. Thus, it appears that individuals who report zero relationships are different from the other two groups to the extent that relational experience results in different memory-structure expectations.

It may be counterintuitive that the only two unique memory-structure behaviors mentioned more by individuals with zero relationships were small talk and marriage. Honeycutt and Cantrill (1991) were unable to determine from their data if the nonexperienced participants expected too much small talk and experienced daters do not expect enough. Furthermore, the omission of marriage by individuals with a relational history may reflect an inability to separate a potential marital relationship from other dating relationships. Thus, this reflects the contrast between the Don Juan and Romeo prototypes.

It is interesting that the two memory-structure expectations (talking about future plans and verbal declaration of love) that emerged as predictors of a relational history were not part of the prototypical, escalating metamemory structure identified using the card-sorting technique. In the study in Box 7.2, talking about future plans was mentioned by only 16% of the subjects and expressing love was mentioned by 18%. However, the subjects who mentioned these expectations were more likely to have had a history of prior relationships.

Individuals reporting one to two and three to five relationships vary on a continuum of relational experiences. Baldwin (1992) discussed the differences between schematic and aschematic individuals. It is rare for a person to be truly *aschematic*, with no representation of relational development, because of the pervasiveness of movies, soap operas, advice-giving newspaper columns, and magazines that present relationships evolving through a series of crises or stages. Movies such as *When Harry Met Sally*, *About Last Night*, *Summer of '42*, and *Love Story* provide fictional models of relationships forming and deteriorating. A few television game shows have been based on expectations for dating (e.g., *The Dating Game*, *Studs*, and *Love Connection*). There are also shows about relational deterioration (e.g., *Divorce Court*). Although few people are truly aschematic because of the widespread availability of these shows, it can be argued that individuals with little direct experience in relationships, who watch movies or television portrayals of personal relationships, reflect cultural expectations when they state their own expectations. The individual expectation contains elements incorporated from cultural expectations. In this regard, Baldwin (1992) discussed that few people in a given domain are highly schematic or aschematic; many people are in an intermediate group, in which schemata are not immediately accessible in the daily processing of social information, but become available after some thought.

DIFFERENCES IN TYPICALITY AND NECESSITY OF ESCALATING ACTIONS

Even though individuals mention a variety of behaviors that characterize developing relationships and are related to history of romances, some of the behaviors may be more typical than necessary for a relationship to grow in intimacy, as well as to decline. Simply having individuals generate a list of actions and using this information to predict the number of relationships a person has been in do not reveal how typical or necessary the actions are. Indeed, behaviors that are seen as necessary but less typical for a developing romance reflect expectations that are not fulfilled.

Graesser et al. (1979) found that scripted actions frequently mentioned during free generation of lists often differ in typicality and necessity. In addition, activities that are seen as very necessary may be inferred in script passages even when they are not there. Pryor and Merluzzi (1985) found that subjects rated actions for getting a date as roughly equal in typicality, contradicting what the researchers knew empirically beforehand—that there were differences in the frequencies that these actions were mentioned in a memory-structure free-generation task. For example, smiling was mentioned by only 20% of subjects when they listed behaviors. Yet when other subjects were asked to rate the typicality of the action, they rated it as being just as typical as other behaviors that had actually been mentioned more often in the script generation task (Pryor & Merluzzi, 1986).

Honeycutt and Cantrill surveyed 61 men and 60 women who were recruited from undergraduate classes in communication studies at Louisiana State University. Their average age was 20.70, with their ages ranging from 18 to 32. The survey contained a description of each of the escalating actions that are listed in Box 7.2. The subjects were asked to indicate if each scripted action was relatively typical (e.g., overcome crisis, talk about future plans as a couple, or say "I love you"), regardless of whether the action had actually been frequently mentioned in the script-generation task (recall that this had been done by a different set of subjects). The students indicated that all of the behaviors were typical, contradicting the actual differences in the frequencies of occurrence of the actions when they were collected. Recall from Box 7.2 that the most-frequently mentioned escalating action is initial meeting followed by dating. Overcoming crisis and talking about future plans as a couple were the least-often-mentioned escalating actions; however, both actions were rated by subjects as highly typical and necessary.

There are interesting differences when contrasting the typicality rating of an escalating action with the report of how necessary the action is. Small talk, showing physical affection, dating, meeting parents, talking about future plans as a couple, exchanging gifts (bonding ritual), verbal commitment, living together, having intercourse, stating interest in one another's goals, and marriage were perceived by subjects as being more typical of than necessary to an escalating relationship. The only exception to this pattern is self-disclosure, which participants believed was less typical of but more necessary for the development of an intimate relationship. Abelson (1981) termed these differences gap-filling, in which individuals report that a given action is typical on seeing it listed, even though it is not frequently mentioned in a generation task.

The gap-filling phenomenon represents the availability heuristic because the base rates of the previous responses are incongruent with subsequent ratings of typicality. Instances of the action may be easier to recall, available in memory, due to recognition of the action. The gap-filling phenomenon is important in explaining how an individual relates to another's personal experiences (Honeycutt, 1993). Thus, memory structures for relationships also exist for recognizing actions as well as generating behavioral expectations. With this in mind, it is possible to predict beliefs about relational development on the basis of the typicality and necessity ratings.

Underlying Dimensions of Relational Development

The ratings of how typical and necessary various actions are can be used to identify underlying clusters of actions. No behavior occurs in a vacuum independent
of other behaviors. Behaviors may occur simultaneously or in quick succession.
Consequently, some actions are more easier interchanged than others. For example, the display of physically affectionate behaviors is more related to consummation than is meeting one another's parents. The underlying dimensions
represent conceptual clusters of co-occurring behaviors.

The idea that some actions are more easily exchanged than others is a
foundation of Foa and Foa's (1976) interpersonal resource theory, in which
resources such as love are more easily exchanged and the exchange sanctioned than the exchange of disparate resources such as love for money.
They argued that the exchange of particularistic resources (e.g., resources
that can only be obtained from particular individuals such as love, services,
and status) and the exchange of universalistic resources for another (e.g., resources that can be obtained from a variety of sources, such as money, information, and goods) are more likely than the exchange of particularistic and
universalistic resources. For example, information tends to be exchanged in
kind. More intimate relationships involve exchanges of love, status, information, and services rather than goods and money (Foa & Foa, 1976). It is
harder to exchange particularistic resources for universalistic resources unless there is a rule or contract for this exchange between individuals (e.g., intercourse for money).

The underlying typicality and necessity dimensions reported by Honeycutt
(1995b) are listed. He found four dimensions for each category.

Typicality Dimensions.   The first dimension contained actions of the
bonding ritual. Verbal terms of endearment such as saying, "I love you," getting married, exchanging gifts, and talking about future plans as a couple
sorted on this dimension. These items were averaged to form an index of
bonding ritual. The second dimension reflected an orientation to one's partner's needs. Sharing informal time together, talking to one's partner on the
phone; talking with one's partner about an exclusive commitment; and communicating an interest in one's partner's goals, values, and needs sorted on
this dimension.

The third dimension consists of reflected physical involvement and consisted of sexual intercourse and displaying physical affection through kissing
and hugging. The final typicality dimension signified personal communication and consisted of actions such as small talk, self-disclosure of intimate information, and overcoming a crisis such as jealousy or high uncertainty from
some event.

Necessity Dimensions.   The initial necessity dimension reflected family bonding and consisted of meeting parents, small talk, and getting married. The second factor was an orientation to one's partner and contained engaging in joint activities together; calling one's partner; and discussing one's partner's goals, values, and personal attitudes. The third factor was dating and cohabitation (or living together). The final necessity dimension was physical involvement and included displaying physical affection, intercourse, and communicating statements of love.

Typicality Versus Necessity in Predicting Beliefs About Relational Development

Gender and the typicality–necessity activity ratings can be used as predictors of relational development in regression analyses that correlate subject's belief that relationships follow a set pattern, that there are expectations about what should occur in the development of an intimate relationship and that relationships can be thought as developing through a series of stages (Honeycutt, 1995b). In addition, data were gathered on the number of intimate relationships that individuals reported having had.

This analysis was different from the results presented earlier, in the discussion of Romeo or Casanova types. In that study, subjects indicated only if they had been in zero, one to two, three to five, or more than five relationships and their various escalating memory structure actions. In this second analysis, a different sample of individuals was asked to report the exact number of close personal relationships the individuals had ever been involved in. Most individuals reported having been in two relationships. The number of relationships ranged from zero to nine, although few individuals reported having been in more than three relationships.

Gender was initially entered in the regression models as a control variable to see whether men and women differed in mentioning any of the escalating activities that, in turn, might be associated with the number of reported relationships. There were no gender differences in predicting developmental beliefs. However, there were significant typicality and necessity predictors, as revealed in the following.

The numbers in parentheses are standardized beta coefficients, ranging from 0 to 1. Scores close to 0 show no association, whereas scores around 1 show perfect predictability. Hence, these coefficients reflect the magnitude of association among each of the escalating relationship activities and beliefs about relationships. The positive or negative sign preceding each activity reveals if the predicted relationship between the behavior and belief is positive or negative.

Typicality Ratings

Relationships tend to follow a set pattern = Show physical affection (0.22) – Self-disclosure (0.19)

I have a lot of expectations of what should occur in the development of an intimate relationship = Other-oriented statements (0.27) + Show physical affection (0.19)

I believe that relationships can be thought of as developing through a series of stages = Overcome crisis (0.26) + Dating (0.21)

Number of relationships = Showing physical affection (0.22) – Getting married (0.18)

Necessity Ratings

Relationships tend to follow a set pattern = No predictors

I have a lot of expectations of what should occur in the development of an intimate relationship = Other-oriented statements (0.25)

I believe that relationships can be thought about as developing through a series of stages = Other-oriented statements (0.27)

Number of relationships = Talk about future plans as a couple (–0.26)–Meeting parents (0.25) + Self-disclosing intimate and personal information (0.19)

It is interesting that self-disclosure was negatively related to the belief that relationships follow a set pattern while it was positively related to the number of relationships an individual reported being in. This is consistent with the earlier finding that self-disclosure is viewed as more necessary, yet less typical, in a developing relationships and that it emerges as a separate phase in the development of relationships (Honeycutt, Cantrill, et al., 1989).

Other-oriented statements emerged as a predictor in three of the equations. Becoming relationally oriented and communicating this to one's partner is associated with having a lot of expectations about relational development. The emergence of a joint identity as a couple can be enhanced by communicating interest in one's partner's interests, opinions, activities, and goals. Further, other research on variables that predict marital happiness revealed that actively signaling attentiveness to what one's marriage partner is saying is related to effective communication, which, in turn, is related to one's spouse's belief that one understands him or her (Honeycutt, 1986). Consequently, communication effectiveness and perceived partner understanding predict the level of marital happiness.

It is interesting that the typicality of overcoming a relational crisis was related to the belief that relationships follow through a series of stages. Overcoming a crisis in the development of a relationship reflects the dialectic view discussed in chapter 6, in which relationships evolve cyclically to the extent that there is continual negotiation about roles (Baxter, 1985). If one person desires a more intimate romance, whereas the other person does not, the nondesiring partner may spend less time with the escalating partner or have to inform the partner of his or her desire not to get any closer. In addition, other strategies designed to communicate the reaction to the potential escalation of romance may be used.

From a dialectic perspective, overcoming a crisis in a relationship could reflect the disengaging of the relationship that has been redefined and the acquisition of memory structures and associated scenes and scripts for relational deescalation. Support for this interpretation is found in a study by Planalp, Rutherford, and Honeycutt (1987), who reported that some relationships became closer after a period of time when uncertainty was temporarily increased by some behavior or event ranging from negative events such as discovering one's partner's infidelity to positive events such as discovering that a friend believed the relationship was closer than one originally believed and the feeling was reciprocated. In addition, there is additional data in which subjects report more often having expectations about what occurs in the development of romance than believing that relationships follow a set pattern (Honeycutt, 1995b). These expectations are not necessarily linear to the extent that individuals are expected to systematically progress through a series of phases while developing intimacy. Rather, the expectations may reflect dialectic periods of bonding or separation.

The display of physical affection is an important activity. It is associated with believing that relationships follow a set pattern, having a lot of expectations of what should occur in the development of relationships, and the number of intimate relationships a person has been in. Recall that mentioning physical affection as a quality of an escalating relationship also characterized Don Juan individuals who reported having had one to five intimate relationships, compared to individuals having had zero close relationships.

The typicality and necessity ratings for escalating actions are intriguing in light of the foregone opportunity to generate any additional actions. The participants also were instructed to write down any additional actions that they believed were typical or necessary but that were not on the survey. Ninety-five percent of the participants did not mention any additional actions. The 5% who wrote additional actions produced paraphrases of already-listed actions. The lack of detailed relational memory structures is related to the speculation by Burnett (1990) discussed in the beginning of this chapter that relationships tend to be thought about frequently but superficially.

UNDERLYING STAGES AND THE PROTOTYPICAL ESCALATING MEMORY STRUCTURE

One of the outcomes associated with having a memory structure for a developing romance is the ability to recognize the actions and arrange them in a sequential order. The sequential ordering of expected actions may reflect stages from a number of developmental models discussed in Chapter 6. Ginsburg (1988) indicated that the discovery of the stereotypical action sequences in a given type of situation in a particular type of relationship would further researcher's understanding of the internal dynamics of relationship and the wide variety of forms in which relationships are manifested.

Although individuals can generate memory structures for an escalating romance, the memory- generation procedure is limited in telling researchers if individuals agree on the order or sequencing of the activities. For example, some individuals may expect meeting the other person's parents to occur before a long-term commitment has been made, whereas others may expect a commitment to occur before meeting the other person's parents. Some individuals may believe that self-disclosure comes early, whereas others believe it comes later in the development of a relationship.

Card-Sorting Experiment

Participants were given a deck of index cards in which each of the actions in Box 7.2 that had been mentioned by at least 25% of the students in the relational schema generation study were listed. Each action was described on a separate card. The participants were given the following instructions.

> We may have expectations for how a romantic relationship should develop. For example, you may believe that there is a typical sequence of behaviors that reflects an escalating relationship. Enclosed in your envelope is a set of 13 index cards that list various relational behaviors. The cards are in a random order. We want you to sort the cards in what you believe is a logical order and then to record how long it took you to sort the deck. (Honeycutt, Cantrill, et al., 1989, p. 75)

A sample of 71 men and 78 women students, in communication studies courses at Louisiana State University, were tested. They ranged in age from 17 to 32, with an average age of 20.42. The students were given response sheets on which to record the rank ordering of the 13 prototypical behaviors. They were instructed to open the envelopes at a specified time, sort the cards, record how long it took to complete the task (in seconds), and write their orderings on the response sheet. On the response sheet, subjects indicated how many intimate relationships they had been involved in.

The time it takes to sort the escalating actions is a measure of a person's ability to access a relational memory structure and use it to recognize actions. Sorting time is correlated with previous relationship history, such that those who had been in more relationships seemed to take less time sorting the cards. Thus, they could more easily relate to the prototypical actions they see on the cards and arrange them in an intuitive order.

The prototypical ordering of the 13 actions is meeting (0.54), small talk (0.52), calling (1.47), dating (1.75), showing physical affection (2.00), sharing time together (2.04), self-disclosure (2.18), sexual intercourse (2.17), meeting parents (2.32), sharing gifts or bonding ritual (1.96), making other-oriented statements (1.88), stating a commitment (2.40), and marriage (2.44). The numbers in parentheses are standard deviations that reveal the extent of disagreement or dispersion on the placement of a given action. They are critical in beginning to demonstrate the existence of underlying stages for developing relationships that exist in the minds of individuals.

The higher the standard deviation, the more individuals disagree on the order for a given action. For example, students agree least on the ordering of verbal commitment and marriage, whereas there was wide agreement on the initial ordering of meeting, small talk, and calling the other person on the telephone. The standard deviations also reflect the degree of interchange among actions. For example, the orders of such actions as small talk and making a verbal commitment are less easily interexchanged, shown by their lower standard deviations, compared to sharing time together, disclosure, intercourse, and meeting parents, which have higher standard deviations.

Cut-off points between clusters of actions were determined by computing adjacent mean difference scores and noting instances of higher differences between adjacent actions. Activities considered to constitute a cluster have lower within mean difference scores compared to the differences between adjacent actions located at the endpoints of respective clusters (Honeycutt, Cantrill, et al. 1989). An example is the mean difference (d) between showing physical affection and calling ($d = 1.82$). This difference is higher than the difference between small talk and calling ($d = 1.03$).

This analysis reveals five underlying phases. Phase one consists of meeting, calling, and small talk. The activities are grouped more closely together and form a cluster that reflects initiation or coming together (Honeycutt, Cantrill, et al., 1989). Small talk is characteristic of what Knapp and Vangelisti (1996) called the experimentation stage. During this stage, potential relational partners experiment using different topics in order to determine if more intimate conversation can develop in particular topical areas. The second phase consists of dating, showing physical affection, and sharing time together. Disclosure also emerges as a separate stage in the story-reading procedure for identifying stages, discussed later (Honeycutt, Cantrill, et al., 1989). The fourth phase consists of intercourse, meeting parents or in-laws, and exchanging gifts or mementos. The fifth phase consists of other-oriented statements, verbal commitment, and getting married. These phases are similar to Knapp and Vangelisti's (1996) social-penetration growth stages of initiation (meeting), experimentation (dating, showing affection), intensifying (disclosure), integrating (meeting in-laws), and bonding (marriage).

Q-Sort Procedure

There is additional evidence of a prototypical, escalating metamemory structure with stages using the Q-sort procedure.

The Procedure. The Q-sort procedure was used by Stephen and Markman (1983) to identify agreement between randomly paired dyads of beliefs about relationships. They used a questionnaire called the Relationship World Index (RWI), which contains 60 statements such as "Relationships should be oriented toward fun, A relationship is a place to escape chaos and strife in life, Both partners should contribute equally to a relationship, Partners don't have to talk about their relationship in order for it to be a good one" (Stephen & Markman, 1983, p. 19).

In using the Q-sort procedure, subjects were given index cards, each containing a statement about relational beliefs. The individuals were instructed to sort the statements into piles in an order that represented their beliefs about the important aspects of an intimate or potentially committed love relationship. The statements were sorted into piles based on how much the subjects strongly disagreed to how much they strongly agreed with them (Stephen, 1984). For example, if one strongly disagreed with the belief that relationships exist only to the extent that there are exciting things to do, one would place this statement in a pile with other beliefs with which one strongly disagreed. There would be additional piles reflecting increasing agreement (e.g., moderate disagreement, minor disagreement, undecided—neither agreement or disagreement, minor agreement, moderate agreement, strong agreement).

This procedure measures convergence or agreement in individuals' orientations to relationships. Relationship convergence is measured by computing the correlation between each relational partner's rank orderings. Each rank order is assumed to reflect a sorting pile. Stephen and Markman (1983) claimed that the correlation coefficient is used "as index of symbolic interdependence, the extent to which partners have constructed a shared view of the world" (p. 18). They found a correlation of 0.31 between randomly paired strangers. They indicate that "this suggests a generalized social reality to which most are aligned in thought and that precedes the development of a relationship world view" (p. 22). Knowledge about relationships is organized at the societal and individual levels. They found agreement about relationship beliefs to a function of increasing intimacy in couples. Engaged couples agreed more on relational beliefs ($r = 0.52$) than did steady daters ($r = 0.49$) and daters ($r = 0.41$). Thus, couples converge in their beliefs about relationships as intimacy increases (Stephen & Markman, 1983).

Q-sort and Stages.   Honeycutt and Cantrill used the *Q*-sort procedure to determine the amount of agreement among subjects about the ordering of prototypical memory-structure expectations. Recall that in the card-sorting experiment each subject was given a deck of 13 index cards that contained descriptions of the escalating actions and was instructed to sort the cards in an intuitive logical order. After this, a *Q*-sort was conducted by randomly pairing men's ranked orders with women's ranked orders, resulting in 71 couples, and computing a correlation coefficient. There was an exceeding high level of agreement at the .001 alpha level between the genders on the ranked ordering of the actions ($r = 0.84$). Thus, randomly paired individuals agree on a prototypical sequence of escalating actions, even though individuals may have more or less complex metamemory structures, may have redundant behaviors, and expect some behavior more than others.

Story-Segmentation Analysis

Further evidence of underlying stages existed in people's relational cognitions was revealed using a story-reading procedure (Honeycutt, Cantrill, et al., 1989). As indicated in chapter 2, metamemory structures subsume memory structures that contain subscenes, with each subscene containing specific scripts (Schank, 1982). The sequence of scripted actions in a subscene can be summarized in terms of a superordinate action (Rumelhart, 1976). Metamemory structures should contain general lines of action that reflect abstract stages of a relationship. Here, the superordinate action represents a breakpoint in an escalating romance. The typical way to measure this is to have individuals read a story containing actions and segment the story into naturally occurring scenes (e.g., Bower et al., 1979; Pryor & Merluzzi, 1985).

Two stories were written containing 13 sentences each, with each sentence representing a prototypical metamemory-structure action (Honeycutt, Cantrill, et al., 1989). These actions were the actions in Box 7.2 that were mentioned by at least 25% of the subjects. Two stories were used to examine the generalizability of results from story to story. A sample of 89 women and 88 men, students at Louisiana State University, was surveyed. The ages ranged between 18 and 30, with an average age of 20.18. Eighty-five students read one romantic story and 92 read a second story. The ratio of women and men readers was balanced for both stories. Readers were given the following instructions.

> Below is a brief story about John (or Linda) and Veronica (or Tom) who are involved in a developing and escalating romance that ends in marriage. Some people feel that romantic stories like these may be divided into several natural parts or stages. We would like you to carefully read the story and decide whether this story may be divided into

different parts. If you think that these natural stages exist please identify them by placing a slash mark (/) at the end of each sentence that you think ends a part. These
slashes are to indicate the boundaries between parts. (Honeycutt, Cantrill, et al.,
1989, p. 84)

Box 7.3 reveals the percentage of subjects marking a boundary after each action in the two stories. Boundary marks were exchanged between sentences 2
and 3 in the two stories. More individuals indicated a boundary after the sentence about discussing a biology course (small talk) in the story about Linda and
Tom, whereas readers of the John and Veronica story placed a boundary after
the sentence about calling for a date. In addition, more readers of the Linda and
Tom story indicated a boundary after the sentence about continual dating.

A statistical analysis of the distribution of the slash-mark locations in each
story revealed that there were significant boundary points, and therefore relationship stages could be identified. The first phase in both stories consists of
meeting and small talk. The second phase reflects dating, the display of physical
affection, and doing informal activities together. The third phase reflects
self-disclosure. The next action, sexual intercourse, was viewed as a separate
unit by a sizable percentage of the readers of the John and Veronica story, compared to readers of the Linda and Tom story. The fifth phase consists of meeting
parents, exchanging mementos, other-oriented statements, and stating a commitment to the relationship. The final phase is marriage. These stages and the
actions within each phase are similar to the phases identified in Box 7.2.

The difference in the percentages demarcating intercourse as a separate
phase may be due to language use and the social desirability of the expression,
"sleeping together." Although this expression is a euphemism for the act of intercourse, "sexual intercourse" sounds more biological or clinical and may not
signal passionate emotion, whereas "sleeping together" has a more intimate
connotation. Because of this connotation, sleeping together slides the relationship into the phase reflecting the intensification or integration of the relationship, as opposed to being a separate phase in itself.

The boundary percentages reinforce the phases identified using the
card-sorting procedure. The first phase reflects the social-penetration stages of
initiation and experimentation. The second phase resembles the penetration
stage of intensifying. The third phase, self-disclosure, was discussed as part of
the intensifying stage (Knapp & Vangelisti, 1996). Sexual intercourse is a separate phase in the stories, whereas the fifth phase appears to represent a combination of intensifying and integrating. The final phase, marriage, simply reflects
a legal-bonding stage in which wedding vows are exchanged.

MESSAGES USED TO ESCALATE INTIMACY

Relational memory structures determine what can be said in a given scene
based on previous experience, instruction from others, or observation of others.

Box 7.3   Phases Within the Prototypical Escalating Metamemory Structure

John and Veronica

John met Veronica for the first time at a party. (8.2%) They engaged in small talk such as commenting on how nice the party was, who they knew at the party as well as learning a little about where each one was from. (24.7%) John asked Veronica for her phone number and if he could call her later to see about going on a date. (81.2%) The first date went well and so they continued dating. (20%) They held hands, kissed, and hugged each other. (20%) They also did informal activities together such as watching TV, studying together, playing tennis, and going to lunch. (69%.4) John and Veronica self-disclosed to each other and revealed personal information such as likes and dislikes, successes and failures, values, and the like. (58.8%) They had sexual intercourse. (64.7%) Veronica took John on a weekend trip to her hometown to meet her parents. (28.2%) They gave each other candy, "love cards," and jewelry. (28.2%) They became more interested in each other's goals and lives since they felt like they needed each other and had an exclusive relationship. (49.4%) They made a verbal commitment so they could make the relationship long-term and stable. (57.6%) They got married. (100%)

Linda and Tom

Linda met Tom in a biology lab during the fall semester. (19.6%) They talked about the course, their majors and what they wanted to do after graduation. (66.3%) Tom asked Linda if he could call her and see about going on a date to one of the home football games. (38.0%) They enjoyed the game and continued going to games as well as having other dates. (43.5%) They held hands and kissed each other. (21.7%) They did informal activities together such as studying, biking, and jogging. (51.1%) They disclosed personal information about such things as family history, failures, and fantasies. (69.6%) They slept together. (47.8%) Tom invited Linda to visit his hometown and meet his parents. (27.2%) They exchanged little gifts and favors such as jewelry and candy. (20.7%) They talked about the other's needs and how to help each other whenever they could. (48.9%) They told each other they were exclusively committed to each other. (63.0%) They got married. (100%)

Note. Numbers in parentheses indicate the percentage of subjects marking boundaries.

Disconfirming experiences may result in the modification of an individual's initial dating expectations. As a result, distinctive messages may be discussed in ensuing dates. Two studies have examined the messages that men and women expect to occur at transitional points in relationships. These studies are discussed in terms of the desire to enhance intimacy and concern for secondary goals such as fear of a rebuff and not wanting the desire for intimacy enhancement to backfire.

Individuals use a variety of communicative strategies to determine the intimacy status of a relationship and where it may be headed. Baxter and Wilmot (1984) found that questioning was not used as often as were other indirect strategies by individuals wanting to find out how intimate their relationship was, such as hinting about more intimacy, determining how much the partner will endure in terms of presenting one's bad side to one's partner, using jealousy tests such as talking about old boyfriends or girlfriends, or introducing oneself and one's partner to outsiders as a couple. These strategies were used more often than direct strategies, such as self-disclosure about the desire for a more intimate romance or questioning the partner about how he or she felt about a closer relationship.

The content of escalating memory-structure messages at transitional points in a relationship was analyzed by Honeycutt, Cantrill, Kelly, and Lambkin (1998). They constructed scenarios that took individuals up to a certain point in a developing romance. These researchers surveyed 538 students from Northern Michigan University and Louisiana State University. The students ranged in age from 18 to 52, with an average age of 21.81. The sample consisted of 43% men and 57% women.

The study examined the (a) effect of knowing where the relationship was currently in terms of the development of intimacy and the effect of the relationship type (self-involvement or personal relationship vs. reading about someone else's or a typical relationship) on the prediction of the next action to occur in the development of romance, (b) the use of compliance-gaining strategies intended to advance a relationship to the next stage, and (c) the justification of secondary goals (why subjects chose the strategies they did as opposed to other alternatives).

To determine the affect of relationship type, the students read two stories in which a relationship was developing and were asked to consider where the relationship stood at a particular point at which the story stopped. The stories differed in terms of personal or typical relationships and the differences in expectation were examined. In this regard, Wish et al. (1976) found that individuals distinguished their own relationships from typical (or others') relationships in terms of intensity and cooperation.

One story was a typical relationship about two characters, Linda and Tom, who met and reached various stages of relational development. These are the same characters in the stories in Box 7.3. A second story was a developing personal romance, in which the subjects imagined they were involved. The order of the typical and personal stories were counterbalanced in the surveys. Each story ended at a particular point in the relationship and the students were queried as to the next major thing they thought would happen in the relationship and what they or the story characters would say if developing the relationship was desired. An open-ended question asked the students why they thought they or the characters would say this instead of something else. This question was posed to determine secondary goals. The points at which each story ended were derived from the stories presented in Box 7.3, containing the prototypical relational memory structure actions.

The results revealed that most students mentioned at least two ensuing actions, two compliance strategies, and concern with one secondary goal. An example of a subject's listing four ensuing actions is the case of a 21-year-old woman who read a story about a personal relationship in which the story ended with sexual intercourse. (The underlined words represent the label for the coded escalating memory-structure action.) She wrote that the next major thing that would happen was, "I think our relationship would grow stronger (inference of relationship growing closer). We would continue to see each other; we would go to church together, spend more free time together (sharing informal activities), and disclose more about ourselves (self-disclosure of intimate information). We may even consider moving in together (cohabitation)."

Students who read stories that ended after initial meeting (initiation stage) expected telephone calling and dating to occur in both typical and personal romantic development. Students who read stories that ended in the intensifying stage, with the story characters dating, expected more sharing of activities in story 1 as well as expecting sexual intercourse as the next action in both stories. Furthermore, students who read stories that ended with disclosure of personal values and failures (disclosure stage) also expected intercourse to ensue.

The most popular strategies to enhance intimacy were ingratiation, direct request, and explanation. A prototypical example of these strategies is a 26-year-old man who read a story about personal romantic involvement. (The strategies are underlined.) He delivered his marriage proposal by saying, "We've been together so long. I can't imagine life without you (explanation). I love you (ingratiation). Will you marry me (direct request)?"

Ingratiation is making statements of love as well as complimenting one's partner and giving gifts or mementos to one's partner. Ingratiation as defined by Schenk-Hamlin et al. (1982) also included supportive listening and showing love or affection. Many of the scripted actions for romantic development discovered by Honeycutt, Cantrill, et al. (1989) reflected Schenk-Hamlin's et al.'s (1982) ingratiation: exchanging gifts, using other-oriented statements to express an interest in one's partner's values and goals, verbal expressions of love, and showing physical affection through touching, hugging, and kissing.

It is intriguing that Honeycutt et al. (1998) also found that a number of partners reported they would do nothing to escalate intimacy. In cases such as these, the persons may be reactive, as opposed to proactive, and may wait for verbal or nonverbal cues from their partners before reinforcing those cues. In a sense, these individuals may simply be waiting for things to happen.

Individuals also reported a secondary choice of strategies. The most popular followup strategy was hinting. An example of hinting is a partner using humor or jokes to indicate his or her desire to pursue more intimacy. Hinting offers cover from rejection, unlike direct request.

Individuals in early stages of relational development used fewer strategies to escalate intimacy than do individuals in more-developed relationships. This reinforces the observation by Knapp and Vangelisti (1996) that there is more flexibility in communicating intimacy in more-developed relationships. There is more rigidity in the early stages of romance because individuals have not learned a variety of nonverbal means to communicate emotion, and so they must be more explicit in order not be misunderstood.

In terms of secondary goals, the data revealed that students reported more identity goals than other types of secondary goals as a justification for not using alternative strategies in order to enhance intimacy at various stages of relational development. Identity goals are defined as attempts to enhance an individual's self-concept. Codes of conduct, ethics, and values symbolize identity. Personal preferences for appropriate behavior are emphasized. Other secondary goals are interaction, resource, and managing arousal. Interaction goals concern the desire to create a favorable impression. Individuals want to avoid threatening another person's self-concept and to ensure smooth communication (Dillard, Segrin, & Harden, 1989). Resource goals concern increasing relational assets in the form of personal rewards that arise from being in a relationship, increasing material assets such as money and goods, and physical assets reflecting health concerns that might be jeopardized in pursing the primary goal (e.g., a person decides after meeting someone when and how to disclose that he or she has some health condition). Arousal management goals concern avoiding strategies that they believe will arouse anxiety or negative emotions when seeking compliance. According to discrepancy-arousal theory, individuals evaluate their arousal as pleasant or unpleasant depending on the status and attractiveness of an interaction partner (Burgoon & LePoire, 1993).

In terms of the effect of personal versus typical relationships, participants cited identity goals when reading about personal romantic developments and less used when reading about typical relationships. However, interaction goals were reported when reading about typical relationships and less used when reading about personal relationships.

GENDER DIFFERENCES IN GENERATING AND PROCESSING ESCALATING MEMORY STRUCTURES

There are significant differences between men and women in generating and processing escalating memory structures. These differences concern the initiation and termination of relationships. Rubin et al. (1981) found that men tend to initiate relationships, whereas women end them. Women also see a breakup coming sooner than do men. Men are more romantic in their beliefs about relationships because they are more emotionally dependent on relationships (Frazier & Esterly, 1990). Traditionally, men have placed more emphasis on sex, game-playing love, and *agape* love (all-giving, selfless, altruistic love) because they have been more economically independent, while being emotionally dependent on the relationship. Coleman and Ganong (1992) found that women expected prospective husbands to make more money; have higher educational achievements; and be more intelligent, successful, and better able to handle things than the women themselves. In contrast, men expected their prospective wives to be relatively similar to the men themselves.

Women are socialized more than men to value interpersonal relationships for their inherent worth. Baxter and Wilmot (1983) analyzed individual diary accounts about specific encounters between relational partners over a 2-week period. They found that women attributed greater importance to encounters in relationships that were characterized as no-growth, compared to low- and high-growth relationships. Females talked more and associated more personableness, satisfaction, and effectiveness to encounters.

Burnett (1990) found that men reported thinking less about relationships, as well as being less involved in communication about relationships. Women were more willing to participate in a relationship study about telling a friend about a relationship with X. Men were less likely to write to a confidant, had difficulty explaining relationships, preferred not to analyze personal relationships, and were more silent regarding talk about relationships.

Burnett (1990) also found that women were more concerned with the assessment of relationships than men, whereas men were more concerned with the business of forming, keeping, and maintaining relationships in the basic sense of meeting and making contact. It appears that men were bothered about the practical aspects that makes relationships possible, regardless of what went on in them, whereas women cared more about monitoring and evaluating the intrinsic relational events. Women also claimed to think, as well as know and talk, more about their closest relationship, even though both sexes claimed to care equally about the relationship. Harvey, Flannery, et al. (1986) also found that women reported more vivid memories of events from their most emotionally significant past relationship.

The gender differences in reflecting on relationships and willingness to communicate about relationships are related. If individuals are unlikely to discuss something, "they may be similarly blocked in their thoughts about it" (Burnett, 1990, p. 89). Therefore, the simpler memory structures about relational development for men are revealed in thought and communication about relationships.

Men are more deeply affected by the termination of relationships than are women (Rubin et al., 1981). Along this line, Rubin (1970) reported that women make more discrete distinctions between liking a man as opposed to loving a man. Rubin et al. (1981) believed that women think about their relationships more carefully than men do. Consequently, women's criteria for falling in love and for staying in love may be more rigorous than men's.

Women's distinctions between liking and love are also supported by data reported in a study of characteristics of same-gender friendships. On the one hand, Duck and Wright (1993) found that both genders meet with same-gender friends most often just to talk for talk's sake, followed by working on some task, and, least often, to discuss relational issues. An example of men doing this is at a bar. (Fig. 7.1). On the other hand, although both men and women were concerned with caring, supportiveness, and encouragement, women were more likely than men to communicate these concerns directly (Fig. 7.2). Duck and Wright (1993) found that women reported voluntary interdependence, supporting one another's ego, affirming a friend's self-concept, security, expressing emotions, and permanence of the relationship as characterizing friendships more often than did men. In addition, they found that women reported same-gender friendships as more important relationships than did men and speculated that when women were asked to identify a best friend or friends, "they may be responding to a better or stronger friend (or friends) than men who are given exactly the same instructions" (p. 724).

The lack of discriminating criteria for men has been suggested by Burnett (1990) to be due to a pattern of socialization of men to not demonstrate emotion for fear of revealing vulnerability. It is considered feminine to demonstrate a need for affection, security, and intimacy. Burnett (1990) wrote:

> Men may be shunned into silence and unawareness about relationships. A passive approach to learning about relationships continues into adulthood and into effortless but often failing personal relationships. Now that it has become an academic discipline, the elevated status of "personal relationships" as a subject to be taught and investigated will perhaps break into this devalue-disregard cycle. (p. 90)

Burnett's statement was supported by data from Rubin et al. (1981). They found that women reported being less romantic than men and more cautious about entering into romance. Women were more pragmatic and sensitive about the development of relationships. If this is true, one would expect women to rate previously generated, common relational meta-MOP (memory organization packet) actions as being more typical than do men because of relational monitoring. Indeed, this is what the data partially reveal.

Women reported having more general expectations of what should happen in the development of an escalating romance (Honeycutt, Cantrill, 1989). Furthermore, women reported being more aware of their reasons for using verbal strategies to escalate intimacy at various stages of relational development (Honeycutt et al., 1998). In addition, women have more developed memory structures for escalating relationships. Women generated an average of 12.11 actions for their escalating metamemory structures, whereas men generated an average of 10.10, without being redundant (Honeycutt, Cantrill, et al., 1989).

FIG. 7.1   Men self-disclosing at a bar.

FIG. 7.2   Women directly disclose their concerns.

However, note how this difference is small. In this regard, Canary and Hause (1993) did extensive reviews of the communication differences between genders and noted that the behavioral differences are often not in evidence and, when they are, the magnitude of differences is small. For example, gender-role stereotypes lead one to believe that women self-disclose more. Indeed, women rate self-disclosure as being more necessary than typical in a growing romance than do men (Honeycutt, Cantrill, et al., 1989). Yet Dindia and Allen (1992), reviewing over 200 studies of gender differences in self-disclosure, found that although women tend to disclose more than men, the difference is small. For example, women disclose more than men in same-gender conversations, but there is no difference between the amount that women and men disclose in opposite-gender conversations.

Canary and Hause (1993) indicated that gender-role stereotypes may be related to gender differences in beliefs about relationships. However, although we have found a number of gender differences in terms of generating expectations, this says nothing about actually doing the behavior. Indeed, the reliance on gender-role stereotypes, in which women are believed to be using strategies to maintain their relationships more than men, may be related to stating actions that support these stereotypes. For example, Honeycutt, Cantrill, et al. found that women rate engaging in joint activities, overcoming a crisis, meeting parents, talking about future plans, verbal expression of love, stating a commitment, and making other-oriented statements as more typical than did men. Women rated meeting one another's parents and talking about future plans as more necessary than did men. The only action mentioned by men as being more necessary in an order for intimacy to develop in a relationship compared to women was sexual intercourse. These self-reports are consistent with traditional gender-role stereotypes of women as having more likely to use relational maintenance than men, even though behavioral studies revealed that both genders use strategies of positivity, disclosure, and giving assurances to one another (Stafford & Canary, 1991).

The expectation of sexual intercourse seems to co-vary with age for women; hence, it loses some of its gender distinctiveness. A study by Collins, Kennedy, and Francis (1976) of men and women 17 to 19, 20 to 24, and 25 to 30 years old investigated expectations about sexual activities, ranging from an initial date to expected behavior in marriage. The study revealed that men and women in the 17-to-19 group had similar expectations about the amount of sexual behavior. The individuals were asked about their levels of expectation for kissing, necking, light petting, petting to orgasm, and full intercourse. Men in the older groups expected women to behave more liberally. After several dates, the men expected women to be more intimate, compared to the women's expectations. Women in the 17-to-19 group expected men to behave less intimately. Collins et al. (1976) surmised that women shifted their expectations over time because they are more aware of the men's motivations. Men may be less understanding of women's expressive orientation because they are less aware of relationship events and activities.

Women monitor their relationships and have more vivid memories of specific events occurring with the relationships. Ross and Holmberg (1992) had spouses tape record descriptions of their first date together, a shared vacation, and argument between them. Subsequently, the partners assessed the clarity of their recall of the event. Wives reported more vivid memories than did their husbands. Similar to the results of Burnett (1990), Ross and Holmberg also found that wives attributed greater personal importance to the events, reported reminiscing about them more often, and expressed more emotions in describing the events than did their husbands. The frequency of reminiscing about the event was associated with clarity of recall. Outside observers who read transcripts of spouses' descriptions of the events also judged the women's recall to be more vivid.

Husbands turn to their wives for help in recalling events of the relationship. When recalling events together, husbands were more likely to report memory failures, whereas husbands' and wives' reports of forgetting did not differ when they recalled relational episodes alone (Ross & Holmberg, 1992). The increase in husbands' forgetting in the dyadic situation and attempts to gain information from their spouses is known as transactive retrieval (Wegner, 1987). When recalling relational events alone, there is no help available and statements about forgetting are infrequent. It was speculated that husbands, with their less-vivid memories, feel a greater need to turn to their wives for aid in recall. Thus, they are implicitly revealing their lack of memory recall.

Ross and Holmberg (1992) noted that the gender effect in the ratings of vividness disappears when the outcome of a recalled argument is considered. Additional analyses of the argument transcripts distinguished between who initiated and who won the argument. Men and women who lost the dispute reported higher vividness ratings than did the winning spouses. Husbands who lost the dispute tended to have the most vivid recall of all. Wives reported more vivid memories because they were more likely to lose the dispute. Losers in marital disputes may be keeping score and keeping in memory the details of how they conceded in hopes of achieving future concessions from their partners. Losers may analyze the dispute more extensively in an attempt to improve their strategies in the future.

A problem with this perspective is that studies of schemata processing revealed that experts in chess, physics, and soccer possess detailed schemata that facilitate memory in the area of specialization (Charness, 1988). Honeycutt, Cantrill, et al. (1989) studies of relational memory-structure processing reveal that individuals who have been in relationships sort randomized actions more efficiently than do individuals who have been in zero relationships. This finding should not be interpreted as implying that individuals in multiple relationships are experts at sustaining relationships. In fact, the very opposite can be surmised, due to the frequent endings of their relationships. In addition, it is possible that the losers in the Ross and Holmberg (1992) study may have analyzed a history of failed strategies. Berger and Kellermann (1986) noted that individuals may use habitual behavioral strategies when trying to gain compliance, even when they are faced with barriers and failure. They speculated that these individuals use a maxim which can be stated as: "Keep doing what usually works even if it isn't and try something new and hope that it will work better" (p. 24).

In general, wives may be more likely than their husbands to evaluate current relational experiences in view of their memories of previous encounters. Ross and Holmberg (1992) provided an example in which a wife exhibits an extreme reaction to an oversight by her husband. He does not understand this. The wife may associate the current disagreement with a previous sequence of actions, whereas the husband may regard her disagreement as an unreasonable response to a single incident.

SUMMARY

The content of relational memory structures for developing romances reveals gender differences in the complexity of the structure. Women report more expectations about the development of romance than do men. Disclosure is seen as a separate phase for women. Men may be rather simplistic in their expectations for romance because in action-generation studies they restate actions and mention few unique activities.

Research has revealed that the number of relationships a person reports having been in can be predicted from what they mention as being characteristic of a developing relationship. In addition, most actions that characterize romance are seen as typical; less are seen as necessary. Individuals often label actions as being characteristic of romance, even though they are unable to generate a list of the actions on their own. In other words, once the action is presented, it is recognized. However, it is an entirely different matter to think of the action in the first place. The only action rated as more necessary than typical was a desire for self-disclosure.

Men and women can readily identify underlying stages of escalating relationships. A prototypical sequence was derived that resembled some of the social-penetration stages in the staircase model of Knapp and Vangelisti (1996). There is more agreement on the ordering of early actions, such as dating, than on later-occurring actions, such as making a commitment.

DISCUSSION QUESTIONS

7.1 Why do women list more expectations for the escalation of romance than men? Are men cognitively simplistic or ignorant about the behaviors that characterize the escalation of romance?

7.2 Look at the list of actions that characterize the escalation of romance. Discuss which of these actions are more easily interchanged or switched in the prototypical sequence. For example, meeting tends to precede marriage, unless cultural mores establish contractually arranged marriages such as in Egypt or India.

7.3 Discuss what may happen if a two individuals meet and one has a diversified set of nonredundant expectations for the development of romance, whereas the other individual has a simple set that is not complex.

APPLICATIONS

7.1 Conduct a mini-experiment by asking three male and three female friends to generate a list of behaviors that characterize a close relationship. Compute the redundancy of the listed actions by counting the number of repeated or similar statements made by an individual. Did the men and women have similar levels of redundancy? When you take redundancy into account, did the men and women generate the same number of unique actions? Can you make any conclusions about difference between the men and women in the complexity of the expectations for a close relationship?

7.2 Conduct a mini-experiment by writing down the descriptions of the behavioral expectations in Box 7.2, each on a separate index card. Shuffle the cards so the expectations are in a random order. Give the deck to three male and three female friends and instruct them to sort the cards in an intuitive logical order. Time them and compare their orders with those in Box 7.2. Was it difficult for them to sort the expectations? Were there any reactions to the experiment? Discuss any gender differences in the sorting times and rank orders of the behavioral expectations.

7.3 Reproduce the stories of John and Veronica and Linda and Tom in Box 7.3, omitting the percentages of subjects marking boundaries after each sentence. Distribute the stories to three men and three women and tell them what to do by following the instructions on pages 121–122. Compare their locations of slash marks with those in Box 7.3. Did the men and women agree on the placement of the slash marks? What do their slash marks reveal about underlying phases in the minds of the individuals you sampled?

8

Memory Structures
for Decaying Relationships

This chapter deals with how the expectations for the development of romantic relationships can cause potential problems. For example, one of the escalating memory structure expectations is overcoming a crisis. This expectation opens the door to potential problems in a relationship insofar as overcoming a crisis results in increased conflict. As indicated in chapters 2 and 6, relationships are characterized by dialectic needs. For example, a commonly mentioned escalating memory structure expectancy is sharing time together or engaging in joint activities; yet it is possible for one partner to believe that the couple is spending too much time together and to want time alone. Another common memory structure expectation is self-disclosure. Yet studies by Burgoon, Parrott, LePoire, Kelley, Walther, and Penny (1989) reveal how privacy maintenance may be a goal in some relationships. Too much disclosure makes some partners uncomfortable, or relational partners may wish to keep confidences in various areas. As a result, they may withdraw from interaction in order to restore a desirable level of privacy.

This chapter examines a series of studies that parallel the studies discussed in chapter 7, except the concern is with de-escalating expectations. Following the outline of the preceding chapter, this chapter discusses the contents of de-escalating memory structures, differences in the typicality and necessity ratings of de-escalating actions, and predictions that can be made about people's beliefs about relational decay on the basis of typicality and necessity ratings. In addition, underlying stages of decay are analyzed in the de-escalating metamemory structures, continuing the stories of the fictional couples presented in chapter 7. Finally, the chapter concludes with discussions of gender differences in generating de-escalating memory structures and the results of a series of studies on individuals' desires to end or redefine a relationship.

CONTENT OF DE-ESCALATING MEMORY STRUCTURES

The script-generating procedure described in chapter 7 was used to measure expectations for relationships that are on the decline. Subjects were asked to list up to 20 actions that they believed were typical in the break up of a romantic relationship (Honeycutt, Cantrill, & Allen, 1992). The participants consisted of 94 men and 121 women who were recruited from undergraduate classes in introductory public speaking at Louisiana State University. They ranged in age from 17 to 28, with an average age of 18.20. The participants had not been exposed to the literature associated with relational decay and communication. They were asked to start the list with two individuals who have a long-term commitment with one another and end the list with the individuals not wanting to have an intimate relationship. Box 8.1 presents the list of de-escalating actions.

The subjects were instructed to report behaviors and to try to avoid reporting emotional inferences that may be associated with the breakdown of a romance. They were told that "a person saying feeling bored, self is unhappy with relationship, doubts the relationship" is reporting on feelings associated with the decay process rather than on behaviors. Even though the subjects were asked to generate behavioral actions and were given examples of actions and inferences, 24% of the lines produced contained inferences. In addition, statistical analysis revealed that individuals generated more redundant inference responses than action responses. (Honeycutt et al., 1992).

Baldwin (1992) noted that interpersonal scripts include thoughts, feelings, and motivations. He notes, "As well as observing the external behaviors of self and other, an individual in an interaction will be aware of his or her own internal states and also quite likely will be inferring something about the internal state of the other person. Included in an interpersonal script thus will be expectations about the thoughts, feelings, and goals of both self and other" (p. 468).

Box 8.1 presents the percentages for each memory structure action. Previous studies have used decision rules as low as 16% (of the participants mentioning an action) in order for an action to be included in the prototypical memory structure (Pryor & Merluzzi, 1985). In this study, a level of 20% was used for a statement's inclusion in the prototypical de-escalating metamemory structure (Honeycutt et al., 1992). This decision was based on an analysis of the number of responses for the actions and a determination of where explicit gaps existed. This revealed that a 20% decision rule provided a clear cut-off point. Four activities ranged between frequencies of 20% and 25%, with a distinct gap coming below 20%.[1]

Box 8.1 De-escalating Memory Structure Expectations

Cluster	Behavioral Expectation*	Percentage of Subjects Mentioning Action
Decreasing intimacy		
	1. Stop expressing intimate feelings* (statements of love, concern, care)	26%
	2. Decrease physical intimacy and withhold affection (such as kisses, hugs, touches, petting, etc.)	14%
Aversive communication		
	3. Argue about little things, pet peeves, recurring irritants*	32%
	4. Disagree about attitudes, opinions, values, roles things to do*	20%
	5. Verbal fighting and antagonization of other* (e.g., shouting, yelling, profanity, whining)	36%
	6. Criticize partner through noting shortcomings in partner, personal attacks	17%
	7. Make sarcastic remarks to partner	13%
Decreasing contact		
	8. Call or phone less	12%
	9. Spend less time together; see each other less often*	39%
	10. Avoid and ignore other in public settings*	40%
	11. Give other excuses for not being able to go out or date	11%

Box 8.1 (Continued)

Cluster	Behavioral Expectation*	Percentage of Subjects Mentioning Action
Reevaluating relationship		
	12. Trial rejuvenation; try to smooth things over through discussion; a period of time for readjustment*	32%
	13. Talk about etiology and why disagreements occur; discuss source of problems/conflicts	15%
	14. Talk about breaking up with partner*	20%
	15. Talk with others or friends about relational problems, issues, or conflicts	10%
Comparing alternatives		
	16. Assess and compare alternatives; think of costs and benefits of other arrangements; become interested in others*	23%
	17. Spend more time with same-gender friends	13%
	18. Start seeing others of the opposite-gender*	23%
	19. Develop more outside interests, hobbies, activities unrelated to relationship	13%
Termination of relationship		
	20. Final breakup and termination of the relationship*	58%
	21. Miscellaneous behaviors	31%

*Asterisk (*) indicates prototypical memory structure actions in which 20% or more of subjects mentioned the behavior.

Based on this rule, 11 actions were identified as comprising the de-escalating metamemory structure (Honeycutt et al., 1992). These actions included reducing or stopping the expression of intimate feelings, arguing about little things, disagreeing with the other person's opinions, verbal fighting, spending less time together, avoiding or ignoring the other person on chance encounter, trying to rejuvenate the relationship, and talking about ending the relationship. Also mentioned were becoming interested in others, actually starting to see others, and finally terminating the relationship.

The memory-structure expectations appear to represent six underlying clusters of behaviors. These clusters were derived by noting conceptual similarities among the activities. For example, the first cluster is labeled decreasing intimacy in which personal communication is decreased. The actions representing this cluster are not expressing verbal feelings and decreasing physical affection. The second cluster is aversive communication, which is arguing about small things and fighting. In addition, criticism and sarcasm may be other aversive behavior toward one's partner. The third cluster is decreasing contact, in which the partners see less of each other and reduce calling. Further, reasons are given for one's not being able to go out with one's partner. This cluster resembles the disengaging strategies identified by Cody et al. (1982), in which they discovered strategies of behavioral deescalation such as the individual avoiding contact with his or her relational partner, as well as not calling the partner. The fourth cluster is reevaluating the relationship. Individuals talk about their relational problems with one another or friends. The fifth cluster is comparing alternatives, in which the individual considers seeing other people. The individual may think about seeing others, as well as developing other interests and spending more time with friends. The final cluster is the terminating the relationship. The next section discusses how some of the actions with these clusters are similar to strategies for relational decline discussed in other research.

De-Escalating Actions Compared to Other Models of Relationship Decline

Many de-escalating actions that are listed in Box 8.1 were observed in a study on breaking up by Battaglia, Richard, Datteri, and Lord (1998). In their study, individuals mentioned lack of interest, noticing other people, acting distant, trying to work things out, avoiding the other person, lacking interest, considering breaking up, communicating feelings, noticing other people, getting back together, considering breaking up, moving on, and breaking up. Communicating feelings included talking with friends or family members, as well as talking about relational problems with one's partner. Of course, the lack of communication was also cited.

The breaking-up process begins when a person loses interest in his or her partner and other people become more attractive. In terms of social-exchange theory, comparison alternatives are noticed and considered. One begins to withdraw emotionally before trying to rejuvenate the relationship. The lack of interest often rekindles the relationship, but the individual begins to consider the final break. The partners talk about the issues that divide them and try to work things out. Yet they continue to notice alternatives to their current relational partners, which may lead to dating others while still dating the current partner. The cycle repeats itself a second time when the couple decides to get back together before considering breaking up for a second time. Emotional detachment allows individuals to experience a sense of having moved on. Finally, gaining a sense of closure through recovering consummates the final step of the relationship-dissolution script (Battaglia et al., 1998).

Some of the de-escalating actions in Box 8.1 are similar to the strategies discussed by Baxter (1984, 1985) for ending a relationship. Baxter distinguished between direct and indirect strategies. Direct strategies include fait accompli—actions indicating that the relationship is over with no opportunity for discussion. Action 14 in Box 8.1 is most similar to this strategy. Baxter discussed a state-of-the-relationship talk strategy in which there is an explicit statement of dissatisfaction and a desire to exit the relationship. Action 13 in Box 8.1 is close to this strategy; partners talk about why disagreements occur between them as well as the sources of relational conflict. Another strategy discussed by Baxter is attributional conflict. This strategy is characterized by anger, yelling, or screaming while attributing blame. This strategy appears in the aversive communication cluster, particularly in action 5 in which there is shouting, yelling, and whining. Another direct strategy is what Baxter referred to as negotiated farewell, in which there is explicit, nonhostile communication that formally ends the relationship. This appears in action 20, the final breakup and ending of the relationship.

Indirect strategies may be used with the intent of accomplishing the dissolution without an explicit statement of the end of the relationship (Baxter, 1985). Withdrawal is an indirect strategy that is characterized by a reduction of intimacy and contact. Actions 1 and 2 of the decrease intimacy cluster represent this strategy. Another indirect strategy is what Baxter referred to as pseudo-deescalation, in which there is a false declaration to the partner that one desires a transformed relationship of reduced closeness. The de-escalating memory structure most similar to this strategy is action 12, involving a period of attempted rejuvenation to discuss a transformed relationship. Cost escalation is another indirect strategy, which involves behavior toward the partner that increases relational costs. Action 7 is most similar to this strategy, in which the individual expects sarcastic language to accompany or even accelerate the decline of relationships. Gottman (1979) also gave examples of unhappily married couples using deliberate sarcasm in order to make their partners feel uncomfortable.

The content of the de-escalating metamemory structure contains actions that are found in the exit-voice-loyalty-neglect model of relational dissatisfaction. Rusbult (1987) discussed four responses to dissatisfaction in relationships: exit (ending or threatening to end the relationship; actions 14 and 20), voice (actively and constructively expressing one's dissatisfaction with the intent of improving conditions; actions 3, 4, 12 and 13), loyalty (passively but optimistically waiting for conditions to improve), and neglect (passively allowing one's relationship to decay; 1, 2, and 8–11).

These categories overlap. Most relational problems extend over time rather than being isolated events and may be associated with several reactions. Rusbult (1987) claimed that exit and neglect are destructive behaviors, whereas voice and loyalty are constructive. Exit and voice are active responses, whereas neglect and loyalty are passive reactions. Rusbult indicated that exit and neglect are destructive of the current relationship, whereas voice and loyalty are constructive to its continuance or reconstitution. On the other hand, Goodwin (1991) found that the responses are not easily classified as active or passive and that the loyalty response contains positive and negative elements. Also, the de-escalating metamemory structure in Box 8.1 reveals no evidence for loyalty; there were no expectations reflecting this type of response. The closest action to this was trial rejuvenation, but this expectation involved an active attempt to work things out in the relationship.

Inferences Associated With Relationship Decay

Box 8.2 contains the inferences that were mentioned by at least 11% of the sample. There was little agreement on the inferences, with the exception of feeling bored with the relationship and feeling an increase in uncertainty. After these inferences, the next most-frequently mentioned inference, anger, only had a frequency of 17%. The finding that boredom was frequently mentioned was also observed in other research to be the most-identified contributing factor to the ending of relationships (e.g., Hill et al., 1976).

One speculation about the mentioning of inferences is that the subjects may be unable to articulate the source or cause of the emotional inference. The inference probably represents an outcome of an underlying action. It was found that individuals are more redundant in generating emotional inferences than actions (Honeycutt et al., 1992). In order to explain this phenomenon, consider Carlston's (1980) dual-memory model of impression formation, which assumes that individuals select distinctive behaviors for analysis as well as drawing on previously stored inferences. Inferences and interpretations may be made about the behaviors; however, there may be an inability to articulate some actions.

Box 8.2 Inferences Interspersed Within the De-escalating Metamemory Structure Actions	
Inference	*Percentage of Subjects Mentioning Inference*
1. Feel angry	17%
2. Feel annoyed, distressed	11%
3. Bitter	11%
4. Feel bored, inattentive, listless, restless	30%
5. Jealousy	11%
6. Moody	12%
7. Feel hurt	10%
8. Feel insecure and loss of confidence	22%
9. Miscellaneous	15%

Baxter (1986) provided an example of a man who cannot find words to express the absence of romance.

In addition, Smith (1997) found that individuals report both behaviors and inferences as justification for their ratings of the intimacy of opposite-gender dyads viewed on videotape. In the study (discussed in chap. 3) viewers were led to believe they were watching either a married couple or a couple just getting acquainted, when in fact each group of viewers watched the same couple. Viewers were asked to rate the intimacy of the couple and note the specific non-verbal behaviors they noticed in support of their judgements. Smith (1997) found that many of the behaviors listed by subjects were inferences, even though they had been clearly instructed to write the specific behaviors that led to their ratings. Nonverbal behaviors listed included touch, smiling, proximity, nodding, forward body lean, gaze, gesturing, leg and arm movements, posture, and body orientation (open, closed, or neutral toward the partner). Inferences listed included relaxed, comfort, being tense, nervous, poor quality of conversation, good quality of conversation, lack of intimacy, relational involvement, and just meeting. Viewers who had been told the couple was married cited on nodding and inferences that the couple was relaxed and relationally involved, even though not interested in one another. Viewers who had been told the couple had just met cited gazing away from each other, gesturing, leg and arm movements, and inferences that the couple was somewhat tense at first, but relaxed over time (Smith, 1997).

Given the frequency at which boredom was cited as an inference and a major cause of relational breakups, the question arises concerning the connotative meaning of boredom. For example, does boredom mean that individuals A and B are doing repetitive behaviors or that A has vast knowledge or interest in a given area, but B does not? Boredom could also refer to an individual's heightened ability to predict another's responses accurately. Because a relatively large amount of an individual's perceptions of relational decay deal with attributions reflecting internal states, a lot of time is spent thinking about emotions or feelings such as boredom. Many times, the pain of the decline of close relationships may be salient and, thus, may result in a variety of inferences ranging from boredom to anger.

Individuals have beliefs about what emotions are appropriate to a relationship and use that knowledge to judge how they feel during interaction in the relationship. Planalp (1987) noted that emotions are one aspect of interaction that are interpreted through conscious and unconscious cognitive processes. The links between cognition, emotional inferences, and interaction need to be examined more carefully before researchers begin to understand the dynamics of personal relationships.

DIFFERENCES IN TYPICALITY AND NECESSITY OF DE-ESCALATING ACTIONS

Similar to their rating the differences between the typicality and necessity of escalating memory structure expectations, individuals also rate de-escalating memory expectations as more typical than necessary. The fact that the actions were seen as more typical than necessary when a relationship started to sour further indicates that there are many ways to redefine or end a relationship. The only de-escalating activity rated as more necessary than typical was discussing why disagreements occur between relational partners. Apparently, this finding points to the lack of communication and direct talk about relational problems. Indeed, other research in the area of marital interaction revealed that many couples withdraw from discussion about serious relational problems (Fitzpatrick, 1988; Gottman, 1994).

Underlying Dimensions of Relationship Decline

Honeycutt et al. (1992) found additional support for the categories comparing alternatives, aversive communication, and decreasing intimacy, listed in Box 8.1. A sample of 54 men and 63 women were surveyed from introductory communication studies courses at Louisiana State University, ranging from 18 to 45 years old, with an average age of 20.92. The students were asked to rate how typical a de-escalating action was in the breakup of a relationship, as well as how necessary it was in order for the relationship to end.

There were four underlying dimensions for rating the typicality of the de-escalating prototypical actions. The first typicality dimension was ending or breaking up the relationship. The second dimension was aversive communication, characterized by arguing about little things or minor aggravations as well as by verbal fighting in which there may be antagonism and profanity expressed toward one's relational partner. The third dimension was the withdrawal of intimacy. The fourth dimension was trial rejuvenation; this most closely resembles the reevaluating relationship cluster found in the memory structure generation task procedure.

The necessity ratings revealed similar factors. However, the first dimension was considering comparison alternatives with the current relationship, indicating the importance of comparing alternatives to the relationship. This dimension is compatible with Levinger's (1966) classic research on attractions and barriers to divorce in, which rewards and costs are analyzed before people decide to remain in the relationship or end it. The second dimension was aversive communication, and the third dimension was breaking up. The fourth dimension, decreasing intimacy, was different from the typicality factor structure in that it reflects the lack of attempts to rejuvenate the relationship (the fourth dimension of the typicality ratings).

Predicting Beliefs About Relational Decay

In chapter 7, the results of various regression models predicting beliefs about relationship development based on ratings of the escalating actions were presented. Similar models were tested for the impact of de-escalating typicality and necessity ratings as predictors of relationship decay in terms of a belief that relationships follow a set pattern, having expectations of what should occur in the deterioration of an intimate relationship, and predicting the number of intimate relationships a person reported having had. Gender was entered in the regression models as a control variable. Recall that there were no gender differences in predicting developmental beliefs.

As in chapter 7, the numbers in parentheses are standardized beta coefficients, ranging from −1 to 1. Scores close to 0 show no association, whereas scores around 1 show perfect predictability. Hence, these coefficients reflect the magnitude of the association among each of the de-escalating actions and beliefs about relationships. The positive or negative sign preceding each activity reveals if the predicted relationship between the behavior and believe is positive or negative.

Typicality Ratings

Relationships tend to follow a set pattern = Sarcasm (0.28) + Arguing (0.27)

I have a lot of expectations of what should occur in the deterioration of an intimate relationship = Arguing (0.23)

Number of relationships = Discuss breaking up (–0.28) + Develop outside interests (0.24)

Necessity Ratings

Relationships tend to follow a set pattern = Develop more outside interests (0.31)

I have a lot of expectations of what should occur in the deterioration of an intimate relationship = Call less often (0.29) – Attempt to rejuvenate relationship (0.25)

Number of relationships = Develop outside interests (0.25)

The beta coefficients in the equations reveal beliefs that sarcasm and arguing over little things are relatively typical in the deterioration of a relationship and predict the belief that relationships following a set pattern. The typicality of arguing also was associated with having expectations about the deterioration of intimate relationships. Arguing about small things over a period of time has cumulative effects, in terms of creating a lot of expectations for the decline of relationships (Honeycutt, 1994). Yet these expectations do not necessarily reflect a linear progression of stages. Recall from chapter 6 in the discussion of relational dialectics that there may be rapidly alternating periods of autonomy versus bonding, disclosiveness versus privateness, and predictability versus spontaneity.

The typicality findings are interesting because they are compatible with findings by Gottman (1994) arguing in and of itself does not predict marital quality over time. Rather, the exchange of anger has only temporary effects and may not be harmful in the long run. It is the style of arguing that is important, in terms of whether the arguing has negative affect. In terms of sarcasm, Gottman (1994) also reported that this may be associated with contempt for one's partner and associated with the long-term dissatisfaction, decline, and termination of marital relationships.

The number of intimate relationships an individual reported being in was predicted by typically not discussing or talking about breaking up, as revealed in the negative beta coefficient. On the other hand, developing outside interests predicted the number of relationships in both typicality and necessity beliefs. This is consistent with social-exchange theory in which individuals may evaluate comparison alternatives with a current relationship and decide if the perceived outcomes from other relationships or activities are more than the outcomes that are currently received (Sabatelli, 1988). Developing outside interests is a way to do activities exclusive of the relationship that may be a desirable comparison alternative.

Developing exclusive interests may be necessary in the pattern of relational decline, while arguing, despite its typicality, is less necessary for the decline of relationships. For example, Fitzpatrick (1988) discussed married couples who have a separate orientation, in which partners are emotionally divorced yet avoid arguing about relational issues. These couples are contrasted with couples who have a traditional orientation about marriage, in which the partners may have arguments about important issues, and an independent orientation, in which the partners are more willing to argue over a variety of issues.

The negative association between attempts to rejuvenate a relationship and having a lot of relational expectations implies that attempts to resuscitate a decaying relationship may be rarer than people think. Indeed, O'Hair and Krayer (1986) found that few couples attempted to rejuvenate a relationship. They found only 16 couples after announcing to students enrolled in communication courses that they were interested in finding couples who had been involved seriously, broken off the relationship, and became involved a second time.[2]

UNDERLYING STAGES AND THE PROTOTYPICAL DE-ESCALATING MEMORY STRUCTURE

Some of the de-escalating memory-structure expectations may occur in a particular sequence with logical antecedents for subsequent activities. For example, talking about breaking up precedes a final breakup, whereas arguing about minor things occurs even earlier in the sequence of events. An attempt to rejuvenate the relationship may occur later. Some behaviors may reoccur (e.g., arguing and fighting), so that the order of events is cyclic, whereas other behaviors are not expected to reoccur, such as a final breakup. Some individuals believe that partners start seeing other people after the final breakup whereas others indicate this comes before the final termination.

Card-Sorting Experiment

Similar to the sorting of randomized escalating actions discussed in chapter 7, subjects sorted the prototypical de-escalating actions into an intuitive, logical order (Honeycutt et al., 1992). The actions in Box 8.1 that were mentioned by at least 20% of the subjects in the schema-generation study were used as the prototypical behaviors. A sample of 48 men and 54 women were tested, recruited from introductory speech communication classes. The students ranged in age from 18 to 41, an average age of 20.45.

The data revealed a slight positive correlation between processing time and the number of relationships previously redefined or ended by the subject, while also taking into account the number of previous relationships ended by both partners or the other partner ($r = 0.16, p < .042$). Even though the magnitude of the correlation is small, this finding is interesting in that an individual who has a number of previous relationships to reflect on may be slowed in processing the actions because each relationship may have gone through the deescalation process differently (Honeycutt et al., 1992). An anecdotal example of this is from a woman who sorted the de-escalating memory structure expectations in 30 seconds. After the experiment, she told the research assistant that the timing of the experiment was ironic because that afternoon she had ended her relationship with a boyfriend after a long struggle.

When reflecting on previous endings of relationships, the individual may be delayed in sorting the actions as he or she considers the alternative de-escalating paths. Consider an individual who has the following thoughts about two relationships, referred to as Y and Z (the other capital letters refer to various behavior). "In relationship Y, I or my partner used behaviors A, B, C, and so on; but in relationship Z, I or my partner used behaviors J, K, L; and so on. Therefore, I have to be careful to sort the typical sequence." To the extent that the de-escalating metamemory-generation task revealed a positive association between relational experience and the absolute number of distinct actions and inferences subjects listed, the relative complexity of an individual's experience-based thought (as opposed to that drawn from movies or novels) may have had a debilitating effect on processing time. No significant associations were found between processing time and number of previous relationships ended by the other partner or both partners.

Following the procedures of Honeycutt, Cantrill, et al. (1989), four clusters were identified in the prototypical de-escalating metamemory structure. The clusters were identified by computing adjacent mean differences, such that behaviors considered to signify a cluster had lower within-mean differences than the behaviors located at the endpoints of tentatively identified clusters.

The prototypical de-escalating order of events (standard deviations are parentheses) includes stopping the expression of intimate feelings (2.38); disagreeing about attitudes, opinions, or values (1.90); and arguing about little things (2.26). These actions constitute the first cluster of interchangeable actions. Verbal fighting (2.32) and spending less time together (2.45) make up the second cluster of behaviors. The third cluster consists of avoiding each other (2.48), attempts to rejuvenate the relationship (2.13), and talk about breaking the relationship off (2.99). The fourth cluster is distinguished by the partners' actively comparing alternatives to the current relationship. This cluster contains becoming interested in others (2.32), actually seeing others (2.33), and the final breakup (2.21).

An intriguing observation is that compared to the prototypical escalating memory-structure actions in chapter 7, there is more agreement on the ordering of escalating actions. In contrast, there is a constant level of dispersion in ordering the de-escalating activities so that the standard deviations are relatively homogenous for the de-escalating actions. "Once a certain action level is reached, there is a spreading activation in which behaviors may co-occur" (Honeycutt, Cantrill, et al., 1989, p. 77).

Q-Sort Procedure

There is additional evidence that individuals disagree more in the sequencing of de-escalating memory structure expectations than on the order of escalating memory structures. Using the Q-sort procedure discussed in chapter 7, each subject was given a deck of 11 index cards that contained descriptions of the de-escalating actions. The subjects were instructed to sort the cards in an intuitive, logical order. Subsequently, the sorts by men and women were randomly paired, resulting in 47 couples. Even though the men and women agreed on the relative ordering of the de-escalating memory structures, the correlation between the de-escalating sorts distinguished by gender was lower ($r = 0.54$, $p <$ .001) than that of the escalating sorts ($r = 0.84$). A test of differences between the values of the correlations was highly significant.[3]

The lack of consensus on the ordering of the de-escalating actions reflects the diversity of scenes that may be used in the generating the relational metamemory structure. A person may recall particular scenes that allow an action to occur earlier in a relationship (e.g., arguing). Schank (1982) claimed that individuals pursuing high-level goals are likely to use personal memory structures that include personal, physical, or societal scenes. He noted:

> We may have our own way of pursuing goals on a date with a member of the opposite sex, that bear no relationship to the way anyone else behaves.... Some personal MOPs can be a variation on a more standard MOP, where some personal scenes are added to, or replace, one or more standard physical or societal scenes. (pp. 97–98)

The ordering of escalating actions have lower standard deviations than the ordering of de-escalating actions. The higher standard deviations for ordering de-escalating actions reflect the easier interexchange or switching of the actions. For example, the de-escalating action "disagreeing about attitudes" is more easily interexchanged with "start seeing others" than is the escalating action "small talk" with "making a verbal commitment." Further, the de-escalating action "stopping the expression of intimate feelings" is more easily interchanged with "final breakup" than is the escalating action "meeting" with "marriage." "Stopping the expression of intimate feelings" and "meeting" were ordered as the first actions in their lists, whereas "final breakup" and "marriage" were ordered as the last occurring actions in the lists.

It appears that cognitive expectations for the breakup of relationships have many interchangeable trajectories. This interpretation is compatible with Baxter's (1984, 1986) findings that there are many trajectories for relationships to follow when breaking up. The constant level of the standard deviations or ordering the declining actions is compatible with memory-structure theory, in that individuals have varied personal expectations for the paths of relationship decline, even though a prototype can be modeled.

Story-Segmentation Analysis

At the conclusions of the stories of John and Veronica and Linda and Tom in chapter 7, they had gotten married. In this chapter, their stories are changed and used to determine how individuals segment de-escalating actions into underlying scenes and phases.

Each new story contained 11 sentences, one sentence for each prototypical de-escalating memory-structure expectation. A sample of 60 men and 63 women were surveyed. They ranged in age from 17 to 34 years, with an average age of 21.25. The subjects were divided into two groups with each group reading one story of a romantic relationship that had started to go sour. Two stories were used in order to generalize beyond the particular characters of one de-escalating story.

The subjects were given one of the stories in Box 8.3 and told that the stories could be divided into underlying parts, as in the instructions in chapter 7 for the escalating stories. The sentences in the stories were derived from the prototypical actions based on the 20% decision rule discussed earlier for the de-escalating schema-generation study. If subjects thought that the story could be subdivided into natural parts, they were asked to place a slash mark at the end of each sentence that they believed ended a part. If they did not think there were parts to the story, then they were asked to put one mark at the end of the story.

A comparison of slash-mark locations between the stories revealed two significant differences between the stories. Readers of the John and Veronica story were more likely to place slash marks after the second sentence about "disagreeing about the other's attitudes" than were the readers of the Linda and Tom story. Apparently, the word "attitudes" in the first story may have more connotative meaning than the word "opinions" in the second story. In addition, readers of the Linda and Tom story were more likely to indicate a boundary after the sentence about rejuvenating the relationship than were the readers of the John and Veronica story.

It is interesting that attempting "to work things out through rejuvenating the relationship" elicited more segments (58.8%) than did trying "to rejuvenate the relationship by talking and attempting to smooth things over (28.3%)." Rejuvenation may not have that much psychological meaning for the readers (Honeycutt et al., 1992).

It is also interesting that readers tended to immediately place boundaries after the first scene, unlike readers in Honeycutt, Cantrill, et al.'s (1989) escalating-relationship study. Therefore, the first de-escalating action may be a critical segmentation point that starts the process. The first scene consists of stopping self-disclosures and seems to be similar to the circumscribing stage described by Knapp and Vangelisti (1996). The second scene involves disagreeing about one's partner's opinions, arguing over small things, and using aversive state-

FIG. 8.1 After a breakup, men may have difficulty communicating about their sorrow.

ments. The third scene represents the decreasing contact cluster (avoiding the other and seeing less of the other) identified in the deescalating metamemory-generation study. This scene is similar to Cody's (1982) behavioral deescalation strategy, as well as the avoidance stage of the social-penetration model (Knapp & Vangelisti, 1992). The fourth scene represents reevaluating the relationship. The fifth scene seems to represent the breaking-up dimensions identified in the factor analyses of the typicality and necessity ratings of the deescalating actions. In this scenes the relationship is ending and interest in others increases. The final scene marks the dissolution of the relationships and is similar to Knapp and Vangelisti's (1992) termination stage, in which the relationship is redefined or ended.

In order to identify central or critical memory-structure actions that are robust in the decline of a relationship, Honeycutt et al. (1992) used five criteria: (a) an action mentioned by at least 20% of the participants in the metamemory structure-generation task, (b) positive loadings on typicality, (c) positive loadings on necessity, (d) signifying the end of a stage in the card-sorting task, and (e) placement of slash marks in the deescalating-relationship stories. They concluded,

> The most important actions seem to be talk about breaking up and final break-up which met all of the criteria. Other robust actions based on meeting four of five criteria were stopping the expression of intimate feelings, arguing about little things, verbal

Box 8.3   Scenes Within the Prototypical Deescalating Metamemory Structure
John and Veronica

John and Veronica stopped telling each other intimate feelings and thoughts. (41.7%) They disagreed about the other's attitudes and opinions as well as things to do together. (38.3%) Veronica and John argued about little things. (11.6%) They fought and antagonized each other through shouting, yelling, and whining. (68.3%) They spent less time together. (20.0%) They avoided and ignored each other when encountering the other on the university campus or in public settings. (91.7%) John and Veronica tried to rejuvenate the relationship by talking and attempting to smooth things over. (28.3%) They talked about breaking up or ending the relationship. (68.3%) They became interested in other opposite-gender individuals. (20.0%) Veronica and John started going out with other individuals. (41.6%) They ended their relationship. (100%)

Linda and Tom

Linda and Tom stopped telling each other their private feelings and thoughts. (52.9%) They disagreed over opinions and what to do together. (8.8%) They argued over small things. (17.6%) They shouted, yelled, and whined as well as antagonized each other. (70.5%) Tom and Linda saw each other less. (18.1%) They ignored each other when coming across one another in public. (91.1%) Linda and Tom attempted to work things out through rejuvenating the relationship. (58.8%) They talked about ending their relationship. (47.0%) They became interested in other potential, relational partners. (27.9%) They started seeing others. (51.4%) They ended their relationship. (100%)

Note. Numbers in parentheses indicate the percentage of subjects marking boundaries.

fighting, avoiding the other, and start seeing others of the opposite sex. To use a metaphor, these actions may be like signposts directing an individual of warnings, hazards, and exit points on the highway of decline. Yet, some relationship drivers may be more attuned to the relationship roadsigns such as those initiating the break-up. On the other hand, persons also tend to believe they began the de-escalating process. (Honeycutt et al., 1992, p. 557)

The memory-structure model emphasizes the importance of the role of thought and cognition in establishing beliefs about appropriate behavior in personal relationships. It is the structure of cognition that resembles phases rather than the nature of the phase concept itself. Studies revealed that internal cognitions resemble thoughts about the rise and demise of relationships found in researcher-imposed stages. Indeed, the expectations represent intrapersonal guides for behavior that help individuals identify behaviors and label their experiences (Honeycutt, 1993). Thus, developmental models of communication serve a heuristic function in conceptualizing interaction phases.

GENDER DIFFERENCES IN GENERATING AND PROCESSING DE-ESCALATING MEMORY STRUCTURES

There are gender differences in generating and processing de-escalating metamemory structures. Women generated more nonredundant behaviors and inferences combined than did men (average actions generated by women = 8.10, average actions generated by men = 7.33; Honeycutt et al., 1992). These findings reinforce other studies cited in chapter 6 indicating that women think about what is happening in their relationships more than do men as well as being aware earlier when relationships are in transition or decaying (Burnett, 1990; Rubin et al., 1981).

Gender differences were also found in rating the typicality of de-escalating behaviors and in processing the behaviors. For example, women rated talking with friends about relational problems as being more typical than did men. Women (average = 91.72 seconds) also processed the de-escalating actions significantly faster than men (average = 124.71 seconds; Honeycutt et al., 1992).

Even though both genders tend to agree on the order of the prototypical de-escalating actions, men ordered arguing about little things before disagreeing about attitudes and opinions. They also placed spending less time together before verbal fighting, whereas women reversed the sequences of these activities.

The finding that women listed more behaviors and inferences is intriguing in light of other research on gender differences in break-up accounts. Overall, Baxter (1986) found that women mentioned more reasons for breakups than did men. In addition, they were more likely to mention desires for autonomy, openness, and equity as reasons for their breakups. The only reason mentioned more by men than women was lack of magical quality. It is interesting that a desire for autonomy was the major reason for given a breakup. Autonomy may reflect an unarticulated, underlying desire to spend time alone. In his research on divorce and marital breakup, Gottman (1994) reviewed studies indicating that the husband is often more lonely and alienated because he no longer has access to the person to whom he disclosed. As revealed in Fig. 8.1, men have not been socialized into communicating their vulnerabilities and isolation and often withdraw.

ATTRIBUTING THE DESIRE TO END OR REDEFINE THE RELATIONSHIP

There is a bias in reporting the desire to end or redefine the relationship. According to Hill et al. (1976), the individual who desires to terminate a relationship is monitoring the problem in the relationship more closely than is his or her partner. The end or redefinition of an intimate relationship should be news to the noninitiator. Lee (1984) reported that it took longer for couples to break up who had been together longer and were more compatible, than for couples who had less well-meshed relationships.

Hill et al. (1976) reported that both genders tended to take responsibility for initiating the breakup. Knapp and Vangelisti (1996) speculated that this is an attempt to offset the stigma of being rejected. Therefore, and individual should report that either the individual or both partners desired to end the relationship more often than that one's partner was responsible. Three studies found that individuals report they themselves had ended more previous relationships than their partners did (Honeycutt et al., 1992). Further, there were few reported cases of mutual desire to end the relationship, the partner moving away, or the death of the partner.

Apparently, individuals want to be the dumper rather than the dumpee. This tendency reflects a type of zero-sum accounting instead of attributing the breakup to a mutual desire. The bias also reinforces the social desirability of reporting that oneself was the terminator of the relationship, rather than being the object of the termination. If matched reports could be obtained from both partners, it would be expected that both individuals would believe they initiated the process. This speculation also reconfirms the notion of gender-specific accounts, (Harvey, Weber, Galvin, Huszti, & Garnick, 1986).

This self-reporting tendency may reflect an attributional bias about responsibility for relational events. For example, researchers observed an egocentric attributional bias in married couples in which spouses take greater responsibility for positive behaviors, rather than ascribing them to their partners (Fincham & Bradbury, 1989). Other researchers noted a partner-centric attribution, in which individuals overestimate their contribution to negative events and underestimate their contribution to positive events (Bradbury & Fincham, 1990; Ross & Sicoly, 1979). A third type of attribution is an equal-responsibility attribution, in which joint responsibility is ascribed to both partners for behaviors. The attributions have been labeled biases only to the extent that individuals report varying tendencies to make attributions away from a midpoint value on Likert-type scales, in which the midpoint value reflects equal responsibility for behaviors and values at the anchors reflect ego-centric or partner-centric attributions.

Additional research revealed that the quality of the marital relationship affects the direction of attributional biases. Weiss (1980) noted that an individual's ratings of his or her and of others' contributions to behavioral actions is determined to a great extent by the general sentiment toward his or her spouse. If negative sentiment toward the spouse was operating, one's partner was also perceived as making more negative contributions than oneself. In this regard, there is research in which happily married spouses attribute positive intentions to their partners' messages, whereas unhappy spouses attribute negative intentions to their partners' messages (Guthrie & Noller, 1988; Noller & Ruzzene,1994).

Fincham, Beach, and Nelson (1987) discussed how unhappy spouses attribute negative motivations to their partners' underlying actions when displeasing events in the marriage were described. There are also studies indicating that unhappy spouses are more likely to make attributions that do not facilitate the relationship than do happily married spouses, even though negative behaviors may not be more prevalent (Baucom, 1987; Holtzworth-Munroe & Jacobson, 1985). People who are happily married are more likely to attribute their partners' positive behavior to internal factors than are people who are less-happily-married (Fincham et al. 1987). This research is relevant because when it comes to attributing responsibility for the ending of a relationship, researchers need to consider the amount of smooth transition or conflict associated with the decline.

SUMMARY

The de-escalating memory structure allows for variation of the sequencing in the breakup of relationships. The de-escalating memory structure may help explain why a number of individuals report not being surprised at the breakup of a relationship they were previously in. Individuals who anticipate the ending of their relationships may be accessing de-escalating memory structures that alert them to an imminent breakup.

In terms of anticipating the ending of a relationship, the data revealed that individuals reported they had initiated more breakups than their partners. This bias reflects a self-serving accounting and does not allow for a joint desire to end the relationship. It may be to one's future advantage in the field of dating eligibles to say that one ended a prior relationship rather than being seen as a deposed individual who was less in control of the situation.

An interesting finding was that individuals generating de-escalating meta-MOPs mixed emotional inferences with reports of actions. For example, boring was an inference. It may be that attributions of boredom reflect an inability to articulate specific behavioral actions. The questions are then What behaviors cause the feeling of boredom? Do repetitive activities or doing unfamilar things result in this short attention span?

Gender differences were evident in the de-escalating studies in which women reported more de-escalating actions and inferences than did men. Furthermore, women processed the prototypical de-escalating actions faster than did men. Women rated talking with friends and verbal fighting higher in typicality than did men.

DISCUSSION QUESTIONS

8.1 Research indicates that both genders tend to take responsibility for initiating the breakup of a relationship. Relate these findings to your own experiences and discuss the nature of this attributional bias.

8.2 Have you ever tried to rejuvenate a relationship? What type of relationship was it? Discuss what you did and the outcome of the attempted rejuvenation.

8.3 Is it really possible for two individuals who have achieved a certain level or type of intimacy in a relationship to go back and just be friends. Is "being friends" a euphemism for saying the current state of the relationship is over?

APPLICATIONS

8.1 Conduct a mini-experiment by asking three male and three female friends to generate a list of behaviors that characterize a deteriorating relationship, following the instructions on page ( ). Be sure to distinguish behaviors and inferences for your sample. Code each of their listed actions as a behavior and inference. Compute the redundancy of the listed actions and inferences by counting the number of repeated or similar statements made by each individual. Did the men and women have similar levels of redundancy for actions and inferences? How many inferences and behaviors were generated? How often was boredom mentioned as a de-escalating inference? After redundancy was taken into account, did the men and women generate the same number of unique actions and inferences? Can you make any conclusions about the complexity of the expectations for a deteriorating relationship for the men and for women?

8.2 Conduct a mini-experiment by writing down the descriptions of the behavioral expectations in Box 8.1 on separate index cards. Shuffle the cards so the expectations are in a random order. Give the deck to three male and three female friends and instruct them to sort the cards into an intuitive, logical order. Time them and compare their orders with those in Box 8.1. Was it difficult for them to sort the expectations? Were there any reactions to the experiment? Discuss any gender differences in the sorting times and orders of the behavioral expectations.

8.3 Reproduce the stories about John and Veronica and Linda and Tom in Box 8.3, omitting the percentages of subjects marking boundaries after each sentence. Distribute the stories to three men and three women and instruct them on what to do, following the instructions on page 31. Compare the location of slash marks with those in Box 8.2. Did the men and women agree on the placement of the slash marks? What do their slash marks reveal about their underlying de-escalating phases?

8.4 Conduct a mini-experiment in which you survey three men and three women on the number of close personal relationships (same- or opposite-gender) they have been in. Ask them who was responsible for break-ing up each of the relationships they report having been in: themselves, the partners, both in a mutual decision, or outside events or people (e.g., death, moving away, or interference of friends or family).

8.5 Conduct a brief case study of the ending of a close personal relationship. Interview the partners from an exclusive relationship that you knew about but that recently ended. Interview each partner individually. Ask each of them why the relationship ended and how they reacted to the ending of the relationship. Ask each of them if the decision to end or re-define the relationship was made by the individual, the partner, or mutu-ally; or if the relationship ended because of outside events or persons interfering with the relationship. Do the ex-partners agree on what caused the end of the relationship? Do the ex-partners see the end of the relationship as being due to a gradual process over time or due to an iso-lated event? If the ex-partners disagree on who is responsible for initiat-ing the breakup, whose version or account is more verifiable, from your own knowledge? What purpose is served by ex-partners telling different versions of relational breakup?

NOTES

[1]Honeycutt, Cantrill, et al. (1989) used a decision rule of 25% in the escalating mem-ory-structure studies. This rule was also based in the examination of frequency responses and determining distinct gaps. In this case, most percentages substantially exceeded the 20% cri-terion.

[2]O'Hair and Krayer (1986) noted that a major limitation of their study was the criteria they used for classifying couples as rejuvenated. The couples had to agree that there had been a definite termination of the relationship, a termination period of at least 2 months involving no dating and little contact, a complete reconciliation process involving exclusive commit-ment to each other that approximated the original relationship, and reconciliation had oc-curred in the last year. These stringent criteria were used in order to standardize what a reconciled relationship might be.

[3]The z test for correlational differences is based on a sample sizes of 517 cases for the de-escalating actions and 923 cases for the escalating actions ($z = 11.20, p < .001$). The unit of analysis is not the couple. There were 47 randomly matched couples for the de-escalating sorts, with 11 actions to be sorted: $N = 47 \times 11 = 517$. There were 71 randomly matched couples for the escalating sorts, with 13 actions to be sorted: $N = 71 \times 13 = 923$.

9

Semantics of Breakups: Claims of Omission and Commission

When an individual ends an intimate relationship, he or she must provide an account of the breakup to members of his or her social network, including work associates, family, and friends. As indicated in chapter 8, research revealed that these accounts tend to place the onus of responsibility on one's partner for the breakdown of the relationship (Cody, 1982; Harvey, & Weber, et al., 1986). People tend to attribute blame to others, absolving themselves of responsibility. This system of allocating blame buttresses self-esteem, helps to save face, and presents a positive image to eligible future partners (Harvey, Weber, et al., 1986). Individuals also develop such accounts to maintain a sense of control over their environment, to aid in emotional purging, and as a reaction to unfinished business (Harvey, Orbuch, & Weber, et al., 1992).

The deescalating-memory structure actions discussed in chapter 8 reveal an additional intriguing phenomenon in terms of linguistic codes. Some of the actions represent what can be referred to as omissions and commissions. This finding was incidental, but significant. Why do people access one language code for a particular action instead of another? Three explanations will be discussed in this chapter in reference to this type of semantic code referencing: attributional, implicit benefit of the doubt, and rules-based. Results of a study revealing gender differences in accessing the codes will also be discussed.

LINGUISTIC CODES OF OMISSION AND COMMISSION

Gergen and Gergen (1992) emphasized the importance of the social construction of relationships based on the language used to describe their events. They stated that relationship events exist in the eye of beholder in such a way that "there are an unlimited number of ways of characterizing the same state of affairs, and no single language can justifiably claim transcendence or status as the one true description" (p. 275). Omissions and commissions illustrate that different linguistic codes can be used to describe the same state of affairs.

The 21 actions in the de-escalating metamemory structure presented in chapter 8 were recorded to reflect either omissions or commissions. For example, one person might write that a typical action indicative of a decaying relationship is that "Individuals do not spend enough time together," whereas another person may write, "Individuals spend too much time on their jobs." The former is an omission, whereas the latter is a commission. Logically, if a person is not spending time with his or her partner, he or she is presumably committing time to something else. But as the example illustrates, some individuals see apples and others see oranges.

Honeycutt et al. (1992) found that one third of the de-escalating actions could be classified as omissions. Words such as "not," "less," "avoid," "decrease," "withholding," and "withdrawal" signal the omission of a behavior. The decreasing intimacy (e.g., stop expressing intimate feelings, decrease physical intimacy) and decreasing contact clusters discussed in chapter 8 (e.g., call less, avoid other, give other excuses for not being able to go out) are omissions. The remaining clusters represented claims of commission to the extent that the language used referred to active behaviors, such as aversive communication, reevaluating the relationship, assessing comparison alternatives, ending the relationship.

SEMANTIC CODING OF ACTIONS

Attributional Explanation

Attributional biases were discussed in chapter 8 in terms of attributing the source of one's relational problems to one's partner in unhappy relationships. Honeycutt et al. (1992) used attribution theory to posit a research question on the existence of omissions. They cited Ross (1977) for his discussion of the fundamental attribution error in which individuals attribute the cause of others' behaviors to dispositional, internal factors and their own behaviors to situational features (e.g., "My boyfriend is late because he is irresponsible." "The boyfriend says he is late because of bad traffic.").

Ross (1977) described a fictional, potentially developing relationship between Jack and Jill in which Jack believes Jill does not like him. He is unable to understand why he feels this way because he can not recall specific actions by Jill that reveal her dislike. But Jack could be focusing on what Jill does not do, such as providing positive feedback and being involved in their interactions. In this fashion, Ross described the informational bias of occurrences versus nonoccurrences.

Individuals tend to notice actions in forming their impressions while neglecting to consider information conveyed when particular actions do not occur. Ross speculated that nonoccurrences may be more noted when an individual has access to active category labels that can be applied to nonoccurring actions, is true of the behaviors associated with intimate relationships. Following this reasoning,

In the breaking up of a relationship, there may be "sins" of commission and omission that reflect attributional conflicts due to actor observer differences. The person is both an actor by being in the relationship as well as an observer by noticing the other's actions. In the former case, there is attribution to what the person is doing (e.g., seeing others). In the latter case, a behavior is omitted because it is *not* occurring (e.g., not seeing me). The difference between these may be a matter of semantics. (Honeycutt et al., 1992, p. 535)

A number of strategies that are used to deescalate a relationship represent nonoccurrences or omissions. Honeycutt et al. (1992) noted that Cody's (1982) behavioral deescalation strategy included some null events: "I *never* brought up the topic," and "I *never* verbally said anything to the partner." On the other hand, two samples in this strategy reflect positive labels for null actions: "I avoided contact," and "I avoided scheduling future meetings with him/her" (p. 163).

Baxter (1984) discussed withdrawal as a unilateral, indirect strategy to end a relationship. The withdrawer reduces contact and intimacy with his or her partner. Some of Baxter's sample accounts involve nonevents. For example, "I *never* answered the notes" (p. 36). Baxter also generated a typology of reasons that individuals gave for their relationships ending. A number of Baxter's categories reflect omissions. For example, the most frequent reasons for a breakup reported by Baxter include lack of similar attitudes or values, lack of supportiveness, lack of openness, lack of fidelity, and lack of romance. Only the desire for autonomy and physical separation were frequent reasons that reflect an affirmative or proactive wording.

Implicit Benefit-of-the-Doubt Explanation

Another explanation for the choice of language to characterize relational failure is the flexibility of null language codes; they allow one to consider other explanations in the hope that omission will end. When a person says, "My partner did not spend enough time with me," it may in the hope that his or her partner will start spending more time with him or her. The null event reflects more tentativeness and is a less definitive statement. For example, someone who says, "My partner was not spending enough time with me" implies that his or her partner could be spending more time with that person. In contrast, the commissive formulation, "My partner was spending too much time doing his hobbies," is more definitive.

Harvey et al. (1992) indicated that one motivation for accounts is to "stimulate an enlightened feeling and greater hope and will for the future" (p. 6). Perhaps, the null event reflects an implicit desire that there could be change, whereas the commission implies that change is not considered. In order to test this idea, it would be necessary to track individuals over time as they go through the process of a relationship breakdown. If this speculation has some foundation, then individuals earlier in the phases of relational decay ought to be more willing to hope for behavioral change than they would be later. Hence, there would be more omissions in early phases of breakdown than in later phases. A Relational Expectancies Survey Test returned by a man (age 28) provides some confirmation that in the early stages of relationship breakdown, when there is still hope for positive changes, omissions predominate over commissions. Under marital status, this respondent checked "married," but placed an arrow directionally toward "separated" with the words "maybe soon" handwritten over the category and "or" with another arrow pointing toward the "divorced" category. Thus he was indicating that at that point he was in a relationship that was beginning to breakdown. His specific responses to a query asking him to list behaviors that are typical of a relationship that has gone sour are found in Box 9.1. Note that of 20 total responses, omissives account for 14 and comissives account of only six. Perhaps this demonstrates "Hope springs eternal," at least in the breast of this husband.

Gottman (1994) conducted a number of longitudinal investigations of the communication behaviors that characterize happily married and unhappily married couples. He posited a cascade model of corrosive communication behaviors that lead to divorce. These behaviors include complaining and criticizing, which in turn leads to contempt. Contempt leads to defensiveness, which results in stonewalling and relational termination. He was able to predict with considerable accuracy which couples would divorce 3 years later.

Gottman (1994) provided examples of these behaviors, and it should be noted that a number of the examples reflect omissions. Defensiveness involves an attempt to protect oneself from perceived attack. Often, defensiveness is reflected through negative mind reading in which there are attributions of motives, feelings, or behaviors to the partner. Gottman (1994) provided examples such as "You don't care about how we live," "You never clean up," "You always embarrass me at parties," and "You get tense in situations like that one" (p. 25).

Box 9.1   Responses of 28-year-old Married, "Maybe Soon Separated" Man

1. Not talking*
2. Not making love*
3. Not being considerate of each other*
4. Not supporting each other's decisions*
5. Avoiding time spent with each other*
6. Not planning surprises*
7. Not helping with household chores*
8. Not kissing goodbye*
9. Not kissing hello*
10. Not checking where you are*
11. Not caring if you return*
12. Spending a lot of time with other people
13. Finding a new partner (male or female)
14. Not ever sending flowers*
15. Not remembering important events*
16. Sleeping separate
17. Rooming separate
18. Living in separate homes
19. Not seeing each other*
20. Divorce or separation

Note. Asterisk (*) indicates an omissive.

In addition, Gottman indicated that mind-reading statements are accompanied by "You always" or "You never" phrases. These types of referents clearly reflect commissions and omissions, respectively.

Gottman discussed whining as a type of defensiveness that reflects dissatisfaction in a childish way. There are several types of whining that he discussed, one contains verbal statements containing omissions. Gottman (1994) provided this omission as an example of the complaint type of whining, "You never take me anywhere" (p. 27).

Individuals may implicitly or subliminally realize that further into the relationship-decay process, their partner is not going to start doing proactive behaviors. In this regard, Gottman (1994) reviewed studies indicating that unhappy couples show greater negativity during discussions of issues in the marriage and also display less humor, less reciprocated laughter, fewer agreements, more criticism, and more putdowns compared to happy couples. This list of differences contains omissions in terms of not showing humor, not laughing together, and disagreeing. Commissions are reflected in the active wording of criticism and the use of putdowns.

It is possible that sins of commission, in proactive wording say, reflect the reduction of uncertainty. Consider the following omission and commission: "Before my partner was not spending enough time with me. Over time, I realized that my partner preferred to spend the time doing God knows what." The omission is ambiguous because the individual does not know what his or her partner is doing; hence, a null event may symbolize a higher level of uncertainty and ambiguity. The wording of commission seems to indicate that a judgment of definitive action has been made and there is less uncertainty.

Rules-Based Explanation

The third explanation is based on the premise that omissions reflect the violation of a rule. The rules-based approach explains language codes for null events in terms of violations of expectations. Hence, a rule violation is noted (e.g., "He or she was not showing me affection."). The actual rule is that an intimate should demonstrate affection to his or her partner. As noted in chapter 3, rules for the rise and demise of relationships may take the form of memory-structure expectations.

Null behaviors reflect violations of expectations and rules for interaction in personal relationships. Argyle and Henderson (1985) created a list of rules that pertain to a variety of relationships (e.g., teacher–student, intimates, acquaintances, best friends). A number of their rules are prescriptive (e.g., Be polite) in that they prescribe what should be done in the given relationship. Other rules are restrictive; that is, they indicate what is not permissible. Research (Jones & Gallois, 1989) revealed that recognizing rule violations may be easier than freely generating rules for relationships.

Examples of Argyle and Henderson's (1985) prescriptive rules are respecting the other's privacy, repaying debts, being polite, and speaking in turn. Restrictive rules include not discussing with others what is said in confidence, not criticizing the other person publicly, not embarrassing the other person, and not lecturing or patronizing the other person. Argyle and Henderson presented a list of the nine most important rules; the breaking of these rules contribute to the collapse of friendships. These rules have been broken when one's friend is jealous of one's other relationships, does not keep confidences, is not being tolerant of one's friends, criticizes one in public, does not confide in one, does not volunteer help in time of need, does not show a positive regard for one, does not stand up for one in your absence, and does not giving one emotional support. It is interesting that seven of the nine are worded to reflect a null event.

Additional research revealed null accounts of why marital and dating relationships ended. Cupach and Metts (1986) conducted a study on the accounts that respondents gave for problems that contributed to the breakups of their relationships. Six underlying dimensions were discovered: the individual's psychological state contributing to relational strain, the enactment of relational roles, relational cohesion, the regulation of interaction, third-party affairs, and external forces beyond the couple's direct control. Each of these dimensions reflects rules for marriage and dating relationships that partners expect to be followed. The breaking of the rules results in relational strain or the ending of the relationship. Note that rule violation is often stated in terms of null events or what is not happening.

In these problems areas, Cupach and Metts (1986) provided numerous instances of omissions stated in the respondents' own words. Box 9.2 contains examples of the underlying problems in relationships. The dimensions are listed, followed by sample omissive statements.

In a factor analysis study of rules for conflict resolution in Australian married couples, Jones and Gallois (1989) reported five factors, two of which were restrictive rules. These restrictive rules appear to be very similar to Cupach and Mett's (1986) dimension of regulation of interaction among divorcees and former partners. The restrictive rules included a dimension reflecting being considerate of one's partner (e.g., Don't interrupt, Don't humiliate the other person, Don't dismiss the other person's issue as unimportant, Don't talk down to the other person, Don't blame the other person unfairly, Don't push one's own point of view as the sole view, Don't be sarcastic or mimic the other person, Don't hurt the other person, Don't make the other person feel guilty, and Don't talk too much or dominate the conversation). The second restrictive-rule dimension, rationality, included rules about keeping conflict rational (e.g., Don't get angry, Don't raise your voice, Don't be aggressive or lose your temper, Don't get upset and keep calm, Don't argue, and Don't bring up issues that tend to lead to arguments). The remaining three dimensions were prescriptive: self-expression (e.g., Get to the point quickly and Be consistent), conflict resolution (e.g., Explore alternatives and Make joint decisions), and positivity (e.g., Try to relieve tension in arguments and Look at each other).

Jones and Gallois (1989), while commenting on rule violation, noted that the married couples in their study "seemed to find it easier to identify rules that they were breaking than to identify the rules they were following" (p. 960). In a study done designed to examine whether Jones and Gallois's rule dimensions extended to an American sample, Honeycutt, Woods, and Fontenot (1993) replicated the restrictive-rule dimensions (rationality and consideration) in samples of engaged and married couples. However, they were not able to replicate the prescriptive rules as clearly as the restrictive rules. Positive understanding and concision emerged as rule dimensions.

Although expectations regarding the rise and demise of relationships can be viewed using a rules-based approach, it is important to note that this approach does not provide the mechanism by which the specific language code is accessed. For example, is it easier to recall restrictive rules? If so, why? Are there individual differences in stating restrictive rules?

Box 9.2 Reasons for Relationships Breaking Reflecting Omissions

1. *References to individual attitudes in the relationship.* Former spouse decided he was *unhappy*. I *never* intended to have a serious relationship. We made plans to go out that night but she *didn't* show up at the place or time. I became *no* fun.

2. *Enactment of relational roles.* I was *not* growing as a person. He found *no* joy in being a father. *No* sexual relations. He was *not* for me an adequate dating partner. He said he *wasn't* ready to become a father. We were *not* ready for the responsibility of marriage.

3. *Relational cohesion.* We *no* longer wanted the same things out of life. Our personalities *didn't* mix. We did *nothing* together as a couple. The feelings of love just *weren't* there.

4. *Regulation of interaction.* He *wouldn't* listen. I learned about a time she was *not* honest with me.

Note: The words in italics reflect the null portion in each response.

GENDER DIFFERENCES IN OMISSIONS
AND COMMISSIONS

A reanalysis of the data presented in the de-escalating metamemory structure generation study of Honeycutt et al. (1992) revealed some interesting results regarding the association of commissions and omissions with gender and other variables associated with relational breakdown. The sample consisted of 197 respondents enrolled in introductory communication courses at a large university. The sample was 44% men and 56% women.

Two frequently mentioned omissions were avoiding the other in public settings and spending less time together. The most-mentioned commission was ending of the relationship followed by verbal fighting/antagonization. Additional analysis, controlling for the degree of redundancy in generating behaviors and inferences, revealed that women came up with a significantly greater variety of commissions (M = 5.13) than did men (M = 4.29) when generating expectations for relational breakdown. There were no significant effects for gender regarding omissions.

Partial correlations that take into account the amount of redundancy in the generated de-escalating memory-structure actions reveal a significant association between the total number of unique behaviors and inferences with commissions (Partial correlation = 0.63, $p < .001$).[1] The partial correlation allows one to describe the association between them, and at the same time to rule out other variables, in this case, the tendency to restate de-escalating behaviors or inferences. The number of omissions was also correlated with the number of unique behaviors and inferences (Partial correlation $= 0.42, p < .001$). The statistical procedure, the z test of correlational differences, was used to determine if the different values of these correlations were statistically significant. Values of z scores equal to or above 1.96 are statistically significant. This analysis revealed that commissions were more common in the generated de-escalating behaviors and inferences than were omissions. The correlation of 0.63 is significantly higher than the correlation of 0.42 ($z = 2.90, p < .004$). Yet, the 0.42 correlation still reflects the subtle incidence of mentioning what is not happening as relationships sour.

SUMMARY

The claims of omission and commission are an intriguing semantic phenomenon. Yet the basic question remains: Why do individuals sometimes reference null events as opposed to active events? More research is needed on the conditions that result in conceptualizing in one code instead of another. We believe that the code accessing occurs subliminally. Rarely does a person say, "I am blaming my partner for what he or she was not doing right, even though I could just as easily have said what they were doing wrong." In this regard, a few theoretical explanations have been offered.

Regarding gender differences, do women notice more null events as relationships are dissolving? This question cannot be answered with these data. However, recall other research with couples on factors leading to the recent breakup of romances indicated that the ending of these relationships is more of a surprise for the men than for the women (Hill et al. 1976). Because women think more about relational problems and the conditions affecting the relationship, they may notice earlier than men what is happening (e.g., "He has been avoiding me. He has not been spending as much time with me as he did a few weeks ago."). If this is case, then they use more omissions because they are simply thinking about the relationship. Recall from chapter 3 of Burnett's (1990) research on the gender differences in thinking about relationships and how this was more difficult for men than women. Men don't know what is going on in terms of noticing and monitoring potential relationship problems.

DISCUSSION QUESTIONS

9.1 How often have you noticed claims of omission and commission when things were going badly in one of your relationships? Was it difficult for you to notice what was not happening? What was the type and nature of this relationship?

9.2 Discuss each of the three explanations for using claims of omission: attributional explanation, implicit benefit-of-doubt, and rules-based perspective. Can you think of examples supporting each of these explanations in a relationship that has some problems? What are the nature of these problems? Can these problems be rectified with good communication?

APPLICATIONS

9.1 Ask three men and three women to generate a list of rules for a happy relationship. Code and compare the number of omissions and commissions between the genders.

9.2 Survey three men and women about how often they notice what a relational partner is not doing when there are tensions or anxieties in the relationship. For example, have they ever thought about or noticed when their partners have quit doing something that they used to do regularly (e.g., "kissing goodbye, asking about events in the day, or doing surprise favors).

9.3 Interview a friend about the breakup of a recent relationship. Ask your friend to make a list of the reasons for the breakup. Code the listed reasons as omissions and commissions. Can you make any conclusions about human cognition in terms of noticing behaviors while a relationship is souring? For example, based on your friend's experience, is it more important what one and one's relational partner are not doing or what both are doing in the course of a relationship?

NOTES

[1]Readers with a background in correlational analyses might be interested in knowing that this partial correlation is also an example of an item-total correlation, which results in inflated correlations because the component of one of the variables (total unique behaviors and inferences) is not independent of the number of commissions or omissions generated by a person. Hence, the number of commissions added to the number of omissions is equal to the total number of behaviors and inferences. The higher item-total correlation for commissions is another indication that more commissions were generated than omissions.

10

Future Research
On Relational Memory
Structures

A major premise of this book is that relationships are the mental creations of individuals, as Duck (1990) argued. They exist in the minds of individuals to the extent that thought is concentrated on someone else. There are American cultural maxims reflecting relationships as mental creations, such as "Absence makes the heart grow fonder," as well as the inverse, "Out of sight, out of mind."

The mental creation of relationships has behavioral effects. Perhaps, the most famous example of this is the self-fulfilling prophecy in which an individual's thoughts influence his or her subsequent behavior. Thus, if someone believes that he or she is in a casual relationship that is not exclusive, the prophecy may end up being fulfilled because that person will choose not to spend a lot of time with the other person.

In addition, as discussed in chapter 4, there is a vast body of literature on information processing indicating that one's expectations influence one's observations of behavior. For example, as discussed in chapters 2 and 3, verbal teasing in the form of putdowns, comments about one's appearance, or sarcasm may be tolerated or even expected to some degree in happy relationships. Yet the same verbal statements could be labeled emotional badgering in an unhappy relationship.

The imaging of relationships in people's minds reflects their expectations for different types of relationships as well as creating expectations for the development, maintenance, and deterioration of relationships. Relationships occur in terms of the behavior and communication between two individuals. Relationships are not mental creations in any simple sense, and the creation of a relationship from a series of interactions is a mental differentiation, not a behavioral one (Duck, personal communication).

Although relationships are mentally created, they occur at multiple levels. Relationships occur in terms of peer and social-network reactions to the dyadic bond or relationship. Recall from in chapter 5 that there are larger societal influences through the media, including television, MTV, magazines, and of classroom socialization. Ultimately, relationships reside in the minds of individuals as individuals think about current or anticipated relationships while recalling events, scenes, and messages from prior relationships.

GENDER DIFFERENCES AND IMAGINING RELATIONSHIPS

In terms of thinking about relationships, research has painted a consistent picture in which gender plays a role in relationship expectations. However, as noted in chapter 7, even though these effects have been consistent, the magnitude of male and female differences in relational expectations may be greater due to gender-role stereotypes, whereas the behavioral differences are smaller. For example, women listed more unique actions for escalating and de-escalating relationships than did men; however the mean differences are small. Further, when the amount of time it took subjects to sort randomized actions of escalating and de-escalating relationships was measured there was no gender difference for sorting escalating-relationship actions, although there was a difference for sorting deescalating-relationship actions. Women rated more escalating-relationship actions as typical than did men, but this difference was not found for deescalating-relationship actions except for the action talking with friends about relational problems.

People's gender-role stereotypes may result in the belief that women think more about relationships and about what is happening in them than about to what is not happening. Recall from chapter 9 that women use more claims of comission in referencing the decline of personal relationships. Also, recall from chapter 6 that women have deeper greater memories of relationship events and often fill in the missing pieces in relational storytelling for the men. Women recall more specific information regarding who, what, when, where, and how than do men about previous relational occurrences. Women have more nonredundant expectations for the rise and demise of relationships and are aware of problems earlier in their personal relationships than are men.

Expectations are revealed in rules for the maintenance of various types of relationships (Argyle & Henderson, 1985). For example, Jones and Gallois (1989) argued that Australian married couples have rules for conflict resolution, such as that spouses expect their partners to be considerate by not interrupting them when they discuss a serious relational problem, to be rational and unemotional in the process of discussion, to be self-expressive by clarifying the problem and avoiding exaggeration, to resolve conflict through exploring alternative solutions, and to be positive by looking at them and being supportive. They also found a number of gender differences regarding the situational applicability of the rules, such as whether a rule applied in public or private contexts, whether it applied only to marriage or other relationships, and how important the rule was. For example, women rated the rationality rule as less important but as applying more in public situations than did men and the conflict-resolution rule as applying more in private than a rule about being considerate of the partner's point of view.

Honeycutt et al. (1993) found that some of these rules, such as being considerate and being rational, also applied to a sample of American engaged and married couples. However, American couples also had rules about positive understanding through praising one's partner, being concise by keeping to the point, and demonstrating consistency in one's viewpoint. It would be worthwhile to examine the endorsement of rules for conflict-resolution and how this is related to expectations for the maintenance of different kinds of relationships (marriage, dating, best friends, competitors, business colleagues). Indeed, the memory structures for personal relationships contain expectations for the kinds of activities that occur in various kinds of relationships.

RELATIONAL STORIES, MEMORY STRUCTURES, AND A RELATIONAL WORLDVIEW

In chapter 3, the functions of telling stories about family events and characters were discussed. Family stories are important in providing a link between cognitive models of relational development and communicative behavior in terms of enduring messages that reflect core values. The stories are accessed in memory such that lines of dialogue may be recalled in the form of memorable messages. In addition, various scenes may be accessed. The actions of the characters may reveal values or themes of life and close relationships (i.e., Hard work pays off, Love conquers all, Commitment is important). The story themes may act as relationship rules and as expectations for current or future relationships.

Researchers need to examine how relational stories reflect people's expectations for the development or maintenance of their current personal relationships. What are the themes of stories as a function of gender, prior relationships, current relationship quality, and complexity of an individual's memory structures for relationships? For example, do people who have been in few or many relationships cite different themes in their most-recalled stories about relational events, activities, or characters? Does relational storytelling inform researchers about the relational partners' hopes and expectations for the future development of the relationship?

Relational storytelling is also important in reflecting a relational worldview as well as expectations for the current or potential relationships. Recall from chapter 1 that Stephen (1994) discussed the notion of a relationship worldview in which "communication between members of ongoing relationships generates a web of shared meaning" (p. 191). This notion emerged out of the fusing of symbolic interactionism and social exchange, thus creating a symbolic exchange framework. Couples construct a shared view of the world as their relationship progresses (Stephen, 1984).

In support of this view, Stephen (1986) reported that geographically separated couples had a higher relationship survival rate over a 2-year period than couples who were able to interact more freely. The worldview is greater than the sum of individual views. Along a similar line, Duck and Miell (1986) speculated that a relationship is a joint construction, such that the relationship is seen by the partners has having certain unique qualities.

In terms of relational memory structures, there is evidence of a relational worldview. The gap-filling phenomenon discussed in chapter 7 occurs when a person is thinking about a particular relational scene and there is a tendency toward the false recognition of nonmentioned action events (Abelson, 1981; Honeycutt, Cantrill, et al., 1989). Individuals may recognize relational actions as occurring once they are locked into a metamemory structure about relationships, regardless of the base rates of occurrence of the particular actions.

The relationship worldview may contribute to the relational gap-filling. Indeed, transactive memory, in which partners rely on one another to fill in pieces of relational stories, reflects gap-filling. The story told by the couple may reflect their relational worldview. An interesting research question concerns the compatibility of the behaviors or events mentioned in the stories and the expectations for a romantic relationship. Other research questions to be pursued are an examination of the association between the content of relational event stories and unfulfilled and fulfilled needs; whether the themes of the stories reflect a relational worldview and the expectations for a romantic relationship, and when individuals change their relational memory structures in order to account for new information.

Effect of Memory Structures on Relational Messages

A critical assumption of relational memory structures is that information processing affects behavior. Baldwin (1992) noted, "Relational schemas should shape the individual's expectations about and interpretations of other people's behavior, as well as beliefs about appropriate responses. The individual bases his or her behavior on this information, to reach valued goals" (p. 478).

Recall from chapter 7, that individuals who have been in more relationships take less time to sort randomized escalating-relationship actions than do individuals having been in zero relationships. Inferences about behavior are made on the basis of people's relational expectations. For example, if an individual believes that a relationship is growing more intimate and his or her relational partner is unsociable on a given day, the new observed behavior may be explained as a situational deviation from the usual pattern of warmth or sensitivity. Hence, as discussed in chapters 2 and 3, the behavior is assimilated into the individual's memory structure for a developing romance.

Relational memory structures determine what can be said in a given scene based on previous experiences, instruction from others, or observation of others. However, the reaction to messages may become assimilated into the memory structure, thus affecting future expectations for relationships (Honeycutt, 1993). For example, an individual may expect the other person to be relatively gregarious, friendly, and attentive on an initial date. Specific initial dates may confirm or reinforce the expectation. Disconfirming experiences may result in the modification of initial dating expectations. As a result, distinctive messages may be discussed in ensuing dates.

Recall from chapter 2 that research indicated that people have an initial interaction memory structure that is relatively stable, while being flexible according to situational needs (Kellermann et al., 1989). The initial interaction memory structure contains sequences of obtaining information, discussing facts, evaluating information, providing interpretations, and discussing intentions. However, people who are more familiar with one another have a greater flexibility to rearrange the order of topics. It would be intriguing to investigate the messages that men and women expect to occur at transitional points in relationships. A start was made in this area in the study by Honeycutt et al. (1998), discussed in chapter 7. In addition, Baxter and Wilmot (1984) found that questioning was not used as often as were other indirect strategies by individuals wanting to find out how intimate their relationship was. Indirect strategies, such as hinting about more intimacy, determining how much the partner would endure in terms of presenting one's bad side to one's partner, use of jealousy tests by talking about old boy- and girlfriends, or introducing the oneself and one's partner to outsiders as a couple, were used more often than were direct strategies, such as self-disclosure about the desire for a more intimate romance.

The content of de-escalating metamemory-structure messages at transitional points could be analyzed by constructing scenarios that take individuals up to a certain point in a souring relationship. Following the procedures discussed in chapter 7, in which messages used to escalate intimacy were examined, individuals could be prompted to reveal what they think would be said next to promote a stage transition toward the demise of relationship, what could be said instead of what had been said, and why something would be said at this point in the relationship. Recall from chapter 5 that this technique invokes a proactive imagined interaction (II).

FORMING CYBER-RELATIONSHIPS ON THE INTERNET

A new source of relationship expectations has arisen through Internet chat lines, in which individuals can initiate conversations with other people online. Relationships that derive from the use of computer networks have been referred to in the popular press as virtual reality or cyberspace relationships. Individuals bring to this medium their experiences from prior relationships. Although the degree to which the Internet is a source of new relationship expectations has not been studied, at the very least it provides a very different environment in which an individual's normal expectations can operate. For instance, using computer networking, an individual has more control over the first impression that he or she makes. Individuals using online dating services (e.g., Match-maker and *love@aol.com*) can scan in their photos and carefully decide which photograph will accompany a written description of themselves. Individuals can create profiles indicating their interests and hobbies, and any personal information they wish to provide.

Individuals can e-mail others, as well as using simultaneous-chat software to communicate, while they are online. Internet users can join a variety of electronic bulletin boards or groups in which the subscribers share common interests. Wildermuth (1999) reported in a study of 83 individuals in an online group interested in romantic relationships that meeting in a chatroom and accessing web-based personal ad services were common. About half the online relationships were successful in that they stayed together for an average of 7 months. Approximately, 45% of the sample was also in a real-life relationship, but said that the real-life relationship was unfulfilling or in danger of dissolving. Of the unsuccessful on-line relationships, 68% of the relationships dissolved after the first face-to-face meeting.

Obviously, there are problems with using the Internet to initiate relationships. The computer screen restricts visual access. Even scanned pictures may be dated or crafted to project the person as being very attractive. Even with the new evolving technology that allows online video conferencing, there is the restriction of the size of the visual frame. Visual information is a primary filter cue that people use in deciding whether to initiate conversations with others (Murstein, 1987). Based on how others look, people decide whether or not they desire to talk to them. There are anecdotal reports of individuals who prefer chatting on the Internet because the visual cue is restricted and they can portray themselves in any personae that they choose. Obviously, the pictures that are posted on the Internet by people with personal web pages or in bulletin-board services are strategically chosen for impression management. Hence, the photographs on the Internet might not reflect a person as he or she currently looks and be even be crafted to make the person more attractive. Indeed, Internet relationships need to be studied and contrasted with real-world offline relationships in terms of expectations for relational development.

ATTACHMENT STYLES AND RELATIONAL MEMORY STRUCTURES

Attachment theory explains individual needs for bonding based on an individual's interaction with his or her primary caregiver (e.g., often the mother) in terms of different attachment styles. For example, individuals may have secure, avoidant, or anxious and ambivalent relations. Other researchers described four styles: secure, preoccupied, dismissive avoidant, and fearful avoidant (Bartholomew, 1990).

Feeney and Noller (1991) analyzed attachment styles in relation to statements about what kind of person a subject's current dating partner was and how the subject got along with his or her partner. Avoidant subjects used more words describing lack of dependence, closeness, and affection in their current dating relationships than did secure and ambivalent subjects. Anxious and ambivalent subjects reported more unqualified affection and idealized their partners more than did the other styles. Secure subjects reported more closeness than did avoidant subjects and less commitment than did anxious and ambivalent subjects. Thus, secure subjects tended to emphasize the importance of openness and closeness while also seeking to retain their individual identities. Secure subjects who were more idealistic made more references to mutual help and support in their relationships. For the avoidant group, having fun and enjoyable times were related to the quality of the relationship.

A number of the verbal reports by these subjects reflect some of the escalating memory-structure actions discussed in chapter 7. There were references to the display of physical affection, commitment, and self-disclosure (openness). An intriguing question to pursue is the relationship between attachment styles and the contents of relational memory structures. For example, do secure people expect more disclosure than avoidant people? Are there attachment-style differences in the complexity of relational memory structures? Are certain actions seen as more necessary or typical than other actions in the different attachment styles?

CURRENT RELATIONAL QUALITY AND MEMORY

Duck (1990) wondered about the influence of talking about the future in the trajectory of relationships. Any relationship may be viewed as an unfolding mental creation based on one's expectations and the recreation of previous encounters. Duck, Pond, and Leatham (1994) found that a couple's reports of the characteristics of communication at different times are related to current relationship satisfaction rather than predicting subsequent relationship satisfaction (cf. Gottman & Krokoff, 1989). It appears that memory about communication is generated in the present in order to be suitable with current relationship happiness.

The memory-structure approach to developmental communication assumes that relationships are indeed mental creations. The imaging of conversations can create expectations for subsequent encounters and relationships. Duck et al. (1994) indicated, "Insofar as subjects clearly invest interactions with their own private and symbolic meanings, researchers will grasp the relational significance of relational events only when they attempt to study and interpret those symbolic meanings that are the arches of the mental creation of relationships" (p. 34).

Research is needed to examine memory structures for different types of relationships. Researchers know little about relational memory structures in business organizations, such as supervisor–subordinate or work associates. Memory structures could also be examined for the relationships including teacher–student, therapist–client, doctor–patient, roommates, brother–sister, brothers, sisters, parent–child, noncustodial parent–child, stepparent–child, and ex-relational partners.

RESILIENCE OF RELATIONAL MEMORY STRUCTURES: STABILITY VERSUS CHANGE

In chapter 2, two modes of information are mentioned—assimilation and accommodation. Recall that in assimilation behavior is interpreted as reinforcing existing categories and that in accommodation behavior results in changing or modifying existing beliefs in order to be compatible with new behavior. Thus, there is tension between certainty about classifying behavior and how certain an individual is that the classification system is correct.

Acredolo and O'Connor (1990) discussed how uncertainty creates vigilance and that people often give the illusion of confidence or certainty. Yet levels of uncertainty are enduring throughout life rather than being situational, as a number of researchers claimed (reviewed in Honeycutt, 1992). Levels of uncertainty are natural and represent the state of a person's knowledge in given areas most of the time. Instances of complete certainty merely represent a preference for one category over another. Without subjective or partial uncertainty there would be no motive for the continued search for knowledge, modification of existing schemata, and reflection. Hence, uncertainty is enduring in various degrees and is thought to be a prime force behind cognitive development.

Uncertainty is a prime force in relational development. Memory structures are used to categorize behaviors and determine the state of a relationship. Behaviors that are not easily classified may cause the creation of new categories and a modification of the existing memory structure. However, it remains an intriguing question to what the extent individuals will persevere in their expectations about the rise and demise of romantic relationships. Recall from chapter 4 that individuals with an ambivalent attachment style are more cynical about the long-term stability of relationships than individuals with a secure style. Yet what happens to the level of optimism about the continuance of the relationship when someone with an anxious style has been in a relationship for a number of years? Does his or her expectations change or is this seen as a rare situational occurrence with the individual's beliefs remaining intact? The latter is revealed in the statement, "Relationships are generally unstable but I was lucky to have found a partner that has resulted in an exception so far. Yet, you never know the future." Hence, researchers should look at individual differences in memory-structure modification in terms of gender, age, number of prior romances, and positiveness of prior relational experiences.

Research is also needed to explore the relationship between the memory-structure action overcoming a crisis and the idea of a relational window of opportunity. Only 13% of the subjects in the study mentioned this as an escalating-relationship action. Yet other subjects in a separate study indicated that it was fairly typical and necessary in the development of an intimate relationship. Hence, this behavior may not easily come to mind, but it is easily recognized when it is stated for the subjects. Our students have debated in seminars whether there is a closing window of relational definition.

Kelley et al. (1983) speculated that there is a critical window of opportunity for relationships to grow more intimate. After this time has passed, it takes a critical event for the window to remain open. People become defined in roles vis-à-vis one another. Berg (1984) indicated that both people in a relationship make decisions about the nature of their relationships early and there is insignificant change over time. It may be harder to alter this role once time has elapsed. For example, there may be a role conflict when a platonic work associate begins to disclose intimate information to one at lunch encounters and one believes that the associate is gazing at one.

It would be intriguing to analyze the relational window of opportunity. We don't believe that the "A-Ha" experience, when all of a sudden, happens very often. A friend is viewed as a romantic interest. How often does this actually happen? What happened to cause the change in perception? How often do relationships escalate due to a critical event? Does the critical event modify relational memory structures or is it seen as a deviation that does not become a part of one's expectations for the growth or deterioration of relationships? Does the critical event accompany some of the escalating memory-structure actions, such as self-disclosure, displaying physical affections, making other-oriented statements, or talking about future plans as a couple?

KEEPING CONFLICT ALIVE THROUGH IMAGINED INTERACTIONS

Recall from chapter 5, that conflict is kept alive in the minds of individuals as they relive old arguments while anticipating new encounters and mentally preparing for them. This is the conflict-linkage function of imagined interactions (IIs). Current II research is examining how everyday conflict is kept alive in people's minds through reliving old arguments that are triggered by environmental cues such as music that may remind them of unresolved conflict (e.g., listening to certain songs may remind one of an old flame). II conflict-linkage theory is an axiomatic theory that seeks to explain why conflict endures, how it is maintained, why it may be constructive or destructive, and why it can erupt at any time during interpersonal communication. The 3 axioms and 9 theorems of II conflict-linkage theory reveal how intrapersonal communication allows conflict to be kept alive in everyday life. This is done through linked IIs that involve a person's recalling a particular conflict episode while anticipating future encounters. Box 10.1 contains the axioms and theorems of II conflict-linkage theory.

SUMMARY

Many avenues for future research are available. Duck et al. (1991) lamented the study of relationships at the behavioral level to the exclusion of individual cognition about relationships. Individuals interpret interactions in terms of their private and symbolic meanings. Researchers will understand the relational significance of relational events only when they "attempt to study and interpret those symbolic meanings that are the arches of the mental creation of relationships" (Duck et al., 1991, p. 34). We concur and believe that the study of relational memory structures provides an intriguing way to examine the mental creations of personal relationships. Perhaps, our readers will be challenged to pursue these questions. Indeed, it is an exciting and worthwhile journey to explore the development of human relationships.

DISCUSSION QUESTIONS

10.1 Discuss the responses that you might make if a friend indicated that he or she wanted to make the relationship more intimate. Have you experienced this?

Box 10. 1   Axioms and Theorems of II Conflict-Linkage Theory

Axiom 1. Interpersonal relationships exist through communication; the communication is the relationship; interpersonal relationships exist through thinking about the relational partner outside of actual interaction.

Axiom 2. An interpersonal relationship is thought into existence through thinking and dwelling on a potential relational partner.

Axiom 3. A major theme of interpersonal relationships is conflict management (e.g., cooperation-competition). Managing conflict begins at the intrapersonal level of communication in terms of IIs.

Theorem 1: Recurring conflict is kept alive through retroactive and proactive Iis.

Theorem 2: The current mood and emotional state of individuals is associated with whether or not their IIs are positive or negative. The better people's moods are, the more positive their IIs will be, as well as the inverse.

Corollary: These IIs serve to amplify these moods such that bad moods lead to negative IIs which makes current moods worse, which results in more negative IIs. Hence, people are caught in a closed, absorbing state of emotional transference and self-fulfilling prophecies.

Theorem 3: When an individual attempts to purposely create positive IIs (i.e., as therapy for a poor marriage), negative intrusive IIs will frequently occur, in many cases with effects that undermine the therapy or positive intent.

Corollary: This intrusion results in dissonance between the negative, perhaps naturally occuring IIs, intrusive IIs, and positive IIs that may be artifically induced through pedagogy.

Theorem 4. Suppressed rage is a result of the lack of opportunity or inability to articulate arguments with the target of conflict.

Theorem 5. Thinking about conflict may be facilitated through exposure to contextual cues including music, chemical dependency, and the media (TV shows and movies).

Theorem 6. Recurring conflict is a function of brain neurotransmitter activity in which neurons are stimulated.

Corollary. There is a biological and genetic component of conflict engagement that is reflected in neural activity.

Theorem 7: In order to enhance constructive conflict, individuals need to imagine positive interactions and outcomes. Thus, intrapersonal communication can be used to mitigate biological determinism.

Corollary: A major function of IIs is to rehearse for anticipated encounters and relieve stress.

Theorem 8: Conflict linkage has the potential of distorting reality because conflict is kept alive in a person's mind and facilitates anticipating a conversation that is most likely to deviate from reality because the actual interaction does not occur as planned.

Theorem 9: People use IIs as a mechanism for escape from societal norms. For example, a person may be expected to talk a certain way in real life, but in his or her IIs, the person can be considerably more bold or liberated.

2. What are the basic rules for interaction between a supervisor and a subordinate in a business organization? How often are these rules violated? Are your expectations for appropriate behaviors in a supervisor–subordinate relationship more or less clear compared to your expectations for the development of a close personal relationship?

3. Discuss experiences in your life that reflect the linkage between expectations for romantic development and behavior. For example, do your expectations reflect a self-fulling prophecy, in that you selectively notice what you expect?

4. Choose one or two axioms from Box 10.1 and apply them to your own life. Provide examples of how the axioms have worked in your relationships.

APPLICATIONS

1. Interview three men and three women about experiencing a critical event after knowing another person for a while that resulted in the relationship becoming more intimate than he or she had expected or planned. What was the nature of the event? Was the event planned or unexpected? How common is this occurrence? Did the respondents de-

cide at one time that this was going to be a platonic or nonromantic relationship? Relate this event to the idea of the relational window of opportunity. In addition, discuss any experiences you have had in which a critical event caused a change in the level of intimacy with someone after you had decided that this would probably be a platonic relationship. Relate your experience to any of the memory-structure actions (e. g., "overcoming a crisis").

2. Go online to *love@aol.com* and observe the messages dealing with romance that are exchanged in a chat room. Note the topics that are discussed. Contrast this medium of chatting with face-to-face interaction.

REFERENCES

Abelson, R. P. (1981). Psychological status of the script concept. *American Psychologist, 36,* 715–729.

Acitelli, L. K. (1992). Gender differences in relationship awareness and marital satisfaction among young married couples. *Personality and Social Psychology Bulletin, 18,* 102–110.

Acitelli, L. K. (1993). You, me, and us: Perspectives on relationship awareness. In S. Duck (Ed.), *Individuals in relationships* (pp. 144–174). Newbury Park, CA: Sage.

Acredolo, C., & O'Connor, J. (1990). On the difficulty of detecting cognitive uncertainty. *Human Development, 728,* 1–16.

Ainsworth, M. D. S. (1989). Attachments beyond intimacy. *American Psychologist, 44,* 709–716.

Altman, I., & Taylor, D. A. (1973). *Social penetration.* New York: Holt, Rinehart & Winston.

Altman, I., Vinsel, A., & Brown, B. (1981). Dialectic conceptions in social psychology: An application to social penetration and privacy regulation. In L. Berkowitz (Ed.), *Advances in experimental social psychology* (Vol. 14, pp. 76–100). New York: Academic Press.

Andersen, P. A. (1993). Cognitive schemata in personal relationships. In S. Duck (Ed.), *Individuals in relationships* (pp. 1–29). Newbury Park, CA: Sage.

Andersen, P. A, & Guerrero, L. (1998). *The handbook of communication and emotion.* San Diego, CA: Academic Press.

Ard, B.N. (1977). Sex in lasting marriages: A longitudinal study. *Journal of Sex Research, 13,* 274–285.

Argyle, M., & Henderson, M. (1985) . The rules of relationships. In S. Duck & D. Perlman (Eds.), *Understanding personal relationships: An interdisciplinary approach* (pp. 63–84). Beverly Hills, CA: Sage.

Arliss, L. P. (1991). *Gender communication.* Englewood Cliffs, NJ: Prentice–Hall.

Askham, J. (1982). Telling stories. *Sociological Review, 30,* 555–573.

Baldwin, M. W. (1992). Relational schemas and the processing of social information. *Psychological Bulletin, 112,* 461–484.

Bartholomew, K. (1990). Avoidance of intimacy: An attachment perspective. *Journal of Social and Personal Relationships, 7,* 147–178.

Batson, C. D., Shaw, L. L., & Oleson, K. C. (1992). Differentiating affect, mood, and emotion. In M. S. Clark (Ed.), *Review of personality and social psychology* (Vol. 11, pp. 294–326). Beverly Hills, CA: Sage.

Battaglia, D. M., Richard, F. D., Datteri, D. L., & Lord, C. G. (1998). Breaking up is (relatively) easy to do: A script for the dissolution of close relationships. *Human Communication Research, 15,* 829–845.

Baucom, D. H. (1989). Attributions in distressed relations: How can we explain them? In S. Duck & D. Perlman (Eds.), *Intimate relationships: Development, dynamics, and deterioration.* Newbury Park, CA: Sage.

Baumeister, R. F. (in press). Gender differences in erotic plasticity: The female sex drive as socially flexible and responsive. *Psychological Bulletin.*

Baumeister, R. F., Wotman, S. R., & Stillwell, A. M. (1993). Unrequited love: On heartbreak, anger, guilt, scriptlessness, and humiliation. *Journal of Personality and Social Psychology, 64,* 377–394.

Baxter, L. A. (1984). Trajectories of relationship disengagement. *Journal of Social and Personal Relationships, 1,* 29–48.

Baxter, L. A. (1985). Accomplishing relationship disengagement. In S. Duck & D. Perlman (Eds.), *Understanding personal relationships: An interdisciplinary approach* (pp. 243–265). Beverly Hills, CA: Sage.

Baxter, L. A. (1986). Gender differences in the heterosexual relationship rules embedded in break-up accounts. *Journal of Social and Personal Relationships, 3,* 289–306.

Baxter, L. A., & Bullis, C. (1986). Turning points in developing romantic relationships. *Human Communication Research, 12,* 469–494.

Baxter, L.A., & Montgomery, B.M. (1996). *Relating: Dialogues and dialectics.* New York: Guilford.

Baxter, L. A., & Simon, E.P. (1993). Relationship maintenence strategies and dialectical contradictions in personal relationships. Journal of Social and Personal Relationships, 10, 225–242.

Baxter, L. A., & Wilmot, W. (1983). Communication characteristics of relationships with differential growth rates. *Communication Monographs, 50,* 264–272.

Baxter, L. A., & Wilmot, W. (1984). 'Secret tests': Strategies for acquiring information about the state of the relationship. *Human Communication Research, 11,* 171–201.

Bell, E. (1999). Weddings and pornography: The cultural performance of sex. *Text and Performance Quarterly, 19,* 173–195.

Berg, J. H. (1984). Development of friendship between roommates. *Journal of Personality and Social Psychology, 2,* 346–356.

Berger, C. R. (1993). Goals, plans, and mutual understanding in relationships. In S. Duck (Ed.), *Individuals in relationships* (pp. 30–59). Newbury Park, CA: Sage.

Berger, C. R., & Bell, R. A. (1988). Plans and the initiation of social relationships. *Human Communication Research, 15,* 217–235.

Berger, C. R., & Bradac, J. J. (1982). *Language and social knowledge: Uncertainty in interpersonal relations.* London: Edward Arnold.

Berger, C. R., & Kellermann, K. (1986, May). *Goal incompatibility and social action: The best laid plans of mice and men often go astray.* Paper presented at the annual meeting of the International Communication Association, Chicago, IL.

Berger, C. R., & Roloff, M. E. (1982). Thinking about friends and lovers: Social cognition and relational trajectories. In M. E. Roloff & C. R. Berger (Eds.), *Social cognition and communication* (pp. 151–192). Beverly Hills, CA: Sage.

Birnbaum, D. A., Nosanchuck, T. A., & Croll, W. L. (1980). Chidren's stereotypes about sex differences in emotionality. *Sex Roles, 6,* 435–443.

Bower, G. H., Black, J. B., & Turner, T. J. (1979). Scripts in memory for text. *Cognitive Psychology, 11,* 177–200.

Bowlby, J. (1982). *Attachment and loss: Vol. 1. Attachment* (2nd ed.). New York: Basic Books.

Bradbury, T. N., & Fincham, F. D. (1990). Attributions in marriage: Review and critique. *Psychological Bulletin, 107,* 3–33.

Burgoon, J. K., & LePoire, B.A (1993). Effects of communication, expectancies, actual communication, and expectancy disconfirmation on evaluations of communicators and their communication behavior. *Human Communication Research, 20,* 67–96.

Burgoon, J. K., Parrott, R., LePoire, B. A., Kelley, D., Walther, J. B., & Penny, D. (1989). Maintaining and restoring privacy through communication in different types of relationships. *Journal of Social and Personal Relationships, 6,* 131–158.

Burke, K. (1962). *A grammar of motives and a rhetoric of motives.* Cleveland, OH: World.

Burleson, B. R., & Denton, W. H. (1997). The relationship between communication skill and marital satisfaction: Some moderating effects. *Journal of Marriage and the Family, 59,* 884–902.

Burnett, R. (1990). Reflection in personal relationships. In R. Burnett, P. McGhee & D. Clarke (Eds.), *Accounting for relationships* (pp. 73–94). London: Methuen.

Buss, D.M. (1989). Conflict between the sexes: Strategic interference and the evocation of anger and upset. *Journal of Personality and Social Psychology, 56,* 735–747.

Buss, D. M., & Schmitt, D. P. (1993). Sexual strategies theory: An evolutionary perspective on human mating. *Psychological Review, 100,* 204–232.

Canary, D. J., & Hause, K. S. (1993). Is there any reason to research sex differences in communication? *Communication Quarterly, 41,* 129–144.

Carlston, D. E. (1980). Events, inferences and impression formation. In R. Hastie, T.M. Ostrom, E.B. Ebbesen, R.S. Wyer, Jr., D.L. Hamilton, & D. E. Carlston (Eds.), *Person memory: The cognitive bias of social perception* (pp. 84–119). Hillsdale, NJ: Lawrence Erlbaum Associates.

Carnelley, K. B., & Janoff-Bulman, R. (1992). Optimism about love relationships: General vs. specific lessons from one's personal experiences. *Journal of Social and Personal Relationships, 9,* 5–20.

Caughey, J. L. (1984). *Imaginary social worlds.* Lincoln, NE: University of Nebraska Press.

Chanowitz, B., & Langer, E. (1981). Premature cognitive commitment. *Journal of Personality and Social Psychology, 41,* 1051–1063.

Charness, N. (1988). Expertise in chess, music and physics: A cognitive perspective. In L. Obler & D. Fein (Eds.), *The exceptional brain* (pp. 399–426). New York: Guilford.

Clark, R. D., & Hatfield, E. (1989). Gender differences in receptivity to sexual offers. *Journal of Psychology and Human Sexuality, 2,* 39–55.

Clore, G. L., Ortony, A., Dienes, B., & Fujita, F. (1993). Where does anger dwell? In T. K. Srulla & R. S. Wyer (Eds.), *Advances in social cognition* (Vol. 5, pp. 57–87). Hillsdale, NJ: Lawrence Erlbaum Associates.

Clore, G. L., Schwartz, N., & Conway, M. (1994). Affective causes and consequences of social information processing. In R. S. Wyer, Jr. & T. K. Srull (Eds.), *Handbook of social cognition* (pp. 323–417). Hillsdale, NJ: Lawrence Erlbaum Associates.

Cody, M. (1982). A typology of disengagement strategies and an examination of the role intimacy reactions to inequity, and behavioral problems play in strategy selection. *Communication Monographs, 49*, 148–170.

Coleman, M., & Ganong, L. (1992). Gender differences in expectations of self and future partner. *Journal of Family Issues, 33*, 55–61.

Coleman, S. (1977). A developmental stage hypothesis for non-marital dyadic relationships. *Journal of Marriage and the Family, 3*, 71–76.

Collins, J. K., Kennedy, J. R., & Francis, R. D. (1976). Insights into a dating partner's expectations of how behavior should ensue during the courtship process. *Journal of Marriage and the Family, xx*, 373–378.

Connolly, J. F. (1991). Adults who had imaginary playmates as children. In R. G. Kunzendorf (Ed.), *Mental imagery* (pp. 113–120). New York: Plenum.

Conville, R. L. (1991). *Relational transitions: The evolution of personal relationships*. New York: Praeger.

Crawford, M. (1989). Humor in conversational context: Beyond biases in the study of gender and humor. In R. K. Unger (Ed.), *Representations: Social constructions of gender* (pp. 155–164). New York: Baywood.

Cupach, W. R., & Metts, S. (1986). Dating and marital accounts of why a relationship ended. *Communication Monographs, 53*, 311–334.

Davis, K. E., & Todd, M. J. (1982). Friendship and love relationships. In K. E. Davis (Ed.), *Advances in descriptive psychology* (Vol. 2, pp. 79–122). Greenwich, CT: JAI.

Davis, K. E., & Todd, M. J. (1985). Assessing friendship: Prototypes, paradigm cases and relational description. In S. Duck & D. Perlman (Eds.), *Understanding personal relationships: An interdisciplinary approach* (pp. 17–28). Beverly Hills, CA: Sage.

Deaux, K. (1976). *The behavior of women and men*. Monterey, CA: Brooks/Cole

Dillard, J. P., Kinney, T. A., & Cruz, M. A. (1996). Influence, appraisals, and emotions in close relationships. *Communication Monographs, 63*, 105–130.

Dillard, J. P., Segrin, C., & Harden, J. M. (1989). Primary and secondary goals in the production of interpersonal influence messages. *Communication Monographs, 56*, 19–38.

Dindia, K., & Allen, M. (1992). Sex differences in self-disclosure: A meta-analysis. *Psychological Bulletin, 112*, 106–124.

Douglas, W. (1984). Initial interaction scripts: When knowing is behaving. *Human Communication Research, 11*, 203–219.

Duck, S. (1977). *The study of acquaintance*. Farnborough, England: Gower.

Duck, S. (1980). Personal relationships in the 1980s: Towards an understanding of complex human socialty. *Western Journal of Speech Communication, 44*, 114–119.

Duck, S. (1982). A topography of relationship disengagement and dissolution. In S. Duck (Ed.), *Personal relationships: Vol. 4: Dissolving personal relationships* (pp. 1–30). London: Academic Press.

Duck, S. (1986). *Human relationships: An introduction to social psychology*. London: Sage.

Duck, S. (1988). *Relating to others*. Chicago, IL: Dorsey Press.

Duck, S. (1990). Relationships as unfinished business: Out of the frying pan and into the 1990s. *Journal of Social and Personal Relationships, 7*, 5–28.

Duck, S. (1991, May). *New lamps for old: A new theory of relationships and a fresh look at some old research.* Paper presented at the third meeting of the International Network on Personal Relationships, Bloomington, IL.

Duck, S., & Lea, M. (1983). Breakdown of relationships as a threat to personal identity. In G. Breakwell (Ed.), *Threatened identities.* London: Wiley.

Duck, S., & Miell, D. E. (1986). Charting the development of personal relationships. In R. Gilmour & S. Duck (Eds.), *The emerging field of personal relationships* (pp. 133–143). Hillsdale, NJ: Lawrence Erlbaum Associates.

Duck, S., Pond, K., & Leatham, G. (1991). Remembering as a context for being in relationships: Different perspectives on the same interaction. *Journal of Social and Personal Relationships,* August issue.

Duck, S., & Wright, P. H. (1993). Reexamining gender differences in same-gender friendships: A close look at two kinds of data. *Sex Roles, 28,* 709–727.

Edwards, R. Honeycutt, J. M., & Zagacki, K. S. (1988). Imagined interaction as an element of social cognition. *Western Journal of Speech Communication, 52,* 23–45.

Edwards, R., Honeycutt, J. M., & Zagacki, K. S. (1989). Sex differences in imagined interactions. *Sex Roles, 21,* 259–268.

Feeney, J. A., & Noller, P. (1991). Attachment style and verbal descriptions of romantic partners. *Journal of Social and Personal Relationships, 8,* 187–215.

Fehr, B. (1993). How do I love thee? Let me consult my prototype. In S. Duck (Ed.), *Individuals in relationships* (pp. 87–120). Newbury Park, CA: Sage.

Fehr, B., & Baldwin, M. (1996). Prototype and script analyses of laypeople's knowledge of anger. In G. J. O. Fletcher & J. Fitness (Eds.), *Knowledge structures in close relationships: A social psychological approach* (pp. 219–245). Mahwah, NJ: Lawrence Erlbaum Associates.

Fehr, B., & Russell, J. A. (1991). Concept of love viewed from a prototype perspective. *Journal of Personality and Social Psychology, 60,* 425–438.

Felmlee, D.H. (1995). Fatal attractions: Affection and disaffection in intimate relationships. *Journal of Social and Personal Relationships, 12,* 295–311.

Fincham, F. D., Beach, S., & Nelson, G. (1987). Attribution processes in distressed & nondistressed couples, 3. Causal and responsibility attributions for spouse behavior. *Cognitive Therapy and Research, 11,* 71–86.

Fincham, F. D., & Bradbury, T. N. (1989). The impact of attributions in marriage: An individual difference analysis. *Journal of Social and Personal Relationships, 6,* 69–85.

Fisher, H. (1994). *The natural history of monogamy, adultery and divorce.* New York: Fawcett.

Fiske, S.T., & Taylor, S. E. (1984). *Social cognition.* Reading, MA: Addison-Wesley.

Fitness, J. (1996). Emotion knowledge structures in close relationships. In G. J. O. Fletcher & J. Fitness (Eds.), *Knowledge structures in close relationships: A social psychological approach* (pp. 195–217). Mahwah, NJ: Lawrence Erlbaum Associates.

Fitness, J., & Fletcher, G.J.O. (1993). Love, hate, anger, and jealously in close relationships. Journal of Personality and Social Psychology, 65, 942–958.

Fitness, J. & Strongman, K. T. (1991). Affect in close relationships. In G. J. O. Fletcher & F. Fincham (Eds.), *Cognition in close relationships* (pp. 175–202). Hillsdale, NJ: Lawrence Erlbaum.

Fitzpatrick, M. A. (1988). *Between husbands and wives.* Newbury Park, CA: Sage.

Fletcher, G. J. O., & Fitness, J. (1993). Knowledge structures and explanations in intimate relationships. In S. Duck (Ed.), *Individuals in relationships* (pp. 121–143). Newbury Park, CA: Sage.

Fletcher, G.J.O., & Fitness, J. (1993). Knowledge structures and explanations in intimate relationships. In S. Duck (Ed.), *Individuals in relationships* (pp. 121–143). Newbury Park, CA: Sage.

Floyd, F. J. (1988). Couples' cognitive/affective reactions to communication behaviors. *Journal of Marriage and the Family, 50,* 523–532.

Foa, E., & Foa, U. (1976). Resource theory of social exchange. In J. Thibaut, J. Spence, & R. Carson (Eds.), *Contemporary topics in social psychology* (pp. 99–131). Morristown, NJ: General Learning Press.

Forgas, J. P. (1991). Affect and cognition in close relationships. In G. J. O. Fletcher & F. D. Fincham (Eds.), *Cognition in close relationships* (pp. 151–174). Hillsdale, NJ: Lawrence Erlbaum Associates.

Forgas, J. P., Bower, G. H., & Krantz, S. (1984). The influence of mood on perceptions of social interactions. *Journal of Experimental Social Psychology, 20,* 497–513.

Forgas, J. P., & Dobosz, B. (1980). Dimensions of romantic involvement: Towards a taxonomy of heterosexual relationships. *Social Psychology Quarterly, 43,* 290–300.

Frazier, P. A., & Esterly, E. (1990). Correlates of relationship beliefs: Gender, relationship experience and relationship satisfaction. *Journal of Social and Personal Relationships, 7,* 331–352.

Frijda, N. (1986). *The emotions.* Cambridge, England: Cambridge University Press.

Gadlin, H. (1977). Private lives and public order: A critical view of the history of intimate relations in the United States. In G. Levinger & H. L. Raush (Eds.), *Close relationships: Perspectives on the meaning of intimacy* (pp. 33–72). Amherst, MA: University of Massachusetts Press.

Gagnon, J. H., & Simon, W. (1973). *Sexual conduct: The social sources of human sexuality.* Chicago: Aldine.

Gergen, M. M., & Gergen, K. J. (1992). Attributions, accounts and close relationships: Close calls and relational resolutions. In J. H. Harvey, T. L. Orbuch, & A. L. Weber (Eds.), *Attributions, accounts, and close relationships* (pp. 269–279). New York: Springer-Verlag.

Giles, H., & Wiemann, J.M. (1987). Language, social comparison, and power. In C.R. Berger & S. H. Chaffee (Eds.), Handbook of communication science (pp. 350–384). Newbury Park, CA: Sage.

Ginsburg, G. P. (1988). Rules, scripts and prototypes in personal relationships. In S. W. Duck (Ed.), *Handbook of personal relationships* (pp. 23–39). New York: Wiley.

Goodwin, C. (1981). *Conversational organization: Interaction between speakers and hearers.* New York: Academic Press.

Goodwin, R. (1991). A re-examination of Rusbult's responses to satisfaction typology. *Journal of Social and Personal Relationships, 4,* 569–574.

Gottman, J. M. (1979). *Marital interaction: Experimental investigations.* New York: Academic Press.

Gottman, J. M. (1994). *What predicts divorce?* Hillsdale, NJ: Lawrence Erlbaum Associates.

Gottman, J. M., & Krokoff, L. J. (1989). Marital interaction and satisfaction: A longitudinal view. *Journal of Consulting and Clinical Psychology, 57,* 47–52.

Graesser, A. C., Gordon, S. E., & Sawyer, J. D. (1979). Recognition memory for typical and atypical actions in scripted activities: Tests of a script pointer + tag hypothesis. *Journal of Verbal Learning and Verbal Behavior, 18,* 319–332.

Grice, H. P. (1975). Logic and conversation. In P. Cole & J. L. Morgan (Eds.), *Syntax and semantics: Vol. 3. Speech acts* (pp. 41–58). New York: Seminar Press.

Guerrero, L. K., & Andersen, P. A. (1998). Jealously experience and expression in romantic relationships. In P. A. Andersen & L.K. Guerrero (Eds.), Handbook of communication and emotion (pp. 156-188). San Diego: Academic Press.

Guthrie, D. M., & Noller, P. (1988). Married couples perceptions of one another in emotional situations. In P. Noller & M. A. Fitzpatrick (Eds.), Perspectives on marital interaction. Cleveland, OH: Multilingual Matters.

Harris, L. M., Gergen, K. J., & Lannamann, J. W. (1986). Aggresion rituals. Communication Monographs, 53, 252–265.

Harvey, J. H., Flannery, R., & Morgan, M. (1986). Vivid memories of vivid loves gone by. Journal of Social and Personal Relationships, 3, 359–373.

Harvey, J. H., Orbuch, T. L., & Weber, A. L. (1992). Introduction: Convergence of the attribution and accounts concepts in the study of close relationships. In J. H. Harvey, T. L. Orbuch, & A. L. Weber (Eds.), Attributions, accounts, and close relationships (pp. 1–18). New York: Springer-Verlag.

Harvey, J. H., Weber, A. L., Galvin, K. S., Huszti, H. C., & Garnick, N. N. (1986). Attribution in the termination of close relationships: A special focus on the account. In R. Gilmour & S. Duck (Eds.), Personal relationships: Vol. 4. Dissolving personal relationships (pp. 107–126). London: Academic Press.

Hays, R. B. (1984). The development and maintenance of friendship. Journal of Social and Personal Relationships, 1, 75–98.

Herold, E.S., & Mewhinney, D. M. K. (1993). Gender differences in casual sex and AIDS prevention: A survey of dating bars. Journal of Sex Research, 30, 36–42.

Hill, C. T., Rubin, Z, & Peplau, L. (1976). Breakups before marriage: The end of 103 affairs. Journal of Social Issues, 32, 147–168.

Hinde, R. L. (1979). Towards understanding relationships. London: Academic Press.

Holladay, S., & Coombs, T. (1991, November). There are plenty of fish in the sea: The exchange of memorable messages about dating. Paper presented at the annual meeting of the Speech Communication Association, Atlanta, GA.

Holmes, J. (1991). Trust and the appraisal process in close relationships. In W. H. Jones & D. Perlman (Eds.), Advances in personal relationships (Vol. 2, pp. 57–106). London: Jessica Kingsley.

Holtzworth-Munroe, A., & Jacobson, N. S. (1985). Causal attributions of married couples: When do they search for causes? What do they conclude when they do? Journal of Personality and Social Psychology, 48, 1398–1412.

Honeycutt, J. M. (1986). A model of marital functioning based on an attraction paradigm and social-penetration dimensions. Journal of Marriage and the Family, 48, 651–667.

Honeycutt, J. M. (1989). A functional analysis of imagined interaction activity in everyday life. In J. E. Shorr, P. Robin, J. A. Connelia, & M. Wolpin (Eds.), Imagery: Current Perspectives (pp. 13–25). New York: Plenum.

Honeycutt, J. M. (1991). Imagined interactions, imagery and mindfulness/mindlessness. In R. Kunzendorf (Ed.), Mental imagery (pp. 121–128). New York: Plenum.

Honeycutt, J. M. (1992). Components and functions of communication during initial interaction with exptrapolations to beyond. In S. Deetz (Ed.), Communication yearbook 16 (pp. 461–514). Newbury Park, CA: Sage.

Honeycutt, J. M. (1993). Memory structures for the rise and fall of personal relationships. In D. Duck (Ed.), Individuals in relationships (pp. 60–86). Newbury Park, CA: Sage.

Honeycutt, J. M. (1995). Imagined interactions, recurrent conflict and thought about personal relationships: A memory structure approach. In J. Aitken & L. J. Shedletsky (Eds.), *Intra personal communication processes* (pp. 138–151). Plymouth, MI: Midnight Oil & Speech Communication Association.

Honeycutt, J. M. (1995b). Predicting beliefs about relational trajectories as a consequence of typicality and necessity ratings of relationship behaviors. *Communication Research Reports, 12,* 3–14.

Honeycutt, J. M., & Brown, R. (1998). Did you hear the one about?: Typological and spousal differences in the planning of jokes and sense of humor in marriage. *Communication Quarterly, 46,* 1–11.

Honeycutt, J. M., Cantrill, J. G., Kelly, P., & Lambkin, D. (1998). How do I love thee? Let me considr my options: Cognition, verbal strategies, and the escalation of intimacy. *Human Communication Research, 25,* 39-63.

Honeycutt, J. M., & Cantrill, J. G. (1991). Using expectations of relational actions to predict number of intimate relationships: Don Juan and Romeo unmasked. *Communication Reports, 4,* 14.

Honeycutt, J. M., Cantrill, J. G., & Allen, T. (1992). Memory structures for relational decay: A cognitive test of sequencing of de-escalating actions and stages. *Human Communication Research, 18,* 528.

Honeycutt, J. M., Cantrill, J. G., & Greene, R. W. (1989). Memory structures for relational escalation: A cognitive test of the sequencing of relational actions and stages. *Human Communication Research, 16,* 62–90.

Honeycutt, J. M., Edwards, R., & Zagacki, K. S. (1989–1990). Using imagined interaction features to predict measures of self-awareness: Loneliness, locus of control, self-dominance, and emotional intensity. *Imagination, Cognition, and Personality, 9,* 17–31.

Honeycutt, J. M., & Patterson, J. (1997). Affinity strategies in relationships: The role of gender and imagined interactions in maintaining liking among college roommates. *Personal Relationships, 4,* 35–46.

Honeycutt, J. M., & Wiemann, J. M. (1999). Analysis of functions of talk and reports of imagined interactions (IIs) during engagement and marriage. *Human Communication Research, 25,* 399–419.

Honeycutt, J. M., Woods, B., & Fontenot, K. (1993). The endorsement of communication conflict rules as a function of engagement, marriage, and marital ideology. *Journal of Social and Personal Relationships, 10,* 285–304.

Honeycutt, J. M., Zagacki, K. S., & Edwards, R. (1992). Imagined interaction, conversational sensitivity and communication competence. *Imagination, Cognition, and Personality, 12,* 139–157.

Honeycutt, J. M., Zagacki, K. S., & Edwards, R. (1989). Intrapersonal communication and imagined interactions. In C. Roberts & K. Watson (Eds.), *Readings in intrapersonal communication* (pp. 167–184). Scottsdale, AZ: Gorsuch Scarisbrick.

Huston, T. L., Surra, C. A., Fitzgerald, N. M., & Cate, R. M. (1981). From courtship to marriage: Mate selection as an interpersonal process. In S. Duck & R. Gilmour (Eds.), *Personal relationships: Vol. 2. Developing personal relationships* (pp. 53–88). New York: Academic Press.

Jankowiak, W. (1995) Introduction. In William Jankowiak (Ed.), *Romantic passion: A universal experience?* New York: Columbia University Press.

Jones, E., & Gallois, C. (1989). Spouses' impressions of rules for communication in public and private marital conflicts. *Journal of Marriage and the Family, 51*, 957–967.

Kellermann, K. (1992). Communication: Inherently strategic and primarily automatic. *Communication Monographs, 59*, 288–300.

Kellermann, K., Broetzmann, S., Lim, T. S., & Kitao, K. (1989). The conversation MOP: Scenes in the stream of discourse. *Discourse Processes, 12*, 27–61.

Kelley, H. H., Berscheid, E., Christensen, A., Harvey, J. H., Huston, T. L., Levinger, G., McClintock, E., Peplau, L. A., & Peterson, D. R. (1983). Analyzing close relationships. In H. H. Kelley, E. Berscheid, A. Christensen, J. H. Harvey, T. L. Huston, G. Levinger, E. McClintock, L. A. Peplau, & D. R. Peterson (Eds.), *Close relationships* (pp. 20–67). New York: Freeman.

King, C. E., & Christensen, A. (1983). The relationship events scale: A Guttman scaling of progress in courtship. *Journal of Marriage and the Family, 45*, 671–678.

Klinger, E. (1987). *What people think about and when they think it.* Paper presented at the annual meeting of the American Psychological Association, New York.

Klos, D. S., & Singer, J. L. (1981). Determinants of the adolescent's ongoing thought following simulated parental confrontations. *Journal of Personality and Social Psychology, 41*, 975–987.

Knapp, M. L., Stohl, C., & Reardon, K. (1981). Memorable messages. *Journal of Communication, 31*, 27–42.

Knapp, M. L., & Vangelisti, A. L. (1996). *Interpersonal communication and human relationships* (3rd ed.). Boston: Allyn & Bacon.

Langer, E. (1978). Rethinking the role of thought in social interaction. In J. Harvey, W. Ickes, & R. Kidd (Eds.), *New directions in attribution research* (pp. 35–58). Hillsdale, NJ: Lawrence Erlbaum Associates.

Langer, E. (1989). *Mindfulness.* Reading, MA: Addison-Wesley.

Lazarus, R. S. (1966). *Psychological stress and the coping process.* New York: McGraw-Hill.

Lee, L. (1984). Sequences in separation: A framework for investigating endings of the personal (romantic) relationship. *Journal of Social and Personal Relationships, 1*, 49–73.

Leigh, G. K., Holman, T. B., & Burr, W. R. (1987). Some confusions and exclusions of the SVR theory of dyadic pairing: A response to Murstein. *Journal of Marriage and the Family, 49*, 933–937.

Levinger, G. (1974). A three-level approach to attraction: Toward an understanding of pair relatedness. In T. L. Huston (Ed.), *Foundations of interpersonal attraction* (pp. 100–120). New York: Academic Press.

Levinger, G. (1980). Toward the analysis of close relationships. *Journal of Experimental Social Psychology, 16*, 510–544.

Levinger, G. (1983). Development and change. In H. H. Kelley, E. Berscheid, A. Christensen, J. H. Harvey, T. L. Huston, G. Levinger, E. McClintock, L. A. Peplau, & D. R. Peterson (Eds.), *Close relationships* (pp. 315–359). New York: Freeman.

Lewis, R. A. (1973). A longitudinal test of a developmental framework for premarital dyadic formation. *Journal of Marriage and the Family, 35*, 16–25.

Lewis, R. A., & Spanier, G. B. (1982). Marital quality, marital stability and social exchange. In F. I. Nye (Ed.), *Family relationships: Rewards & costs* (pp. 49–65). Beverly Hills, CA: Sage.

Lykken, D., & Tellegen, A. (1996). Happiness is a stochastic phenomenon. *Psychological Science, 7*, 186–189.

Lynn, D. B. (1969). *Parental and sex role identification: A theoretical formulation*. Berkeley, CA: McCitchan.

Mandler, G. (1975). *Mind and emotion*. New York: Wiley.

Markman, H.J., & Floyd, F. (1980). Possibilities for the prevention of marital discord: A behavioral perspective. *American Journal of Family Therapy, 8,* 29–48.

Martin, P., Hagestad, G. O., & Diedrick, P. (1988). Family stories: Events (temporarily) remembered. *Journal of Marriage and the Family, 50,* 533–541.

Martin, R. W. (1991). Examining personal relationship thinking: The relational cognition complexity instrument. *Journal of Social and Personal Relationships, 8,* 467–480.

Miller, L., & Read, S. J. (1991). On the coherence of mental models of persons and relationships: A knowledge structure approach. In G.J.O. Fletcher & F. Fincham (Eds.), *Cognition in close relationships* (pp. 69–99). Hillsdale, NJ: Lawrence Erlbaum Associates.

Miell, D. K. (1987). Remembering relationship development: Constructing a context for interactions. In R. Burnett, P. McGhee, & D. Clarke (Eds.), *Accounting for relationships* (pp. 60–73). London: Methuen.

Mercern, G.W., & Kohn, P. M. (1979). Gender difference in the integration of conservatism, sex urge, and sexual behaviors among colege students. *Journal of Sex Research, 15,* 129–142.

Montgomery, B. M. (1993). Relationship maintenance versus relationship change: A dialectical dilemma. *Journal of Social and Personal Relationships, 10,* 205–224.

Murstein, B. I. (1974). Clarification of obfuscation on conjugation: A reply to a criticism of the SVR theory of marital choice. *Journal of Marriage and the Family, 36,* 231–234.

Murstein, B. I. (1986). *Paths to marriage*. Beverly Hills, CA: Sage.

Murstein, B. I. (1987). A clarification and extension of the SVR theory of dyadic pairing. *Journal of Marriage and the Family, 49,* 929–933.

Myers, D. E., & Diener, E. (1995). Who is happy? *Psychological science, 6,* 10–19.

Nisbett, R. E., & Ross, L. (1980). *Human inference: Strategies and shortcoming of human judgment*. Englewood Cliffs, NJ: Prentice-Hall.

Noller, P. (1984). *Nonverbal communication in marital interaction*. New York: Pergamon.

Noller, P., & Ruzzene, M. (1991). Communication in marriage: The influence of affect and cognition. In G. Fletcher & F. D. Fincham (Eds.) *Affect and cognition in close relationships*. New York: Lawrence Erlbaum Associates.

Notarius, C., & Johnson, J. (1982). Emotional expression in husbands and wives. *Journal of Marriage and the Family, 44,* 483–489.

O'Hair, D., & Krayer, K. J. (1986, November). *Reconciliation strategies in interpersonal communication relationships: A discovery and link to disengagement methods*. Paper presented at the annual meeting of the Speech Communication Association, Chicago, IL.

Olson, D. H. McCubbin, H.I., Barnes, H.L., Larsen, A. S., Muxen, M. J., & Wilson, M. A. (1983). *Families: What makes them work*. Beverly Hills, CA: Sage.

O'Keefe, B. J., & Delia, J. G. (1979). Construct comprehensiveness and cognitive complexity as predictors of the number and strategic adaptation of arguments and appeals in a persuasive message. *Communication Monographs, 46,* 231–253.

Pearson, J. C., Turner, L. H., & Todd-Manchillas, W. (1991). *Gender and communication* (2nd ed.). New York: Wadsworth.

Pepper, T., & Weiss, D. L. (1987). Proceptive and rejective strategies of U. S. and Canadian college women. *Journal of Sex Research, 23,* 455–480.

Peters, R. S. (1969). Motivation, emotion, and the conceptual schemas of common sense. In T. Mischel (Ed.), *Human action*. New York: Academic Press.

Piaget, J.(1983). Piaget's theory. In P. H. Mussen (Ed.), *Handbook of child psychology* (4th ed., Vol. 1). New York: Wiley.

Planalp, S. (1985). Relational schemata: A test of alternative forms of relational knowledge as guides to communication. *Human Communication Research, 12*, 3–29.

Planalp, S. (1987). Interplay between relational knowledge and events. In R. Burnett, P. McGhee, & D. Clarke (Eds.), *Accounting for relationships* (pp. 173–191). London: Methuen.

Planalp, S. (1999). Communicating emotion: Not just for interpersonal scholars anymore. *Communication Theory, 9*, 216–228.

Planalp, S., & Honeycutt, J. M. (1985). Events that increase uncertainty in personal relationships. *Human Communication Research, 11*, 593–604.

Planalp, S., Rutherford, D. K., & Honeycutt, J. M. (1987). Events that increase uncertainty in personal relationships, II. Replication and extension. *Human Communication Research, 14*, 516–547.

Price, S. J., & McKenry, P. C. (1988). *Divorce*. Beverly Hills, CA: Sage.

Pryor, J. B., & Merluzzi, T. V. (1985). The role of expertise in processing social interaction scripts. *Journal of Experimental Social Psychology, 21*, 362–379.

Rosch, E. H. (1978). Principles of categorization. In E. H. Rosch & B. B. Lloyd (Eds.), *Cognition and categorization* (pp. 27–48). Hillsdale, NJ: Lawrence Erlbaum Associates.

Rosch, E. R., Mervis, C. B., Gray, W. D., Johnson, D. M., & Graem, P. (1976). Basic objects in natural categories. *Cognitive Psychology, 8*, 382–439.

Roseman, I. J., Spindel, M. S., & Jose, P. E. (1990). Appraisals of emotion-eliciting events: Testing a theory of discrete emotions. *Journal of Personality and Social Psychology, 59*, 899–915.

Rosenblatt, P. C., & Meyer, C. (1986). Imagined interactions and the family. *Family Relations, 35*, 319–324.

Ross, L. (1977). The intuitive psychologist and his shortcomings: Distortions in the attribution process. In L. Berkowitz (Ed.), *Advances in experimental social psychology* (Vol. 10, pp. 173–220). New York: Academic Press.

Ross, M., & Holmberg, D. (1992). Are wives' memories for events in relationships more vivid than their husbands' memories? *Journal of Social and Personal Relationships, 9*, 585–604.

Ross, M., & Sicoly, F. (1979). Egocentric biases in availability and attribution. *Journal of Personality and Social Psychology, 37*, 322–336.

Rubin, Z., & Levinger, G. (1974). Theory and data badly mated: A critique of Murstein's SVR and Lewis's PDF models of mate selection. *Journal of Marriage and the Family, 36*, 226–231.

Rubin, Z., Peplau, L. A., & Hill, C. T. (1981). Loving and leaving: Sex differences in romantic attachments. *Sex Roles, 7*, 821–835.

Rumelhart, D. E. (1977). Understanding and summarizing brief stories. In D. LaBerge & J. Samuels (Eds.), *Basic processes in reading: Perception and comprehension* (pp. 265–303). Hillsdale, NJ: Lawrence Erlbaum Associates.

Rusbult, C. E. (1987). Responses to dissatisfaction in close relationships: The exit-voice-loyalty-neglect model. In S. Duck & D. Perlman (Eds.) *Intimate relationships: Development, dynamics, and deterioration* (pp. 209–237). Newbury Park, CA: Sage.

Sabatelli, R. M. (1988). Exploring relationship satisfaction: A social exchange perspective on the interdependence between theory, research, and practice. *Family Relations, 37,* 217–222.

Schacter, S., & Singer, J. (1962). Cognitive, social, and physiological determinants of emotional state. *Psychological Review, 65,* 379–399.

Schank, R. C. (1982). *Dynamic memory.* New York: Cambridge University Press.

Schank, R. C., & Abelson, R. P. (1977). *Scripts, plans, goals, and understanding.* Hillsdale, NJ: Lawrence Erlbaum Associates.

Schenk-Hamlin, W. J., Wiseman, R. L., & Georgacarakos, G. N. (1982). A model of properties of compliance-gaining strategies. *Communication Quarterly, 30,* 92–100.

Schutz, W. C. (1958). *FIRO: A three-dimension theory of interpersonal behavior.* New York: Holt, Rinehart & Winston.

Scott, C. K., Fuhrman, R. W., & Wyer, R. S. (1991). Information processing in close relationships. In G. J. O. Fletcher & F. D. Fincham (Eds.), *Cognition in close relationships* (pp. 37–67). Hillsdale, NJ: Lawrence Erlbaum Associates.

Sherman, S. J., & Corty, E. (1984). Cognitive heuristics. In R. S. Wyer, Jr. & T. K. Srull (Eds.), *Handbook of social cognition* (Vol. 1). Hillsdale, NJ: Lawrence Erlbaum Associates.

Shields, S. A. (1987). Women, men, and the dilemma of emotion. In P. Shaver & C. Hendrick (Eds.)., *Sex and gender.* Beverly Hills, CA: Sage.

Sillars, A.L., Weisberg, J., Burgraff, C. S., & Wilson, E.A. (1987). Content themes in marital conversations. *Human Communication Research, 13,* 495–528.

Simpson, J. A., Gangestand, S. W., & Lermann, M. (1990). Perception of physical attractiveness: Mechanisms involved in the maintenance of romantic relationships. *Journal of Personality and Social Psychology, 59,* 1192–1201.

Singer, J. L. (1979). *Proceedings, international year of the child.* New Haven, CT: Yale University Press.

Singer, J. L. (1985). Private experience and public action: The study of ongoing thought. Henry A. Murray Lecture, *Symposium on Personality.* Symposium conducted at Michigan State University, East Lansing.

Singer, J. L. (1987). Reinterpreting the transference. In D. C. Turk & P. Salovey (Eds.), *Reasoning, inference & judgement in clinical psychology* (pp. 182–205). New York: Free Press.

Smith, C. W., & Lazarus, R. S. (1990). Emotion and adaptation. In L. Pervin (Ed.), *Handbook of personality* (pp. 609–637). New York: Guilford.

Smith, S. W. (1997). Perceptual processing of nonverbal relational messages. In D. E. Hewes (Ed.), *The cognitive bases of interpersonal communication.* Hillsdale, NJ: Lawrence Erlbaum Associates.

Spanier, G. B. (1976). Measuring dyadic adjustment: New scales for assessing the quality of marital adjustment. *Journal of Marriage and the Family, 42,* 15–27.

Sprecher, S., & McKinney, K. (1994). Sexuality in close relationships. In A. L. Weber & J. H. Harvey (Eds.), *Perspectives on close relationships* (pp. 193–216). Boston: Allyn & Bacon.

Stafford, L., & Canary, D. J. (1991). Maintenance strategies and romantic relationship type, gender, and relational characteristics. *Journal of Social and Personal Relationships, 8,* 217–242.

Stafford, L., & Daly, J. A. (1984). The effects of recall mode and memory expectancies on remembrances of natural conversation. *Human Communication Research, 10,* 379–402.

Staines, G. L., & Libby, P. L. (1986). Men and women in role relationships. In *The social psychology of female-male relations* (pp. 211–258). New York: Academic Press.

Stephen, T. (1984). A symbolic exchange framework for the development of intimate relationships. *Human Relations, 37,* 393–408.

Stephen, T. (1987). Taking communication seriously: A reply to Murstein. *Journal of Marriage and the Family, 49,* 937–938.

Stephen, T. (1994). Communication in the shifting context of intimacy: Marriage, meaning, and modernity. *Communication Theory, 4,* 191–218.

Stephen, T., & Markman, H. J. (1983). Assessing the development of relationships: A new measure. *Family Process, 22,* 15–25.

Stets, J. E., & Henderson, D. A. (1991). Contextual factors surrounding conflict resolution while dating: Results from a national study. *Family Relations, 40,* 29–36.

Stets, J. E., & Straus, M. (1990). Gender differences in reporting marital violence and its medical and psychological consequences. In M. A. Straus & R. J. Gelles (Eds.), *Physical violence in American families: Risk factors and adaptations to violence in 18,145 families* (pp. 151–165). New Brunswick, NJ: Transaction Books.

Stohl, C. (1986). The role of memorable messages in the process of organizational socialization. *Communication Quarterly, 34,* 231–249.

Surra, C. A. (1990). Research and theory on mate selection and premarital relationships in the 1980's. *Journal of Marriage and the Family, 52,* 844–865.

Swann, W. B., Jr. (1987). Identity negotiation: Where two roads meet. *Journal of Personality and Social Psychology, 53,* 1038–1051.

Taylor, D. A., & Altman, I. (1987). Communication in interpersonal relationships: Social penetration processes. In M. E. Roloff & G. R. Miller (Eds.), *Interpersonal processes: New directions in communication research* (pp. 257–277). Newbury Park, CA: Sage.

Tennov, D. (1980). *Love and limerence.* New York: Stein and Day.

Thompson, S. C., & Kelley, H. H. (1981). Judgements of responsibility for activities in close relationships. *Journal of Personality and Social Psychology, 41,* 469–477.

Tversky, A., & Kahneman, D. (1974). Judgment under uncertainty: Heuristics and biases. *Science, 185,* 1124–1131.

VanLear, C. A. (1987). The formation of social relationships: A longitudinal study of social penetration. *Human Communication Research, 13,* 299–322.

Watzlawick, P., Beavin, J., & Jackson, D. D. (1967). *Pragmatics of human communication: A study of interactional patterns, pathologies and paradoxes.* New York: Norton.

Weber, A., Harvey, J. H., & Stanley, M. A. (1987). The nature and motivations of accounts for failed relationships. In R. Burnett, P. McGhee, & D. Clarke (Eds.), *Accounting for relationships* (pp. 114–133). London: Methuen.

Wegner, D. M. (1987). Transactive memory. In B. Mullen & G. R. Goethals (Eds.), *Theories of group behavior* (pp. 185–208). New York: Springer-Verlag.

Weiss, R. L. (1980). Strategic behavioral marital therapy: Toward a model for assessment and intervention. In J. P. Vincent (Ed.), *Advances in family intervention, assessment, and theory* (Vol. 1, pp. 229–271). Greenwich, CT: JAI.

Weiss, R. L. (1984). Cognitive and strategic interventions in behavioral marital therapy. In K. Hahlweg & N. S. Jacobson (Eds.), *Marital interaction: Analysis and modification* (pp. 337–355). New York: Guilford.

Wildermuth, S. (1999, June). *Love on the line: A study of romantic relationships in an on-line context*. Paper presented at the joint meeting of the International Network on Personal Relationships and the International Society for the Study of Personal Relationships, University of Louisville, KY.

Wilson, S. R. (1994). Elaborating the cognitive rules models of interaction goals: The problem of accounting for individual differences in goal formation. *Communication Yearbook, 18*, 3–25.

Wish, M., Deutsch, M., & Kaplan, S. J. (1976). Perceived dimensions of interpersonal relations. *Journal of Personality and Social Psychology, 33*, 404–420.

Zagacki, K. S., Edwards, R., & Honeycutt, J. M. (1992). The role of mental imagery and emotion in imagined interaction. *Communication Quarterly, 40*, 56–68.

Zajonc, R. B., & Markus, H. (1984). Affect and cognition: The hard interface. In C. E. Izard, J. Kagan, & R. B. Zagonc (Eds.), *Emotions, cognition, and behavior* (pp. 73–103). London: Cambridge University Press.

Zippin, D. (1966). Sex differences and the sense of humor. *Psychoanalytic Review, 53*, 45–55.

Author Index

A

Abelson, R. P., 14, 18, 25, 113, 169
Acredolo, C., 173
Acitelli, L. K., 65, 72, 75, 76
Ainsworth, M. D. S., 7
Allen, T., xxii, 130, 135
Altman, I., 86, 87, 88, 90, 92
Andersen, P. A., 48, 51, 53, 96
Ard, B. N., 28
Argyle, M., 161, 168
Arliss, L. P., 99
Askham, J., 88

B

Baldwin, M. W., 6, 10, 53, 54, 55, 112, 135, 169
Bartholomew, K, 172
Batson, C. D., 50
Battaglia, D. M., 138, 139
Baucom, D. H., 153
Baumeister, R. F., 28, 34
Baxter, L. A., xxiii, 86, 87, 88, 92, 94, 108, 110, 117, 124, 127, 139, 141, 147, 151, 158, 170
Beach, S., 153
Beavin, J., 93
Bell, E., 29, 31, 64
Berg, J. H., 174
Berger, C. R., 11, 64, 87, 95, 96, 132
Birnbaum, D. A., 48
Black, J. B., 18
Bower, G. H., 18, 20, 58, 106, 107, 121
Bowlby, J., 7
Bradac, J. J., 87
Bradbury, T. N., 152
Broetzmann, S., 23
Brown, B., 86
Brown, R., 79
Bullis, C., 108
Burgoon, J. K., 20, 21, 126, 134
Burke, K., 18

Burleson, B. R., 13
Burnett, R., 103, 117, 127, 128, 151, 164
Burr, W. R., 89
Buss, D. M., 28, 55

C

Canary, D. J., 130
Cantrill, J. G., xxii, 99, 104, 106, 107, 111, 113, 116, 118, 119, 121, 122, 124, 125, 128, 130, 131, 135, 146, 148, 155, 169
Carlston, D. E., 140
Carnelley, K. B., 7
Cate, R. M, 29
Caughey, J. L, 65, 66, 67
Chanowitz, B., 21
Charness, N., 131
Christensen, A., 90
Clark, R. D., 29
Clore, G. L, 49, 50
Cody, M., 138, 149, 156
Coleman, M., 88
Coleman, S., 127
Collins, J. K., 130
Connolly, J. F, 69
Conville, R. L., 91, 94, 103
Conway, M., 49
Corty, E., 70
Coombs, T., 37
Crawford, M., 80
Croll, W. L., 48
Cruz, M. A., 48
Cupach, W. R., 161, 162

D

Daly, J. A., 23
Datteri, D. L, 138
Davis, K. E, 39
Deaux, K., 100
Delia, J. G., 12

193

Subject Index